TOO TIRED TO
KEEP RUNNING,
TOO SCARED
TO STOP

TOO TIRED TO KEEP RUNNING, TOO SCARED TO STOP

Change Your Beliefs, Change Your Life

Joyce Nelson Patenaude, Ph.D.

E L E M E N T
Boston, Massachusetts • Shaftesbury, Dorset
Melbourne, Victoria

Element Books, Inc. 1998
Text © Joyce Nelson Patenaude, Ph.D. 1998

First published in the USA in 1998 by
Element Books, Inc.
160 North Washington Street
Boston, Massachusetts 02114

Published in Great Britain in 1998 by
Element Books Limited
Shaftesbury, Dorset SP7 8BP

Published in Australia in 1998 by
Element Books Limited for
Penguin Books Australia Limited
487 Maroondah Highway, Ringwood, Victoria 3134

Library of Congress Cataloging-in-Publication Data
Patenaude, Joyce A.
    Too tired to keep running, too scared to stop : change your
beliefs, change your life / Joyce A. Patenaude. – 1st ed.
    p.   cm.
  ISBN 1-86204-349-3
    1. Schemas (Psychology) 2. Change (Psychology) 3. Self
-actualization (Psychology). I. Title.
  BF313.P37 1998
    158–dc21   98-13575
                                                          CIP

British Library Cataloguing in Publication Data available.

First Edition
10 9 8 7 6 5 4 3 2 1

Printed and bound in the United States by Edwards Brothers

ISBN 1-86204-349-3

CONTENTS

To my mother, Ruth DeBoer Nelson,
and father, Roy A. Nelson, who gave me
the gift of believing in myself and encouraged me
to be all that I could be

ACKNOWLEDGMENTS

This book is the product of many years of my life's experience. Through these years, many people's paths have crossed my own on our shared journey. We have been teachers and healers in each other's lives. We have laughed and cried, cared and been cared for, supported and encouraged, but most of all loved. These people have enriched my life and made it possible to write this book, which I hope will enrich many other lives.

First of all, I dedicate this book to my mother and father. They were good people who saw good in others. Their caring spirits reached out to others with concern and compassion. It is this gift of caring that led me to be a teacher and a healer. I wish they were both alive to share with me this work that I offer the world.

I thank my family for their love and support. My husband, André, my partner and friend, gave sound feedback on the content of this book. The chapter on men and beliefs was his special gift to this work and came from his experience as a fellow healer. This chapter could not have been written without his full support. To my dearest daughter, Helene, her husband, Bob Nemchik, and my two loving granddaughters, Alexandra and Gabrielle, I thank you for your encouragement and daily prayers in the completion of this book (which I wrote while maintaining my full practice) and your blessings for my continued good health. My brother, Dick Nelson, and his wife, Sandi, read every chapter and made wonderful suggestions. Their weekly encouragement meant very much to me. To my sisters, Jean Beck and Arlene Olson, and their families, who also held me in prayer with constant encouragement, thank you. I also want to thank Alex Patenaude, my stepson, who never ceased to inquire with enthusiasm about my book. To this list of caring souls I add my sisters-in-law, Monica Woolgar, Huguette Patenaude, and Diane Ketchum. To my mother-in-law, Blanche, thank you for your prayers.

Let me also include and thank my dear friends Duncan and Catherine Regehr, who believed in my work and opened the door to this publication. To Dario and Michelle Campanile, thanks for your encouragement. I love you both. To Stuart Hoffman and Tara O'Driscoll, your listening ears and loving support were great. To Larry Cooper, who believed in and promoted me for the last six years in lecturing and teaching, your encouragement to put into words what I offered in my lectures was the push I needed to write this book. Thank you so much. To my long-time dear friend Ulla Anneli, Maj Brit, and goddaughter Ingrid, thank you for your loving support. Raul Rodriguez provided inspiration and encouragement not only through this venture, but also over the last thirty years. In addition, thanks to Bonnie Collins, my business partner —you have been a real friend. And thanks to the many more friends and relatives who called or wrote with congratulations and best wishes on my writing.

I offer my thanks to Harville Hendrix, who was my mentor and teacher in Imago Relationship Therapy. What you offered me not only has changed the lives of all the couples and families who have come to me, but it also has given me the tools to have a marvelous relationship with my beloved husband, André. Thanks also to Mel Suhd, who was the academic adviser for my doctorate. Our wonderful long conversations inspired me to learn, to grow, and to share with others my gifts. Thanks to all those teachers living and dead who showed me the spiritual way through their teachings, and to Maharaji, who showed me how to find the source of Divine grace within me. I am grateful for God's grace and presence in every experience in my life, including this book.

These acknowledgments would not be complete without thanking the many wonderful clients and students who have been the inspiration for this book. Your stories of pain and growth will hopefully help others to heal their wounds. Thank you for blessing me with the opportunity to be a part of your life and healing.

I would also like to thank those who worked directly with my writings. To Mitch Sisskin, who gave me the push in putting my proposal together and my ideas on paper. Other than my journals, I had never written much professionally before and needed your guidance. Thank you. To my dear, dear Liz Leshin, I couldn't have done it without you. Thank you for lovingly editing each page of the manuscript with magnificent insight and clarity. To Roberta Scimone at Element, who gave me, a first-time author, a chance, thank you so very much. And I thank the copyeditor, Dianne Woo, who clarified the meaning of my writing and never lost my voice.

FOREWORD

I am proud to be writing the foreword to Joyce Patenaude's book *Too Tired to Keep Running, Too Scared to Stop.* It is my kind of book born from the depth of painful human experience and forged in the quest for life's meaning. I consider this one of a new breed of books which is ushering in a renewed consciousness. I call this renewed consciousness *"deep democracy."*

Deep democracy is not a new phenomena. It is part of every great spiritual tradition, the part which teaches nonjudgmental sharing and the utter uniqueness of every single being.

What is new about deep democracy is its challenge to the old monarchal patriarchal cosmology that has ruled the west for centuries. The monarchal cosmology is hierarchal and based on authoritative power. It spawns rigid belief systems which demand the conformity of one's mind and will to the mind and will of the authority, whomever that authority may be. Monarchal patriarchy also demands the repression of all emotions save fear which becomes for many (the militia movement) the paranoid fear of authority.

Paradoxically, participatory democracy has existed with monarchal patriarchy, but deep democracy cannot. Because of its emphasis on individual uniqueness, deep democracy demands the critical examination of belief systems and challenges all adjectival modifiers that attempt to define a mysterious unique human being.

Many of us are waking up from this patriarchal trance and are exercising our right to practice the "examined life." Many of us have found that the belief systems we have defined ourselves by are shame-based and narrow fueling a vicious cycle of self-hate which pushes us away from ourselves in a frantic attempt to achieve and acquire more and more. I describe this as becoming a "human doing" rather than "being a human being." Joyce Patenaude describes it as *Too Tired to Keep Running, Too Scared to Stop.*

If you are too tired of running, but too scared to stop, this book will help to transform your beliefs about yourself. Since we are limited by our beliefs, it will help us discover the negative beliefs that hold us prisoners.

Joyce's book is rich with clear, precise and practical exercises that you can do to challenge and change your own belief system. Remember that belief governs all other systems. My boss didn't like or trust himself and projected that on others. He had never learned what wise people have taught for generations–that all love begins with self-love and respect.

I promise you this is a transformational book that can bring you new and exciting beliefs about yourself and the world. It is chock-full of treasures that are fully within each person's reach. The joy that comes from honest effort and discovery awaits you. On your part, you do have to make a commitment by not just reading the book, but also by doing the exercises Joyce suggests. This is a small price to pay for personal transformation. Keep in mind that these exercises are not contrived clinical fictions. They were born from the pain of a terrible car accident with the debilitating depression and sense of loss that follows such a trauma.

In short this book is a journey to self-worth and freedom tested in the fires of experience. Every page celebrates the new life each of us can have when we, as Joseph Campbell puts it, drop the dragons of should, ought and must. Start reading. Believe me you won't be able to stop until you're finished.

JOHN BRADSHAW
April 30, 1998

INTRODUCTION

On June 4, 1978, my life underwent a radical change when I made a left-hand turn into the path of a speeding car. The speed at which my personal life had been moving came to a sudden, screeching halt.

Before that June day, my life was frantic. I was teaching in the evenings, developing a psychotherapy practice, and going to graduate school to finish my master's degree. I was always exhausted. If I did anything for pleasure, I was too tired to enjoy myself. I felt constantly overwhelmed. Besides the external pressure, I had an internal pressure that pushed me to achieve perfection in every area of my life.

That feeling of external and internal pressure had been there for as long as I could remember, along with a deeper feeling of inadequacy and never measuring up. I believed that I always had to prove my worth. And I had learned to do more, give more, acquire more, achieve more, and have more at the expense of my own health and sanity. Yet no matter what I did, it was still never enough. I lived in a pattern of my own making that I could never seem to understand or resolve.

The major head trauma that I sustained from the accident totally transformed my life. For months I could remember very little. It was as if the slate of my mind and brain had been wiped clean. I had no memory of events even five minutes before. I forgot how to do simple things. I was filled with anxiety and fear during the day and terror and nightmares every night. I will always be grateful to my therapist, Dr. Hugh Beaton, who supported me through the darkness of my soul's journey.

For the next two years, I struggled to recover. I found myself frightened of many things that I previously could handle with relative ease. I avoided any experience I felt I could not cope with. Being with strangers or in a crowd filled me with overwhelming anxiety. Talking to people brought up fears because the words weren't always there and my memory often failed me. I could no longer teach or work as a psychotherapist. Riding in a car filled me with terror. Shopping in a mall, even a market, brought me to tears. The only way I felt safe was to be alone. I lived in the moment and prayed unceasingly. And when I was able to write, I found great comfort making entries in my journal.

While I was healing physically and emotionally, I began to unravel my own destructive patterns of beliefs. In my journal writing, I recognized the limiting beliefs I had about myself. What was it in me that kept telling me to do more and to achieve more? Though my parents no longer had an influence on my life, I could constantly hear messages in my head—messages from them and from others about every area of my life. I had to be perfect, attractive, smart, and a good cook. I had to keep a perfect house, be a great therapist, and have money and material things. Somehow, all my life I had always felt I wasn't enough.

The accident stripped me of the energy I had previously used to fill my constant self-demands. I could now turn my focus and energy inward. I began to keep a False Belief notebook about all the limiting beliefs I had about myself and about others. I wrote in it daily, and each day I discovered new things about myself of which I had been unaware. Night after night, I had dreams and recorded them the next morning. Some deeper part of me was directing me toward a wonderful discovery. And in my writings I experienced Divine revelations and clarity about life itself.

In time I recognized that I had created a blueprint made up of false beliefs about what I should and ought to be. The blueprint wasn't me; it really wasn't even about me. It came from those who I had trusted, and I *believed* it was mine. It was during this recovery and discovery period that the title of this book came to me. Throughout my life, I had been too tired to keep running and too scared to stop. The accident stopped me. Though the experience was the most painful one in my life, it was also a wake-up call and a precious gift to me.

When I was well enough to practice psychotherapy again, my life had changed. Self-discovery held new meaning for me. In my clients I saw the same unfulfilling drive that had kept me running and afraid to stop. Like me, each of them longed for something that made sense in her or his life. Their self-discovery brought them to recognize the limiting beliefs that made up their blueprint, and gradually their lives began to change. They could now stop running, face the fears that their belief blueprint triggered, and make sense of their lives.

Our natural state is one of peace, joy, and happiness, of contentment and fulfillment. Yet most of us never experience this state. Neither did our parents, and subsequently they created an environment for us that did not nurture this experience. We continue to live as if stress, suffering, and pain is our natural state. Each of us must ask, What is it that I am doing to block the natural flow of joy and peace in my life? A river has a natural flow. If we block this natural flow, it will become stagnant and polluted, or the intense stress created by the block will in time cause a tremendous breakdown. The internal collection of toxic waste will be expressed as a powerful energy force that brings about illness, accidents, and disease.

We are born whole and filled with potential, with innate gifts that are like seeds waiting to germinate and grow. To develop these gifts, we must depend on our caregivers and their environment. The environment we grow in, however, does not always nurture and support these gifts. Our caregivers have their own agenda and nurture us in the only way they know how. Their agenda is made up of beliefs that came from the cultural, religious, and social environment in which they were raised. These beliefs have been passed down from generation to generation.

Because our caregivers provide the only world we know, we come to believe and assimilate what they believe. Even as adults, we continue to adapt to our world as we did when we were children. We continue to believe that who we are is determined by an external authority and that we must live up to its expectations. When the pain becomes intolerable and our adaptation skills no longer work, out of desperation we seek new mates, new careers, and so forth, hoping that the changes will bring us what we long for. But eventually we find ourselves back in the "same old, same old." We are changing horses on a merry-go-round when what we really need to do is get off. The problem is, we don't know how. *We are too tired to keep running and too scared to stop.*

What can we do? First, know that change is possible. We can change our negative, limiting beliefs that make up our core blueprint, which tells us that we are *not enough.* To break these negative patterns requires a shift in consciousness. It necessitates jumping off the merry-go-round with a willingness to let go of everything in order to find ourselves. But it is not a journey without risks. We must leave behind familiar places and move into the unknown. Change never happens overnight. Self-discovery takes time.

Twenty years ago, I knew that someday I would write about my own journey. In 1987 I met my husband, André, and decided to make room in my life for him. My journals, stacked on top of one another, were now more than three feet high. I decided to throw them away knowing that what I had learned through them could never be lost. *Too Tired to Keep Running, Too Scared to Stop* is a composite of my many hours of personal journaling about my healing path and the journeys of my clients and students. To protect their privacy, their names have been changed, and some are amalgams of those who carry similar wounds. I am grateful for the fulfilling and healing relationships I have developed with my clients and students. Sometimes I am not sure who is the mentor and who is the student, as I have had the privilege of growing and learning in each of these special encounters.

My goal in this book and in the transformational workshops that I will be presenting with my husband, André, is to bring awareness to those who are tired of running and want to stop. If they are ready to change their limiting beliefs, they can change their lives. I have written *Too Tired to Keep Running* to share my knowledge and experience that came from self-discovery in order to help others in their own self-discovery. This book is really an autobiography. It is not only my story, however; it is a story to which all of us can relate.

In these pages, I wish to help others find what they long for: the true self that is buried under generations of beliefs. Chapter 1 launches the reader on the path of self-discovery by explaining the core belief blueprint that is in each of us. In chapter 2, I address how our limiting beliefs create our personal reality. Chapters 3 and 4 focus on cultural, societal and familial beliefs about men and women and how they in turn affect our own attitudes about the sexes. The beliefs we bring to relationships and marriage, and how our impulse to love and be loved is affected by them, are examined in chapter 5. In chapter 6, I explore the family system, uncovering patterns we learn in childhood. The mind-body connection and how our beliefs help us adapt to stress and crisis is the subject of chapter 7, and the world of work and careers is examined in chapter 8. Chapter 9, on how our lives are affected by religion and spirituality, lays the foundation for the final chapter, which emphasizes that once we recognize and embrace our positive and negative beliefs, we can then embark on a return to wholeness—our true selves.

For clarity and change to happen in our lives, we must each do our own work. At the end of each chapter are various exercises that serve as a series of helpful guideposts on the journey to self-discovery. For example, the reader will learn how to explore limiting beliefs from childhood, how to start a False Belief notebook, how to communicate more effectively, and how to create a vision for life.

Awareness is the beginning of change. The change will happen when we explore and examine our past, our family of origin, our childhood experiences and our decisions, and return to wholeness. The next step is to commit daily to living our lives free of crippling limiting beliefs so we can be liberated to be who we really are. As Socrates said, "The unexamined life is not worth living."

The journey we take must be our own. To take this journey, we must trust that we will always know *what* we need to know, *when* we need to know it. The answers to life's questions exist within ourselves. It is an individual quest. It is the hero's journey.

Chapter 1

OUR CORE BELIEF BLUEPRINT:
A Guide to Self-Discovery

Sharon is in her early forties and married with two children. Throughout our session she's agitated and anxious, and sighs continuously.

"I'm so bored with my life," she begins. Then she adds, "It's more than just boredom."

"Bored with what?" I ask.

"Everything!" she blurts out. "Especially David! We've been married for fifteen years."

She says it as if it were an eternity.

"What about David?" I ask.

"I feel stuck and trapped. I've been thinking of leaving him. Thinking seriously about it."

"Tell me more."

"I can't stand it anymore. I want to leave, but I'm scared. Part of me feels like I should stay. What will happen to my two kids? And if I leave, what will I do? I feel so confused, so scared."

After a moment of silence, Sharon starts to cry. We've been over this before. Sharon is confused and unclear about her priorities. She doesn't know what she wants and doesn't know what to do.

In many respects, Sharon is quite comfortable. She has a lovely home, two kids in private school, a new car, weekly lunches with girlfriends, a "perfect" body and a beautiful wardrobe. On the one hand, she admits she has everything she thought she wanted and believes she'd be a fool to leave it all behind. On the other hand, she is miserable. Sex with her husband is rare these days, as infrequent as she can get by with, and whenever they do have sex, it's joyless and unsatisfactory.

Sharon believes the source of her unhappiness is her relationship with David. She is always finding fault with him and sees him as lacking. Although David has provided her with everything she has, she is resentful because she feels obligated as a result.

Her dissatisfaction has launched her on a search. She buys tapes and books on self-discovery and personal development. Many of her days are filled with spiritual and self-help lectures, workshops and seminars. In fact, it was at one of these seminars that Sharon met Richard. He seemed attracted to her, and that made her feel good about herself. A telephone relationship with Richard evolved. Over time, it became intimate and sexual.

Richard's home is a long distance from Sharon's. They talk every day. Usually Sharon is uncomfortable talking about herself, even with her husband. But with Richard, it feels easy and safe. He listens to her and validates her. He seems to care about her. They share sexual fantasies on the phone while mutually masturbating. She soon began to structure her life around the calls. Their relationship has become an addiction, obsessive as well as gratifying. Lately they have been fantasizing about becoming more deeply involved.

Meanwhile, her marriage to David is falling apart. She has stopped trying to make it work. It's too much effort, she says. Yet she feels guilty—close to panic sometimes. And this morning, just before she left for our session, David asked her about the phone bill.

■

Paul, a prominent and successful physician, attended the best colleges and medical schools and now shares a thriving practice with two other doctors. Married with three children, Paul has accumulated a battery of worldly goods that bespeak success: a big house in an upper-middle-class neighborhood, expensive cars and private school for his kids. He has all the accoutrements of wealth, yet he hates his life. In our session, he says that at times he feels like "just walking away from it all." His responsibilities at home and at work overwhelm him. He feels burned out and wants to stop and to try to make sense of his life, but he fears stopping because his world as he knows it will fall apart.

"Empty" is the word Paul often uses in our sessions. Again and again he says, "My life is so empty. I feel constant pressure and dissatisfaction, a feeling that never goes away. I have everything, and yet I feel empty inside."

Paul admits he has developed a drug habit. As a doctor, it's easy for him to get drugs. He takes sleeping pills at night, uppers during the day, antidepressants and other drugs to keep him going and to block the emotional pain. The drugs seemed to work for a while, but lately they have left him feeling even more unfulfilled and empty.

I ask him if he remembers ever feeling fulfilled.

He hesitates, searching his memory. "I remember my happiest time was when I was a teenager at camp. It was great. I felt at one with nature."

Then he smiles sadly. "That was over thirty years ago."

■

There have been many changes in Lora's life over the past few years, but to her everything always seems the same. A few years ago her company transferred her to New York from her hometown in the Midwest. Now she's been transferred again, this time to Los Angeles. A new city, a new apartment, perhaps a new start—but the same old problems arise.

Lora is employed by a large public relations agency and enjoys her work. She arrives early, stays late and occasionally works on weekends, but she feels her bosses take advantage of her. Yet she never says no to extra work. And though she wants a raise and feels she deserves it, she's afraid to ask for it.

Away from the office, Lora's life is the same as it was in New York. She hasn't made friends, and it seems as though she doesn't know how. She feels safer alone in her apartment, watching television and eating to fill the emptiness inside her. She's severely overweight but thinks it would take too much effort to do anything about it.

Lora tells me that she wants friends and that she wants a special man in her life—"a special man like Bob was." She often talks about Bob, the things they did together, the moments they shared. She can even repeat entire conversations they had; it's all very clear in her mind. Bob left her for someone else eight years ago, and Lora still feels depressed and hopeless. Now she is thirty-eight years old, and she wonders if there will ever be another Bob.

Sharon, Paul and Lora have much in common. Obviously, they are unsatisfied with their lives, they are miserable and they feel helpless. What may be less obvious is the fact that they are all miserable for the same reasons. I know this because, in more than twenty years of practice as a psychotherapist, I have worked with hundreds of clients and students who shared the same inner pain and longing for fulfillment. I know this because for a long time I was frustrated and unfulfilled in much the same way. In this chapter, I am going to show you the real source of this dissatisfaction. And I am going to show you how you can heal the pain of dissatisfaction. Sharon, Paul and Lora are now opening themselves to finding joy, satisfaction and fulfillment in their lives. We can all find the same joy, satisfaction and fulfillment in our lives, no matter how difficult or far-reaching it might appear.

MY LIFE'S BELIEFS

In the introduction to this book, I talk about the car accident that changed my life. My car was totaled in the head-on collision, and I was knocked unconscious and sustained severe head trauma. For two months, everything was a blur. I was completely disoriented and no longer able to teach or see clients. For the next two years, I struggled to reconstruct my life, but I never was able to put it back together the way it had been. The world I had known was changed forever.

Before the accident, my life had been filled with ever-increasing stress and pressure. A few years earlier I had ended a marriage that had left me feeling burned out. I was still experiencing a lot of guilt over my decision to leave my mate and felt like a failure. I had done everything I knew how to do to make the marriage work. Now I carried that fear of failure into every potential relationship. I believed there must be either something wrong with me, or something wrong with the people I selected.

At the time of the car accident, I was teaching classes at night, attending graduate school and starting a psychotherapy practice. I felt constantly overwhelmed and exhausted. It seemed I was about always trying to prove something, and I wasn't sure what it was. Just surviving became a struggle. I lived with a constant fear of failure and hoped that somehow everything would be fine when I achieved my goals—even though I didn't know what those goals were.

I knew a great deal about psychology, but throughout my life I knew very little about myself. I always had the feeling everyone else knew more about me than I did: my parents, teachers and others who seemed to have authority. In fact, I lived in fear of exposing myself to anyone because I believed they would judge me. I felt as if I had something to hide, and again, I wasn't sure what it was. I pretended a lot. I thought I would learn who I was by getting a college education and reading a flurry of academic and self-help books. But no matter how many classes and lectures I went to or how much I studied or read, I never seemed to reach a clear understanding of myself. At that point I didn't realize that life's lessons are the best teacher.

The constant drive to prove myself had always been a part of me. As long as I could remember, I had feelings of inadequacy and of *not being good enough.* I pretended to others and, at times, even to myself that those feelings weren't there. I felt like a horse constantly whipped by its rider to go faster and jump higher. No matter how much I accomplished, I still never felt good enough. It wasn't for lack of trying, though. I did all the right things, was educated, dressed attractively, kept my body in shape, dated interesting men, had many friends and worked hard, but still there was something missing. To others I appeared self-sufficient and "together," but inside I felt empty and desperate. Gradually, through my own inner discovery, I realized that my despair was not about *not being good enough,* it was about *not being enough,* period.

I longed for fulfillment and peace of mind, but it seemed to elude me. There were moments of contentment and joy, however. I went to church and prayed. I'd find solace in my prayers and in the spiritual music. I studied yoga and began to meditate. It felt great—for a while. My painting, drawing and sculpting always brought me joy. There were moments I spent in nature when I felt truly at one with everything around me. I'd even had mystical experiences that held no explanation, experiences that gave me momentary bliss. But the contentment didn't last. I always had to do something, achieve something or have something in order to feel good about myself.

When I hit that other car, some part of me died. It was the death of the old and the birth of the new. I was scared. I had no idea what would happen next. This experience was an unknown for me. I lived with the fear of surviving. I was in an utter state of confusion. What's more, I could no longer sustain my abilities, defenses and adaptations that had kept me from feeling my fears and inadequacies.

Perhaps my story is familiar to you. Perhaps you are striving to find your way, pushing and driving yourself to exhaustion and feeling unfulfilled and hopeless. Or perhaps you are on an aimless path trying to find answers and feeling desperate, as if you're going nowhere and possibly even sabotaging yourself. Sometimes it takes a major crisis to wake us up: a traumatic accident, an illness that seems to take over our lives, the end of a loving relationship, the death of a relative or a dear friend, an addiction that gets out of control, or the loss of a career built over the course of a lifetime.

TWO MESSAGES, A NETWORK OF BELIEFS

What is it that pushes us, drives us, yet denies us the fulfillment and happiness we so desperately need and want? What is it that makes us give up out of sheer frustration and stop trying? In my own life, and in working with hundreds of clients and students, I have discovered two inner messages—messages that keep us searching but never finding. These fateful messages are learned early in life, and they leave our souls branded as if by a hot iron:

You are not enough just the way you are.

and

If you follow certain paths, they will lead you to being enough.

These messages are programmed into our subconscious mind. We accept them as truths in early childhood, even in infancy. They leave us feeling unworthy, inadequate, lacking and at times hopeless that we will ever measure up. They are the foundation for all our limiting and negative beliefs. They were passed down to us from our parents, who received them from their parents before them, and they are found in every culture and society.

Our very existence is darkened by these limiting beliefs. They remind us constantly that we are *not enough*. They generate feelings of powerlessness, helplessness, hopelessness and shame. Whenever we succeed at something, these beliefs cheat us out of our success by reminding us of what we are lacking. Whenever we fail, these messages tell us we don't deserve to succeed. For a while, we may be able to block these beliefs and the feelings they create, but when we least expect it, the messages resurface, along with the pain.

We avoid exploring these negative messages about ourselves because we are afraid of discovering that they might be true. In order to deal with these fears, we develop a false self. We hide our fears and pretend they don't exist because we believe that if others ever found out how inadequate we really are, they would abandon us, and we would be shamed. We then adapt to these beliefs by either doing more or doing less. Eventually we become exhausted trying to prove our worth and overwhelmed with fear to stop trying.

Core Belief Blueprint

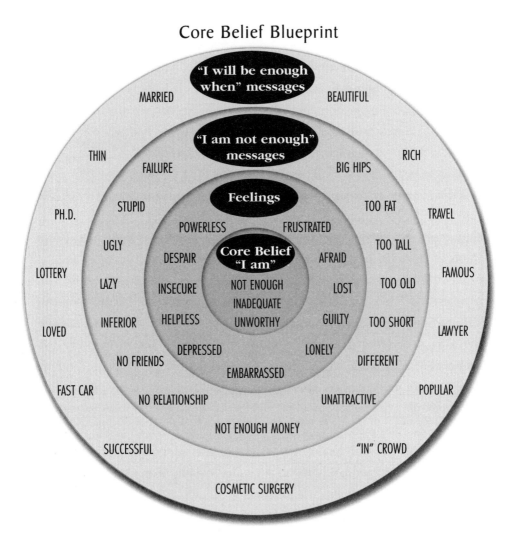

Figure 1 shows a blueprint of our limiting beliefs. From richest to poorest, from most successful to least successful, each of us has such a blueprint. At the center is our core belief of our "not enoughness." The second circle represents feelings generated from this core belief. The third circle displays the messages of our limiting beliefs that support the core belief. The outer circle contains the messages that bombard us internally and externally, telling us how to "be enough." This is our blueprint of life. It creates our personal reality and is the foundation for our present life's experiences.

Though the original messages that formed our core belief and limiting beliefs may have been long forgotten, we continue to send similar messages to ourselves through our thoughts, interpretations, assumptions, judgments, ideas, prejudices and in our inner voice and self-talk. We become so conditioned by these messages that we are no longer aware that they are there. They cover up our real self and our wholeness like clouds cover the sun. Soon we begin to feel a longing, even if we don't always know why. We long to connect with our self and our wholeness, that place within us that holds our true potential, that deep part of ourselves from which we separated long ago. We believe there is something basically wrong with us and that we need to be fixed. *The truth is, there is nothing to fix.*

SUSAN

When Susan first began seeing me, she said her life was "a mess." She felt hopeless that it would ever change. Fear that her world was collapsing and the belief that she had to "keep it together" kept her in a constant state of anxiety. She believed she was at the mercy of a hostile world she could no longer control. When I asked her to describe her life, she said she was a "survivor." But she wanted more from life than just surviving.

After several sessions of therapy, Susan began to realize that her pain and frustration were not about her relationship with her boyfriend, John. Nor were they about her job, which she hated, or her boss, who abused her. Throughout her life here had been a continuing negative pattern of relationships and jobs. Each would start out promising and end in disappointment. Susan blamed herself and thought there was something wrong with her because she could not find fulfillment and satisfaction. She also blamed her parents, an alcoholic, abusive father and a needy mother. She was confused and discouraged.

Susan felt helpless because she didn't know how to get what she wanted. She had a good education, stayed physically fit and contributed greatly to both her job and her relationships, but still she believed something was terribly wrong with her. Feeling empty and burned out, Susan wanted to give up. She didn't have the strength to endure the same frustrating experiences over and over.

In our sessions, as Susan began to pull on the thread of her despair and confusion, free of judgment and blame, she unraveled many limiting beliefs about herself that had been with her as long as she could remember. She recalled an incident at Christmastime when she was five years old. She had wanted a bike, and she had wanted one for a long time. All of the other kids in the neighborhood had bikes. Susan waited anxiously for her father to come home with presents for the whole family, but he didn't come home for three days. There were no gifts because he'd spent the money on alcohol. Her mother broke down crying. When Susan told her mother how upset she was about not getting a bike, her mother responded angrily, "What's wrong with you? Can't you see how upset I am? You are selfish and inconsiderate and think only of yourself." Susan felt ashamed and guilty.

More beliefs unraveled. Whenever Susan's parents gave her something, they reminded her that they were making a sacrifice for her and that "you'd better be good enough to deserve it." She felt like a burden. She felt anxiety about asking for what she wanted because it always had strings attached. Soon she stopped asking. It felt better to get nothing.

Susan also remembered many times standing next to her mother at the window, waiting for her father to come home, comforting her mother and reassuring her. She became the "good girl" and the caregiver at a very young age.

At my encouragement, Susan began keeping a False Belief notebook (see the exercises at the end of this chapter). In it, she wrote comments, judgments and criticisms she made to others about herself. She started listening to her critical inner voice and wrote down what she said about herself: *"My thighs are too big," "I look awful today in this outfit," "I really am inadequate and I hope others won't notice," "Others are smarter than me."* After a few weeks, she was amazed at how many times a day she reminded herself of the false and limiting beliefs she held. As she explored where those messages came from, she often heard one of her parents' voices in her self-talk, mostly her mother's. She began to write daily in her personal journal (separate from her False Belief notebook) about her feelings, what she did when she had those feelings and how she adapted to them. In therapy we dialogued with the adapted parts, the false self, that she created to survive: *the People Pleaser, the Good Girl, the Critic, the Caregiver.* Susan also dialogued with those parts in her journal.

Over time, Susan realized that the beliefs she carried from childhood were the source of her discomfort, frustration and pain. She carried hundreds of false beliefs about herself and her world: "Other people are more important than me; don't make waves; if I speak up for what I want, I will be shamed and abandoned; if I report my feelings, others will invalidate me and may even punish me; I don't deserve to get what I want in life; something about me isn't OK; I have to prove my worth." This was her blueprint. At the core was a basic feeling of inadequacy and unworthiness. She had made many decisions in childhood that she had never explored or corrected as an adult: "I will never get what I want unless I am perfect enough, good enough, smart enough or attractive enough." "Other people always come first, and to have what I want I must put others first." "I can never measure up."

The process of changing limiting beliefs is gradual and takes time and commitment. An awareness of our core belief blueprint and how we adapt to it marks the beginning of this process. It isn't about fixing something that is wrong with us; it is about revealing the truth that lies under the blueprint of limiting beliefs. It is like laundering to remove the dirt that hides our true fabric.

When Susan became aware of the power her limiting beliefs had over her life, she began to change. One of the changes she made was to validate herself and her feelings. She began asking others for what she wanted. It was difficult at first, but it became easier as people responded positively to her. She left her job because she was no longer willing to work in an abusive environment; it sacrificed her integrity. Susan began trusting that she could become a successful screenwriter, something she had always wanted to be. Until then, she had always believed someone else would make things happen for her if only she was *good enough, smart enough and perfect enough.* When she discovered there was nothing to overcome, she let go of old, limiting beliefs and self-sabotaging behaviors, like being the Caregiver and the People Pleaser, and her life began to change. She sold a screenplay. And, as she began to have a loving relationship with herself, her relationship with John became closer and more intimate.

HOW FALSE BELIEFS DEVELOP

The longing for contentment, fulfillment and satisfaction is inherent in every human being. We long for a peace and joy that we vaguely remember once feeling. As infants, we experienced a wholeness and a oneness with the world. We felt bliss and joy just being alive. Each of us was and is filled with a unique potential, innate gifts like seeds waiting to germinate and grow. The environment we grew up in did not always nurture and support our unique gifts, however. Our caregivers had an agenda for us even before we were born, an agenda made up of their own beliefs that came from the culture, society and religion in which they lived. They passed these beliefs down to us as a blueprint that we unconsciously accepted.

As infants, our bliss was soon replaced with messages of what was expected of us. Very early in life, we learned what was acceptable and what was unacceptable, what was good and what was bad to our parents. We learned that to survive in our parents' world, we must abandon a part of ourselves and hold their beliefs as ours. To do that, we had to split off from that part of us that felt bliss, joy and contentment. This caused a rupture in our development. We never forgot that part of ourselves that held our innate wisdom and joy, and unconsciously we long to return to it.

By the age of seven, we have become conditioned and have assimilated and internalized our parents' beliefs and the beliefs from their culture, society and religion. The messages that carry these beliefs are both explicit and implicit. We get them from our parents, relatives and siblings, in religious and nonreligious settings and from our teachers and peers. Messages bombard us from the television we watch and the stories we read. Like sponges, we absorb everything, and soon we become so conditioned that we are unaware that these beliefs control our lives.

Most of us carry these unexamined beliefs into our adult lives. We live in bodies that look grown-up, but inside we are children with an unresolved clarity of who and what we really are. We continue to follow the same beliefs from childhood that tell us we are *not enough.* Desperately seeking financial success, power positions, fame, material accumulations, relationships and academic achievements, we discover that the emptiness remains. Under it all, we still feel inadequate and *not enough.*

Even as adults, we still adapt like children, complying to some amorphous external authority whom we believe will reward us if we do enough, give enough or try harder, so that at last we will *be enough.* Or, we rebel against authority, known and often unknown, only to find that after the rebellion is over we have achieved nothing. Or, as many do, we give up: We settle for empty relationships and dead-end jobs, barely existing, becoming depressed, ill, helpless and hopeless, waiting for someone to come along and rescue us, or we turn to alcohol or drugs, contemplate suicide or perhaps even end up on the streets.

We gave away our power and authority as children before we knew we even had any. This is how we survived—by trusting an external authority. As adults, however, we continue to give our power away to those we consider superiors—bosses, the corporations we work for, leaders, managers, religious figures—believing that through them we will be knighted into our own power. But it never happens, and we continue to feel powerless, inadequate and helpless.

Our feelings are triggered by our beliefs. Feelings, then, are actually information that can lead us to discovering the limiting and false beliefs we have about ourselves and our world. Our feelings are reactions to deeper messages we tell ourselves about the events in our lives. It isn't the events that cause our reactions, it is the beliefs that we have about the event.

All behavior is based on beliefs: If our core belief is "I am not good enough," it will be demonstrated in our actions. If we believe we must be the CEO of a large corporation in order to find our worth, we will act accordingly. If our belief is "I must be thin enough, attractive enough to be accepted," we will do everything to be thin enough and attractive enough, or we will hate ourselves for not doing everything we think we should. But when is enough enough?

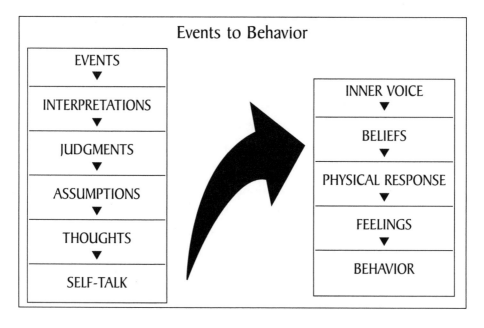

Figure 2 shows how events lead to behavior. The events in our lives are catalysts that trigger inner and outer reactions. These reactions come from how we interpret and view the event. They cover up our beliefs, opinions and judgments about the event. Often the events reopen old wounds from childhood and bring up old fears and insecurities.

If we continue to live in this constant reactive state, it will in time compromise our health, our relationships and our lives. At some point we begin to experience difficulties. We feel overwhelmed and confused.

The stresses of our life are manifested in depression, anxiety, high blood pressure, heart problems and disease. We feel out of control. Sometimes we reach a total breakdown and are filled with terror. Our careers and jobs are unfulfilling, and our marriages are abusive or emotionally dead. We live with the belief that if only "I had more money, had chosen differently, had a better education, was younger, prettier or thinner, someone would discover me." We scramble for answers. We decide to change our situation or seek intervention, hoping to get our life back in control.

Out of desperation, we change jobs, seek new mates, look for new gurus and teachers, immerse ourselves in old religions that we no longer practice or find new religions, hoping that they will bring us the desired results. We decide we need to lose weight, join a gym or get plastic surgery. And we long to feel contentment and joy. For a while, the changes may make a difference. But in time we are back in the "same old same old," because we carry our old belief blueprint into our new experiences. The Bible says we can't put new wine into old bottles. Changing external experiences is like changing horses on a merry-go-round, when what we really need to do is get off. Unfortunately, we don't know how to stop our emotional feelings and behavioral patterns that keep us going round and round.

We seek out doctors, therapists, healers and psychics, hoping they have the answers. But even if they do, we filter the answers through our limiting belief system. We try herbs, vitamins and prescription drugs. We drink more or less, stop smoking, go on diets, start exercising, take up hobbies, golf, play tennis or go back to school. We try everything we can think of to rid ourselves of the pain we are experiencing. That pain is a symptom, however, and to ignore or remove it is like removing the warning light on the dashboard of our car. Until we let go of our old limiting blueprint of beliefs, the symptoms will remain, and we will exhaust ourselves running on a treadmill going nowhere.

Often we will get caught up in blaming men, women, our parents, our culture, former lovers, advertisers, the commercial world, the corporate world, religion and so on. If we blame others for our problems, we will find friends and groups to support our blaming, and the cycle will remain unbroken. If we blame ourselves, the cycle of pain and despair will still continue. Blame only drives us further away from finding the answers.

Support groups form around pathological behaviors that are really symptoms: "I am an alcoholic, a drug addict, a codependent, an overeater, an anorexic, a neurotic." This is who we believe we are, so we learn to modify our behavior and form what is called *symptom substitution*. We substitute old behaviors for new behaviors as a way of creating more acceptable adaptations to the same old problems. But the source of the pain and problem remains untapped, and the sense that there is something deeper that needs to be healed continues to haunt us. We can no longer ignore our problems, have someone else take responsibility for them or wait for them to magically disappear, for the messages will only get louder, and the pain and discomfort will only increase.

DIGGING DEEPER: THE JOURNEY TO SELF-DISCOVERY

Our psyche is that part of us that constantly works to bring us back to wholeness, to heal the wounds that were created when we abandoned ourselves in childhood. We will be attracted to experiences that give us the information we need. The answers always lie in the problem. We just need to learn how to decipher the hidden messages in our experiences and the reactions we have to them: our self-talk, interpretations, feelings, emotions and behavior. This discovery will expose the underlying beliefs that keep us stuck, chasing wearily after pipe dreams. It can open doors to the revelation of our true self.

Remember, there is nothing to fix. To change what we perceive as imperfection does not mean we need to achieve a believed perfection. *The opposite of imperfection is not perfection; it is wholeness.* We can return to our wholeness. It will be revealed to us when the cloud of limiting beliefs has been cleared away. To break the negative patterns in our life requires a shift in consciousness, a jumping off the merry-go-round with a willingness to let go of everything in order to find ourselves. The journey to self-discovery is one we must take alone. It is not a journey without risks. We must leave behind familiar places and people and move into an unknown. And we must keep in mind that change never happens overnight; it is a process. Self-discovery, once it is achieved, will lead to our wholeness and offer us an opportunity to express our true gifts and manifest our potential, the potential that was there before we were born.

To find a way out of our conflict, we must find a way in. First, we must realize that each of us is exactly where we are supposed to be, and that this place is neither good nor bad. There are precious gifts and lessons to be revealed in all of our experiences. The journey to self-discovery requires looking nonjudgmentally at where we are now. We need a map to show us not only our destination, but also our starting point. The exercise that follows will help you get started. The path to wholeness and potential has always been there—we just lost our way.

Next, we must remove the obstacles to finding our way by examining our core belief blueprint (see figure 1). If we have the desire and the intent to free ourselves from the prison of our false beliefs, we can. And if we have the courage to let go of the false self we developed in reaction to our belief blueprint, we can open the possibility of experiencing the joy, contentment, peace and well-being that is our natural state. We each have our own gifts that have been covered up by someone else's agenda. Change is possible for all of us. It means, however, that we must move from an unconscious to a conscious way of living, from being reactive to being intentional. It is our personal hero's journey.

EXERCISES

Making changes in your life involves more than just reading about it. You must do your own work by evaluating where you are now and exploring your limiting beliefs.

WHERE ARE YOU NOW?

To make changes, you first must be aware of your present life experiences. How do you prioritize your life? Time awareness gives you clues to living your life fully. Using a 1 to 10 scale (1 lowest, 10 highest), evaluate how much time and energy you spend in the eight different areas of your life listed below. Some of these areas will overlap. Write the numbers on a separate sheet of paper.

1. Self (time alone, relaxing, resting, contemplating, reading, writing, journaling, listening to music).

2. Family (wife, husband, children, parents, siblings).

3. Friends (socializing, partying, sharing, talking in person and on the phone).

4. Work (job, career, profession, education, housekeeping, parenting responsibilities).

5. Pleasure (playing, creating, hobbies, games, movies, theater, classes, vacations).

6. Spirituality (prayer, meditation, church or synagogue, spiritual reading, retreats).

7. Health (emotional, mental and physical—diet, massages, therapy, regular checkups, health seminars and retreats, reading).

8. Exercise (walking, running, jogging, swimming, biking, skiing, golfing).

On the following diagram, place a dot on each line corresponding to the number you wrote down. Connect the dots.

Now repeat the same exercise, this time using the 1 to 10 scale to evaluate the fulfillment you have in the same eight areas. Use a different color to record the dots on the diagram, or circle the previous dot if the number is the same. Again, connect the dots.

Imagine a wheel that is shaped like your time/energy chart. How far could you travel on it? If the connected dots form a circle your life is closer in balance. To create a healthy and fulfilling life we must create balance. We must invest our time and energy in things that fulfill us. *Your beliefs determine how you spend your time and energy.* If for

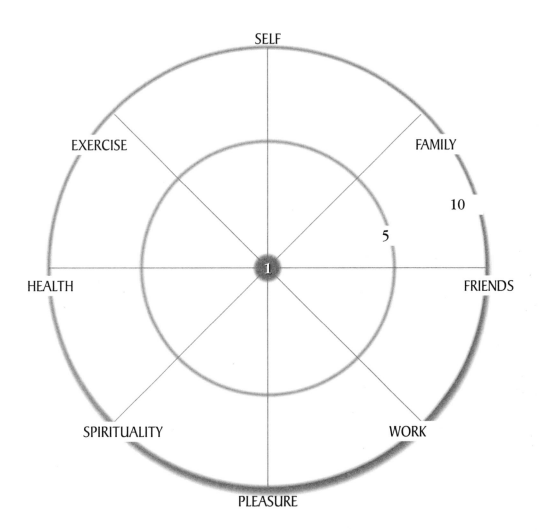

example, on the work scale you are close to a 10 on how you spend your time and a 3 for fulfillment it is time to evaluate your beliefs.

FALSE BELIEF NOTEBOOK

Start a False Belief notebook, recording all the false beliefs you have about yourself and others as you become aware of them, including limiting beliefs gleaned from the following exercises. Any spiral-bound notebook will do, or you can purchase a more elegant journal or blank book at a bookstore.

SELF-KNOWLEDGE INVENTORY

■ Circle the "Not Enough Messages" that apply to you.

I'm not smart enough

I'm stupid

I'm dumb

I'm lazy

Other people are smarter than I am

I am inadequate

I am poor

I don't have enough money

I don't know how to make
    enough money

There is something wrong with me

I don't have a good job

I am inadequate at what I do

I am inadequate in relationships

I have no friends

I am inadequate at games or
    sports

I am not perfect enough

I am too short

I am too tall

My body isn't perfect

I am too fat

I am too thin

My breasts are too small

My thighs and hips are too big

There is something about my body
    that is not OK

My penis is too small

I don't have a good build

I am not attractive enough

My eyesight is bad, and
    I need glasses

I am bald

I am gray

I am too old

I don't look good in my clothes

I live in the wrong neighborhood

My parents were poor

My parents had little education

I came from a dysfunctional family

I am the wrong color, race
    or religion

I am different

Others are better than I am

I have disabilities that make
    me less

I have health problems

I am sick

I don't own a lot of material things

I don't drive the best car

I always fail

I always make mistakes

Others will find out I am a failure

I can never measure up

I don't deserve

[Add any other messages]

■ **Circle the feelings you have about not being enough.**

depressed • helpless • insecure • lonely • ashamed • despondent • inadequate • hopeless • sad • sick • lost • afraid of abandonment • afraid • embarrassed • ambitionless • frustrated • angry • worried • determined • hurt • devastated • pained • dumb • dense • confused • anxious • nervous • empty

[Add any other feelings]

■ **I will be enough when ... (circle the messages that apply)**

Someone loves me

I marry the right person

Someone who is rich marries me

I'm rich enough

I get the best education at the best schools

I'm a professional

I'm a doctor or lawyer

I'm the CEO of a big corporation

I have a Ph.D.

I know the right people

I have a beautiful home in the right neighborhood

I drive the right car

I have material things

I wear expensive clothes

I shop at the right places

I have the right labels (Gucci, Fendi, Jaguar)

I belong to the right clubs

I go to the "in places"

I have a perfect body

I work out enough at the gym

I have great legs

I have a big penis

I have a flat stomach

I have no cellulite on my thighs or hips

I'm good in bed

I develop a charismatic personality

I have big breasts, a small waist or small hips

I look thin like a model and wear a size 6

I have plastic surgery, a facelift or a nose job

I am young enough

I dye my hair a different color

I get over my baldness or wear a toupee

I become famous and recognized

I have power

I achieve success

I struggle hard enough

I try hard enough

I belong to the right (and only) religion

I am saved by the right religion

[Add any other messages]

■ Circle how you adapt to these beliefs. (See "The Emergence of Subpersonalities" in chapter 2 for more details.)

Example: I become a People Pleaser, and I give more.

People Pleaser	Controller	Manipulator
Victim	Victimizer	Pusher
Judge	Know-It-All	Critic
Superachiever	Good Boy or Good Girl	Bully
Caregiver	Intellectual	Snob
Show-off	Con artist	Rebel
Competitor	Recluse	Macho
Withholder	Withdraw	User
Doormat	Loner	Martyr
Pretender	Complier	Defier
Do more	Do less	Give up
Abuser	Give more	Give less
Dieter	Anorexic	Bulimic
Overeater	Sabotager	Alcoholic
Drug user	Become sarcastic	Yeller
Become homeless	Get violent	Fanatic
Behave criminally	Have fantasies	Go crazy
Prejudiced	Become depressed	Fall apart
Become neurotic	Become ill	Act pious
Act out anger	Get hysterical	Try harder
Overspend	Hoard	Lie and cheat
Have affairs	Rationalize	Have denial
Become passive	Blame others	Become cynical
Attack verbally	Analyze	Get suicidal
Bragger	Get physical	Bossy

The following questions will help you see the limiting beliefs that form your personal blueprint. Answer these questions deliberately and with careful attention. This information will be developed in further chapters.

Keep in mind that some of the messages you received were verbal, others were implied. These messages formed your "I'm not enough" core belief. *They are the basis for your thoughts, your self-talk, your interpretations, assumptions, judgments, reactions, physical responses and behaviors.*

■ "I am not enough" messages

My mother's limiting messages about me were: (Example: *You're lazy.*)

_____

_____

My father's limiting messages about me were: (Example: *You'll never amount to anything. No matter what you do, you'll never be enough.*)

_____

_____

My sibling's (or siblings') limiting messages about me were: (Example: *You're selfish and greedy.*)

_____

_____

Limiting messages from my teachers about me were: (Example: *You're stupid and don't try hard enough.*)

_____

_____

Limiting messages from my peers about me were: (Example: *You're a sissy and a crybaby.*)

_____

_____

Limiting messages from the opposite sex about me were/are: (Example: *You're too emotional and moody. You're too needy.*)

_____

_____

Limiting messages from religion about me were/are: (Example: *You're bad and a sinner. You're guilty.*)

_____

_____

Limiting messages from culture, race and society were/are: (Example: *You're not thin enough. You don't have enough money. You're skin is the wrong color.*)

_____

_____

Limiting messages I tell myself are: (Example: *I am a failure. I am inadequate. There must be something wrong with me.*)

_____

_____

■ "I'll be enough if and when" messages.

Review the not enough messages you circled on page 21 and review your answers on pages 23 and 24. Below, write down the messages that tell you what you need to do to be enough. For example: If your father's message was *You'll never amount to anything,* the verbal or implied message on how to be enough may be *People who amount to anything are smart, get good grades in school and have an education. If you want to amount to anything, you need to get all As.*

I will be enough when:

_____

_____

_____

_____

_____

■ Your Core Belief Blueprint

Fill in the worksheet below with your responses from the exercises above.

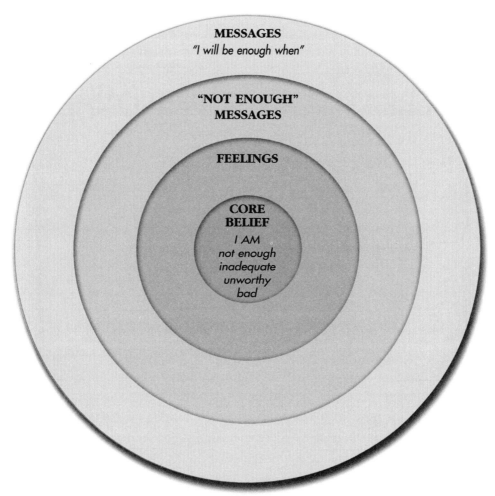

1. The core belief "I'm not enough" remains in the center circle.
2. In the second circle, write down the feelings generated by the "not enough" message on page 21.
3. In the third circle, fill in the limiting "not enough" messages from page 20 and pages 23 and 24.
4. In the fourth circle, fill in the "I will be enough when" messages from page 21 and page 24.
5. Outside of the circles, write down all your adaptive behaviors from page 22.

This is your core belief blueprint that creates your personal reality. Use it as your guide in your journey to self-discovery.

Chapter 2

CREATING OUR PERSONAL REALITY

Remember Lora from chapter 1? Although she was hoping for a fresh start, when she moved to Los Angeles she brought the same emotional baggage with her that she'd had in New York. She found similar bosses who took advantage of her. Her financial rewards were not commensurate with what she gave. She longed for friendships and a relationship but kept re-creating the same scenario that sustained her loneliness because she was ignorant of how to do anything different. Though Lora had moved thousands of miles, life for her remained the same. She felt like she had no control of her own life.

I often tell my clients the story of the panda that was brought to the United Staes from China. When the panda arrived, its compound was not yet ready. Three additional months were needed to complete a huge compound that would emulate its habitat in China. During that three-month period, the panda was placed in an $8' \times 10'$ cage. When the compound was completed, the animal was moved to its new huge surroundings. The panda, however, continued to pace in a small $8' \times 10'$ area.

We each have an internal $8' \times 10'$ space, a self-made prison of past conditioning of which we are unaware. Like Lora, we stay there because it feels familiar and gives us a false sense of security. But it is a prison filled with limiting beliefs and decisions established by our child's mind and unmended by our adult reasoning. Though we live a limitless existence with multiple choices and opportunities, we unconsciously limit our experiences by the choices we make. In each new experience we continue to re-create the same old patterns based on our previous conditioning. The limits we place on our lives come from our beliefs. This is our personal reality. To change our life, we must move out of the $8' \times 10'$ space that is our belief blueprint.

My car accident was an abrupt interruption of my $8' \times 10'$ space. My life had been filled with past conditioning that distorted my reality. I had a core belief that constantly reminded me that I wasn't enough just the way I was. I wasn't even aware that my discomfort and pain stemmed from that belief. All I knew was that I had an obsessive drive to prove myself. It pushed me to achieve more, do more, have more. And yet I was left feeling empty, unfulfilled and exhausted. The accident catapulted me into an unfamiliar space that forced me to face the fears I was running from.

HOW WE LOSE THE CONNECTION WITH OURSELVES

Each of us is born filled with the seeds of potential, free of limiting beliefs. As infants, we were free of judgment, duality, prejudices, social status, rights and wrongs and religious convictions. Our inner life force filled us with joy, peace and contentment. This was, and is, our natural state. Somewhere along the way, we lost that experience of bliss. We were helpless and dependent on our parents to care for all our needs. We experienced a natural anxiety and fear when our needs were not met and our survival was threatened. Unmet needs are perceived as a danger to our existence and create a rupture in the peaceful connection with our selves. These are our emotional wounds that were inflicted in our earliest stages of development. Though we usually have no recollection of this time in our lives, we still have a deep longing that we cannot explain. We never lose the longing; we just forget what we are longing for: that part of us that we separated from to survive.

PARENTS AS AUTHORITY FIGURES

To a child, parents are the absolute, unchallenged authority, and we model ourselves after them. When they are ignorant of their own inner wholeness and potential, they ignore our inner wholeness and potential, and we learn to do so as well. If our parents knew different, they would act different. Even though they have our best interests at heart, our parents inevitably reinforce the belief that certain parts of us are acceptable and other parts of us have to be extinguished and denied. By the time we are two years old, most of us believe something in us is *bad* or *wrong,* that we are not enough just the way we are and that something in us is unacceptable and inadequate. We spill our milk and are told we are bad. In a short period of time, the spilled milk is a reminder of our badness. It's not the *act* that is bad; we believe *we* are bad. That belief becomes our shame and reinforces our low self-worth. We are punished for being bad and rewarded for being good. Our beliefs are assimilated with the milk we drink and the pabulum we swallow. Our parents' judgments and agenda are communicated in their interactions with us. It shows on their faces. It is how they control us and probably how they were controlled by their parents. We begin to internalize their messages about us and our world. Eventually, a part of us acts and another part judges those actions.

From these early teachings, we learn to establish a hierarchy of good and bad based on our parents' beliefs, and we start to judge others as well as ourselves. Consequently, we develop a social self that meets our parents' and our world's agenda and expectations. The world, as we have learned to view it, is a dichotomy between good and bad. That view is reinforced by society, religion, education, the movies and TV. Soon, we align ourselves accordingly. Out of the fear of not measuring up to others' expectations, we develop a false self. Robbed of our spontaneity, we are no longer free to fully express who we are. This fear of being vulnerable and exposing our emotions traumatizes and paralyzes us.

By the time we are seven years old, we have already established a belief blueprint, a map for life. Unfortunately, it is not a map of our true selves. Rather, it is a map that is outdated and outmoded, and it distorts our perception of ourselves and our world. Our beliefs, perceptions, thoughts, judgments, interpretations, decisions and feelings come from this blueprint. We unconsciously follow this blueprint until we decide to update it or create a new one. The blueprint that lays the foundation for our lives is called a *paradigm*. The dictionary meaning of *paradigm* is "an example that serves as a pattern or model." To experience more options and choices in our lives and to find greater opportunities that lead to fulfillment, we must make a *paradigm shift*.

THE SELF-FULFILLING PROPHECY

Our blueprint is filled with messages about every aspect of our lives. From it we establish a complete belief system. We attract experiences that match our beliefs, or we interpret experiences based on our beliefs. This is called *selective focus*. If we believe that we have to struggle to get what we want, we will attract countless ways to struggle. If we believe we don't deserve a happy relationship, we will choose and create a relationship in which we will be unhappy. If we believe all men are users, we will attract men who are users. If we believe all women are bitches, guess what we will attract? A person who believes she is a victim will always attract a victimizer. A controlling personality will always attract someone who believes he needs to be controlled. Caregivers always find people who are in need of care. What we attract is about ourselves. It is how we create our own personal reality determined by our blueprint.

In working with couples, I have found that one attracts in the other what one has disowned in oneself. If anger is something one partner has repressed, she will attract someone whose anger is out of control. The angry partner carries the other partner's repressed anger. If we are a caregiver or enabler, the needy part of ourselves will attract that same part in others. This is the foundation of codependent relationships.

That which we dislike or even hate in others is about ourselves. All prejudices are about our disowned, hated parts that we project onto others and despise. To heal, we must own those parts in ourselves. We must learn to love and nurture the part we hate in others.

THE EGO

Let's talk for a moment about the part our ego plays. Our ego is the caregiver of our blueprint. It sits at the window of our existence, a window that looks out and looks in. What we perceive from the outer world and the inner world through our senses—hearing, seeing, tasting, touching, smelling and intuition—is what our ego relies on. Our perceptions, however, are often distorted from past conditioning and the limiting beliefs we carry. The ego connects this information to beliefs in our blueprint. Like a clerk placing mail into cubbyholes, if the information doesn't match, the ego sorts through the material to see if it is similar to something else in the blueprint. And if the information doesn't make sense, the ego discards it.

Our ego is not our true self. It is what we have learned in order to survive. It constantly tries to protect us from the things in life that threaten us by rigidly following old patterns from our belief blueprint. The ego pretends it is better than others to overcome our insecurity and our core belief of worthlessness. It brags and competes to prove our self-worth. When we speak from the ego, we simply want to hear ourselves talk, looking for approval of everything we say. The ego is built on the false beliefs we have of ourselves, our world and everyone in it. A healthy ego creates boundaries to protect us from invasion or harm. It works for our highest good.

THE REPTILIAN BRAIN

Everyone adapts differently. How we adapt to the events in our lives is based on our beliefs. Our parents modeled adaptive responses and often we copy our parents' adaptations. If our parents withdrew or became angry and attacked when faced with a conflict, we will usually choose the same reactions. How we adapted as a child is usually how we continue to adapt as adults.

In our brain lies a timeless place where present experiences are the same as past experiences. It is called our reptilian brain. It doesn't analyze danger, it just experiences it and reacts, often in the same way it reacted in the past, when we felt small and powerless and the feared threat seemed large and powerful. As adults we may be successful in many of life's challenges, but when an experience replicates a similar one that traumatized us in childhood, our reptilian brain will cause us to respond in the same way as we did then. Take Glen and Elaine's situation, for example.

As a child, Glen was verbally abused by his alcoholic father. When his wife, Elaine, yells at him out of frustration, he feels overwhelmed by fear. He withdraws, stays late at work, keeps himself busy to avoid her. He believes she is controlling his life. Elaine, however, feels helpless and abandoned. Whenever she calls Glen at work, he is always too busy to talk to her. As her frustration increases, so does her anger, as it did when her parents worked constantly and never found time for her. She rebels and acts out like she did as a child, but all it does is drive Glen further away. Elaine feels it is Glen who is controlling her life. There are enough good times to keep them together, and at those times they comply with each other. Glen and Elaine are enmeshed. They give their power away to each other and fear emotional honesty; they fear growth and change.

OUR DEFENSE MECHANISMS

At a very early age we develop coping strategies, creative ways to deal with conflict and anxiety. The mind generates many coping skills and defenses to protect us from anxiety-provoking experiences. It edits, deletes, reorganizes and makes something new out of old experiences. It adds and subtracts from perception to fill memory gaps and creates new memories. These strategies are called ego *defense mechanisms.* We find ways to adapt in order to defend, or protect, ourselves when we feel our survival is threatened. These methods are habitual and based on unconscious mental and emotional patterns. Thus, defense mechanisms are unconscious patterns that dominate our behavior in situations in which we fear we are going to be attacked and need to protect ourselves.

Our responses to danger are the same whether the threat is real or imagined. If we believe an event threatens us, and it triggers old, unresolved wounds, we will react by defending ourselves in the adaptive ways we unconsciously learned. Our interpretation comes from our belief blueprint. The reactions to the events in our lives belong to us. They are ours, and we must own them.

We use defense mechanisms every day. Often we are unaware that we are using them. Events and experiences threaten us in different ways and to different degrees, from someone cutting us off while driving, to a fight with our mate, to getting fired by our boss, to a major illness that threatens our life. Though there are many types of defense mechanisms, we will explore those we most frequently recognize in ourselves.

DENIAL. What are the defense mechanisms we use to protect us under threat? After one of my seminars, a friend and I walked out to the lobby of the hotel, where her husband and her four-year-old son were waiting. My friend noticed her son had very noticeably wet his pants. "What happened?" she asked him.

"Nothing," he replied.

"Your pants are wet."

"No, they're not."

Her son absolutely believed his *denial*. To him, his pants were not wet. With denial, we do away with facts as if they don't exist, because we believe this will protect us. Denial is used when the loss of security and love is feared. It is usually the first defense that children use. The following example comes from a client of mine named Cindy.

Cindy told me of her lunch date with her mother. Though mother said everything was fine, Cindy knew differently. Her mother had returned from her vacation to find that her desk at the office had been cleaned out. She had been a bookkeeper for thirty years. The company was under new management. Her mother wasn't sure what was going on. Was she fired? Was she moved? Cindy suspected her mother would be upset and asked her what she was going to do. She said, "I don't want to talk about it. Everything is fine." Cindy remembered this was how her mother dealt with conflict all her life. She just denied there was a problem. In fact, it was only after years of blatant clues that she discovered her husband's affair. Even then, she denied there was a problem.

■

Denial is often what alcoholics and drug users practice when partners or friends try to get them to face their addiction. It is used when we face major life-threatening crises in our lives. All of our defenses are founded on our beliefs, and we use denial to protect ourselves.

RATIONALIZATION. When my friend suggested to her son that he look at himself and feel his pants, he said, "Someone spilled their drink on me when they walked by." He now believed this was the truth. In *rationalization,* responsibility is transferred somewhere else. We make our own creative rationalizations, for instance, when we are late for an appointment: "Oh, traffic was terrible." "The bus broke down." "My alarm didn't go off." "I couldn't find my watch."

REPRESSION AND PROJECTION. *Repression* is what we do when we force unwanted thoughts out of our mind. We repress thoughts that bring up shame, guilt and humiliation. Repression occurs when an experience or a memory conflicts with our self-image. If we were shamed or made to feel guilty for our anger as a child, we may not permit ourselves to feel anger as an adult. We believe our feelings are unacceptable and that there is something wrong with having or expressing angry feelings. So, we repress those feelings and even project them onto others, judging *them* as hostile, when that is not the truth.

A friend of mine told me of a co-worker who decided to become a born-again Christian. This man now struggles with any feelings that conflict with his newfound religion. He represses his sexual feelings, which he judges as "bad," and makes critical remarks about every woman in the office who wears a short skirt or a low-cut blouse. He is projecting his "unacceptable" sexual thoughts onto the women to whom he is sexually attracted. His projection and shaming comments of others reduces the anxiety provoked by his own impulses. He judges others rather than himself.

Projection is how we cope with our unwanted feelings. Those feelings and emotions that we deny and repress are projected onto others. We attribute our private meanings of events that come from our blueprint and assign them to others. Parents often project their thoughts and beliefs onto their babies: "Look how happy she is." "She wants you to hold her." "She doesn't like the little dress she is wearing." In working with couples, I often see one partner projecting onto the other his or her own thoughts and feelings and then reacting to what they have projected. In most cases it isn't what the projected partner is thinking or feeling at all. No one's thoughts, feelings, interpretations, or beliefs are the same as anyone else's, even in the same family. To find out the truth about what our thoughts are and what someone else's thoughts are, we must test our reality, as I tried to encourage Dianne to do.

Dianne temps as an executive secretary. The temporary agency gives her assignments in the corporate world that last for a week or more. Within a short time, at each assignment, she is convinced none of the other employees likes her. She is sure her bosses think she is inadequate and incompetent. It fills her with great distress. She wants to be liked and appreciated for her abilities, but invariably she finds herself in the same situation over and over. Even if they tell her she is doing a good job, she is certain they are just trying to bolster her ego because they feel sorry that she is so incompetent.

The same problem arises in her social life. Dianne has friends for a while until she thinks they don't like her, and then she ends the relationship. I encourage her to test her reality and ask them how they feel about her. But she has such a fear of rejection and the possibility that her beliefs are true, that she would rather abandon the friendship. She has moved many times because she believes landlords dislike her and her neighbors are unfriendly. She longs for an intimate relationship but has herself convinced no man would be attracted to her.

Dianne's life is filled with pain and loneliness. Tears run down her cheeks as she tells me of her deep sadness because she can't find anyone who appreciates her or even accepts her. In therapy, she is beginning to see that perhaps what is happening in her world is about her. She confesses that she has always felt there is something wrong with her. Dianne feels she is not enough and inadequate and projects those beliefs onto others.

In her childhood, Dianne was often criticized by a perfectionistic and judgmental mother. She was a chubby child and began wearing glasses at an early age. She had learning difficulties that left her feeling dumb and stupid. The other kids at school made fun of her. Her mother thought her younger sister was perfect and pushed Dianne away because she didn't measure up to her expectations. As a child, Dianne had no one to comfort her pain.

At forty-two years of age, her wounds remain. She assumes everyone finds fault with her because she feels that she can't measure up to anyone's expectations. She interprets every event in her life from this perspective. This is her belief blueprint, and until she changes it she will continue to project onto others the judgments she has about herself.

When we project our repressed beliefs onto others, we expect those people to mirror our thoughts and ideas. We believe others should think like us, believe like us, act like us and be like us. We attract people with a similar belief system and challenge those who have a different belief system than ours. Projection is the foundation of prejudice. Throughout history, scapegoats have carried the projections of others' disowned and hated parts. Conflicting belief systems are also the cause of power struggles among individuals, societies, races, countries, nations and religions. Our blueprint determines how we decide who is right or wrong. We want to convince *them* to think like *us*.

DISPLACEMENT. Another defense in dealing with anger is to *displace* it. If we believe we can't express our frustration and anger in one place, we dump it elsewhere, on employees, store clerks, our spouses, children, the family pet. On the road, all of us have seen drivers express their displaced anger by yelling at strangers, swearing and making obscene gestures. Their anger comes from some other area of their lives where it is not safe for them to express it, so they dump it on others. A recent article stated if you have more than three such driving incidents in one year, it is time to see a therapist to work through displaced anger.

In our belief system, there are messages that tell us what feelings we can have and what ones we can't have, which ones can be expressed and which ones must be repressed. If we don't repress them or project them, we displace them. Displaced anger can be the basis of abuse and violent behavior.

IDENTIFICATION. The opposite of projection is *identification*. It helps us overcome our feelings of inadequacy and beliefs of "not enough." Power is a common goal of identification. For example, corporations like all employees to identify with a certain look and style. If we don't measure up to that image, we are suspect. To be successful and "good enough," we must wear Brooks Brothers clothes, live in the right neighborhood and drive a fancy car because it is the "in" thing—we emulate people we admire or would like to be. In the late fifties and early sixties, thousands of women copied Marilyn Monroe. In 1967, Faye Dunaway started the latest look in the film *Bonnie and Clyde*. Madonna inspired her share of wanna-be's in the eighties. And the list goes on. Identification is a way to allay our fears of not being enough by pretending to be someone else.

Teenagers dress alike, ironically, to find their own identity. But they tend to dress the same as those they identify with as having popularity and power. Gangs dress alike as a mark of mutual identity. It gives members a feeling of belonging and group power.

INTELLECTUALIZATION. We deal with our fears of inadequacy by *intellectualizing*. This defense is respected in the left-brain community. Politics, academics and business honor the intellect and are uncomfortable with feelings. Men are raised to develop their intellect and shut off their feelings. Intellectualization represses the emotional components of an experience and restates it in an abstract, analytical way. We cut ourselves off from our feelings because we judge them according to our belief blueprint and interpret them as unacceptable. By analyzing and intellectualizing the events in our life, however, we never really understand our reactions because we have cut ourselves off from our beliefs, our feelings and our emotions.

REGRESSION. One client told me that when her new baby came into the family, her four-year-old daughter, Emily, began wetting her bed and talking baby talk. That was how Emily dealt with her fear and anxiety of abandonment and losing her parents' love. This coping mechanism is called *regression*. People can regress at any age when insecurity and the fear of abandonment surfaces. I see regression often in working with couples. They use childlike ways of relating to each other. Though they are in adult bodies, they function like five-year-olds, talking baby talk, screaming, crying, yelling, hitting, spitting and having temper tantrums. They regress out of their fears and insecurities.

THE EMERGENCE OF SUBPERSONALITIES

In addition to defense mechanisms, we create *subpersonalities* at a very young age. It is how our ego protects itself based on our belief system. These personalities are modeled on our parents' adaptive behavior. They make up the False Self that we present to the world. Eventually they become integrated into our personality, and we believe that these subpersonalities are who we are. We use them to cover up our fears of *not being enough* and to give us a false sense of power in a world where we feel powerless. The following is a list of some common subpersonalities (see also the exercises in chapter 1):

The Pusher keeps us and everyone else in line.

The Critic and Judge remind us of our lack and the lack in others.

The Superachiever keeps us striving.

The Good Boy or Good Girl complies to get the approval of others.

The People Pleaser puts everyone else's needs first.

The Caregiver cares for everyone else's needs except our own.

The Intellectual analyzes everything to show others how smart we are.

The Know-It-All challenges everything and everyone.

The Snob wants others to think we are superior.

The Controller takes over every situation.

The Victimizer is immune to boundaries and invalidates the experiences of others.

The Victim allows others to cross boundaries and invalidate us.

The Rebel acts out against others but not in our best interests.

The Macho controls others with physical or verbal abuse.

The Recluse checks out.

The Withholder hoards feelings and objects.

The User uses others for our own benefit.

The Doormat lets others walk all over us.

The Martyr goes to any length to get appreciation for how much we sacrifice.

The Bully reacts to others by intimidating them.

The Show-off is constantly in need of attention.

The Con Artist manipulates to get what we want.

The Bragger embellishes our accomplishments for praise.

Many of these subpersonalities come in clusters. For example, that part of us that is the Know-It-All will join the Critic, the Judge and the Controller. This gives us the illusion of power. The more insecure we are, the more controlling we will be. If we go back to our childhood, we see the seeds of each subpersonality planted as an unconscious decision we made to survive. If, for instance, we began at a young age to take care of others around us, we would become a caregiver. These subpersonalities are often fashioned after one of our parents. If our parents used control, abuse or people-pleasing to deal with their world, we may behave in the same way.

FINDING THE MEANING IN OUR ADAPTIVE BEHAVIOR

All adaptive behavior has meaning. Everything from antisocial behavior to the behavior of saints depends on the individual's belief system. In his book *Violence: Our Deadly Epidemic and Its Causes,* James Gilligan, M.D., states his belief that the root of all violent crime is the belief in one's own shame. Shame is the cause of social breakdown. As clinical director of psychiatric services for the Massachusetts state prison system, Gilligan worked to prevent the humiliation of the inmates in order to heighten their self-esteem. The result? The level of lethal violence in the prison dropped to nearly zero. Gilligan has come to the conclusion that "the emotion of shame is the primary or ultimate cause of all violence, whether toward others or toward the self." As the meaning behind our adaptive behavior changes, so will our behavior.

REACTIONS ARE COVER-UPS

When an event happens in our lives, it is never the event that causes the reaction, it is our interpretation of the event. We experience an emotional and visceral response in a fraction of a second. Our reactions are instinctual and come from that part of our brain that is concerned with survival. We are usually unaware of why we react the way we do. Our reactions are always cover-ups. What they cover up are our interpretations, thoughts, judgments and beliefs.

The event itself is only a catalyst and is neither good nor bad. We perceive the event through our blueprint and *interpret* it as good or bad. Our reactions cover up our wounds from our childhood and the traumas and hurts throughout our life. Sometimes the emotional and physical responses can seem disproportionate to the event. In my work I often tell couples, "Imagine that you have a bad sunburn and you cover up with a shirt. Your partner cannot see the burn under the shirt and lovingly pats you on the back. You immediately feel the pain. You react by yelling, blaming, crying, getting angry, withdrawing or any number of other reactions. Though the pat may not have been intentionally hurtful, the reaction will be as if it were. When Elaine yells at Glen, he becomes six years old again, traumatized by a father who terrorized him. He re-experiences the same fears with the same physical responses: trembling, a dry mouth and heart palpitations. His rational mind cannot make sense of his reactions.

There is also a secondary reaction, a reaction to our own feelings. As children, we learn that some feelings are acceptable and others are not. Even in adulthood, we continue to judge our feelings as good or bad. This can add to the distortion of the event and determines how we adapt. In our reptilian brain, the present experience triggers our past experience and distorts our perception. Reactions seem to have no sense of linear time. We become children again and react to protect ourselves.

The reaction chart in figure 3 shows our chain of reactions to an event. As you study it, think of an event in your life. What do you tell yourself about it? What are your interpretations and judgments? What

Reactions Are Cover-ups

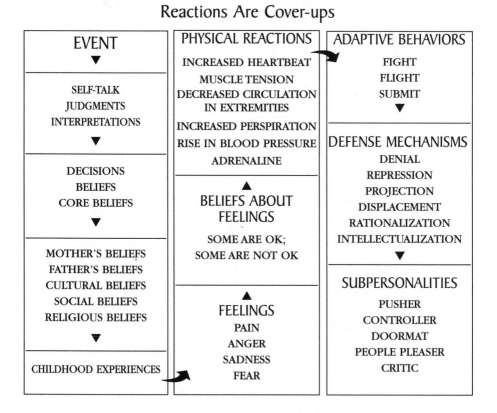

EVENT ▼	PHYSICAL REACTIONS	ADAPTIVE BEHAVIORS
	INCREASED HEARTBEAT	FIGHT
SELF-TALK JUDGMENTS INTERPRETATIONS ▼	MUSCLE TENSION DECREASED CIRCULATION IN EXTREMITIES	FLIGHT SUBMIT ▼
	INCREASED PERSPIRATION RISE IN BLOOD PRESSURE ADRENALINE	DEFENSE MECHANISMS
DECISIONS BELIEFS CORE BELIEFS ▼	▲ BELIEFS ABOUT FEELINGS	DENIAL REPRESSION PROJECTION DISPLACEMENT RATIONALIZATION INTELLECTUALIZATION ▼
	SOME ARE OK; SOME ARE NOT OK	
MOTHER'S BELIEFS FATHER'S BELIEFS CULTURAL BELIEFS SOCIAL BELIEFS RELIGIOUS BELIEFS ▼	▲ FEELINGS PAIN ANGER	SUBPERSONALITIES PUSHER CONTROLLER DOORMAT PEOPLE PLEASER CRITIC
CHILDHOOD EXPERIENCES	SADNESS FEAR	

beliefs do you have about the event? Does it reopen an early wound from childhood that is similar? What decisions have you made in the past about events like this? What beliefs from others do you remember about such events? What are you feeling? Are your feelings acceptable? How do you react? How do you usually adapt to similar events? Bringing your reactions into awareness and owning them is the beginning of change. Write your answers to the above questions in your personal journal.

How can you tell if you are reacting? Here are some indications:

- You feel fear.
- You feel anxious.
- You feel threatened.
- The event feels familiar.
- You feel uncomfortable.
- You are not in the present.
- You blame yourself or others.
- You feel like you have to fight or run.
- You think about the event over and over.
- Your thoughts are in the past or the future.

Let's return to Lora's story. When Lora's boss asks her to stay an extra two hours after work, she feels resentful and used. She's afraid that if she says no, she might lose her job and may not be liked, so she reacts by acquiescing and says yes. The People Pleaser in her does what another part of her doesn't want to do. She stays the extra two hours but believes she will never get what she wants and that she will not be appreciated no matter how much she gives. Lora feels helpless, inadequate and not in control of her own life.

Lora is in fact maintaining an *illusion* of control by remaining a little girl, hoping someone in authority will recognize her if she tries hard enough. She learned to *people please* because it is what she saw her mother model. Lora ignores her feelings and fears expressing them. She feels like a victim and is afraid to ask for what she wants. Figure 4 is a diagram of Lora's unconscious reactions.

Diagram of Lora's Unconscious Reaction

EVENT

Male Boss asks her to work overtime

▼

SELF-TALK	*"If I say no, I might lose my job."*
JUDGMENTS	*"I'll get in trouble if I make waves."*
INTERPRETATIONS	*"He scares me—I have to do what I'm told so that I don't upset him."*

▼

DECISIONS	*"Other people have authority over me, and I must please them to get what I want."*
BELIEFS	*"When I'm rich or have a rich husband, I'll be better than the others."*
CORE BELIEFS	*"I'm not enough just the way I am."* *"I'm inadequate."*

▼

MOTHER'S BELIEFS	*"To get ahead, you have to knuckle under and please others."*
FATHER'S BELIEFS	*"Life is a struggle and a sacrifice."*
CULTURAL BELIEFS	*"You'll be enough if you're smart enough, good enough, attractive enough and have enough money."*
SOCIAL BELIEFS	*"Wealth is power." "Men are superior."*
RELIGIOUS BELIEFS	*"You're a sinner and need to be saved."*

▼

CHILDHOOD EXPERIENCES	*Father unavailable, sometimes warm, sometimes abusive and authoritative.*
	Mother submissive, fearful, sometimes warm; people pleaser; victim; martyr.
	Family struggles financially.

SUBPERSONALITIES

PUSHER
CONTROLLER
DOORMAT
PEOPLE PLEASER
CRITIC

▲

ADAPTIVE BEHAVIORS

SUBMIT–FLIGHT
COMPLIES
GIVES MORE/DOES MORE
IGNORES HERSELF
WITHDRAWS
OVEREATS
REPRESSES FEELINGS
RATIONALIZES
INTELLECTUALIZES
DENIAL

▲

BELIEFS ABOUT FEELINGS

"My feelings are not OK."
"I have to hide them."

▲

FEELINGS

RESENTFUL
FRUSTRATED
POWERLESS
FEARFUL
ANXIOUS
USED

THE NEED FOR CHANGE

Our reactions, feelings and behavior are not who we are. They are adaptations of the distorted perception of who we believe we are. Not only do our beliefs affect us individually, but they also affect us collectively. If we can heal the basic causes of our behavior and return to the wholeness that is inherent within each of us, our world and future generations will change.

Change is possible for all of us. Our dissatisfaction, discomfort and unhappiness tell us that something needs to change. The limiting beliefs we have integrated and believed to be true have brought us to where we are now. Sometimes it takes a major life crisis for us to take the responsibility of letting go of the false self that we have created and begin a commitment to the journey of self-discovery. Embarking on this journey takes intention and courage. It is a journey that can give birth to who and what we are. We can't wait for permission or expect someone to go with us, and we can't compromise, even with ourselves. It is a risk, a leap of faith, a jump into the unknown. We can choose to take an active role in our own process. As we have the courage to change, others will also have the courage to change. In all of us there is an unconscious recognition that life has more to offer, and on a deeper level we already know the way. The discovery of ourselves leads to wholeness and the seeds of innate potential within us that are waiting to be expressed and manifested in our lives.

EXERCISES

JOURNALING YOUR REACTIONS

Your personal journal is a learning tool to help you move from being reactive to acting with intent and from being unconscious into being conscious in your life. Like your False Belief notebook, any blank book or spiral-bound notebook will do.

■ In your journal, write down a recent event that triggered a reaction. Example: Your boyfriend said he was going to call you, and he didn't. Your boss gave the promotion to someone else. Your husband is late coming home. Refer to the diagram in figure 4 for guidance. Be a detective. Note that your reactions are about *your* interpretations.

1. Write down the self-talk, the chatter that goes on in your head about the event.

2. Write down your judgments about the event.

3. Write down your interpretations of the event.

4. What decisions have you made in the past about this same type of event?

5. Identify your beliefs, especially your core beliefs. Write down the beliefs that are triggered by the event.

6. What do you think the beliefs of your father, your mother, your culture, your religion and society would be in the same or similar event?

7. What similar experiences did you have in childhood? Describe them in your journal.

■ Explore your feelings. Unprocessed feelings from childhood will be triggered by similar events. Go back to #7 above and write down the feelings you have from childhood that were triggered by these events. Also, notice the feelings you judge as acceptable and unacceptable and record that information.

■ Explore your behaviors.

1. How did you adapt as a child to experiences that threatened you?

_____

_____

2. What threatened you?

_____

_____

3. How do you adapt now?

_____

_____

4. What threatens you today?

_____

_____

5. Circle all that apply: When you feel fearful and insecure, do you become a:
   * Know-It-All • Controller • Judge or Critic • Pusher • People Pleaser
   * Caregiver • Victim • Bully • Bragger • Show-off?

   These are the *subpersonalities* you developed to protect yourself.

6. Now, write in your journal a dialogue process with one subpersonality. Remember your subpersonality is not the real you. It is what you developed to survive when you were feeling powerless. A sample dialogue appears below. Ask your subpersonality the same questions and allow that part to answer you. Let the answers be an uncensored reaction and write whatever comes to you. Record the dialogue as though you are writing a script.

Me: So what age was I when you first appeared?

Subpersonality (The Critic): I came in when you were about six years old.

Me: What was going on in my life when you first appeared?

The Critic: You started school, and you had to measure up to the teacher's expectations, and you were afraid you would fail.

Me: What purpose did you serve?

The Critic: Like a parent, I kept reminding you of all the things you had to do so you wouldn't forget or make mistakes. I kept you in line so you didn't goof off. If you did well, the teacher approved. If you made a mistake, the teacher criticized you. I protected you by criticizing you to keep you in line. When I tell you about everyone else's mistakes and failures, you feel better and not so dumb.

Me: What percentage of the time are you there now?

The Critic: Probably about 60 percent of the time.

Me: When are you there in my life?

The Critic: Anytime you might make a mistake and fail, and around anyone you are dating who might judge you. I tell you all the things that are wrong with you that I think they might think: "You're too fat, you look awful in a bathing suit, glasses look awful on you, others are more attractive than you." At work, I remind you of all your mistakes so you will learn how to measure up and not earn approval from your boss. If you are having difficulties with others, I criticize them and find their faults.

Me: What purpose do you serve?

The Critic: I am here to protect you from making mistakes and failing. I keep reminding you to work harder to improve yourself. I know I am hard on you and remind you of all your faults, but without me you would have failed. I make your life predictable by telling you everyone else's faults.

Me: Who are you like from my past?

The Critic: I am like your mother. She always kept you in line by criticizing you. She also criticized everyone else. I'm also like your third-grade teacher. Her criticism made you spell better.

Me: Why are you still in my life?

The Critic: Because you believe you are inadequate and not enough, and without me you believe you would fail in everything you do.

Me: What triggers you?

The Critic: I come into your life whenever you feel unsure of yourself, whenever you are afraid you won't measure up, when you want someone's approval, when you feel down and bad about yourself. I tell you what is wrong with you so you'll improve.

Me: How do you feel about me?

The Critic: I think you still don't measure up and maybe never will.

Me: How do you think I feel about you?

The Critic: Though you listen to me, sometimes you don't know how to shut me up. I think you hate me for my constant criticism. But that is the job you gave me, to keep you and everyone else in line.

Me: What would happen to me if you weren't there anymore?

The Critic: Part of me thinks you'll fail without me. Another part thinks you could survive without me, you're not a child anymore.

Me: What do I need to do to manage my life without you?

The Critic: I've taught you everything you need to know, and now you can just start trusting yourself. The information is always there.

Me: Thank you for protecting my life when I needed it. I am grateful. However, I am now willing to trust my ability to manage my life without limiting beliefs and limiting rigid adaptive patterns and sub-personalities.

We are multidimensional and usually have several subpersonalities. We develop them because we don't trust ourselves and our ability to deal with life's challenges. Repeat the above dialogue for each of your remaining subpersonalities. Some personalities continue to serve you, and you may choose to keep them until a later time. In trusting ourselves, we come to know what we need to know, when we need to know it. By accepting, embracing and even thanking the subpersonalities we have created to survive, we will integrate our lives and heal ourselves.

HOW TO CHANGE BELIEFS AND DECISIONS

1. In your False Belief notebook, record information you gathered in the previous exercise. Examples: *I need approval from others to be a success. I can't handle it if others are angry at me. Others know more about me than I do. I can't fail.*

2. Start a Creative Awareness notebook in which you substitute new, more meaningful beliefs for each of the old ones. Write down your new beliefs. Example: *I believe in myself and trust in my ability to succeed, and I am open for support and encouragement from others.* Print these messages on $3'' \times 5''$ cards.

Read them at least three times a day, including just before bed. You are reprogramming this new information into your subconscious mind.

3. Act in light of the new belief. In other words, *act as if.* There once was a time I was terrified to speak in front of a crowd. I felt fear that something awful would happen, and others would judge me unfavorably because I didn't measure up. Because I wanted to be a teacher, however, I chose to face my fears and to take the risk of speaking in a classroom. In the beginning I was anxious and uncomfortable. But, by *acting as if,* the fears left and I am now quite comfortable teaching and lecturing. In fact, I enjoy it. Changing your behavior will change your attitude.

4. Continue to act in new ways, even if it feels uncomfortable or phony. If you persist, in time the new belief will become part of your natural behavior. Take risks even if it feels uncomfortable. Growth comes from stretching beyond your comfort zone.

HOW TO TEST YOUR REALITY: TAKE A RISK

Sometimes you project onto others your own beliefs and incorrectly interpret a facial expression or tone of voice in others as anger or judgment. You can clarify the situation and help improve communication by being upfront. For example, if you believe another person doesn't like you or is angry with you, you can ask, "I'd like to do a reality check. It seems to me you are angry with me. Am I correct?" This will clarify your confusion about your reality.

Here are more steps you can take:

- If the other person *is* angry at you, ask him to tell you what is upsetting him.
- Remember that others' reactions are about *them.* Invite conversation. Stay open and contained. Put your reactions and judgments aside so you can hear what it is like for the other person. Be curious.

- At some point, let the other person know from her point of view that what she is saying makes sense. You don't have to agree.
- Empathize. Tell him how you think he must feel.
- Remember, apologies are not necessary, but listening, validating and empathy are.

Testing your reality and sharing your feelings and observations are good ways to discover the beliefs you carry about the events and experiences in your life. Additional communication skills are covered in chapters 5 and 6.

Chapter 3

WOMEN AND
BELIEFS

Nina is a designer and manufacturer of her own line of ladies' sportswear. She grew up in the fashion industry and started working in her dad's factory as a teenager. When she grew older, she worked in the factory's New York showroom. After graduating from the fashion institute, she became a designer. She developed much confidence in her work.

Her husband, Brian, was representing her father's line when they met and married. Nina and Brian decided to become manufacturers themselves. The dress line they developed became a success. Though Nina stayed home when their kids were little, she continued to work the trade shows with Brian, and she approved all the designs. Once the kids got older, she designed the line for each season and was in the factory every day.

The marriage lasted until the kids were in high school. Nina discovered her husband was having an affair with a showroom worker more than twenty years younger than he was. It was a shock. Nina had grown secure in their marriage. She thought they would be working together for the rest of their lives. She gave so much to make their marriage work. Brian traveled more than she did, so Nina always held down the fort. At times she felt overwhelmed and exhausted with so much responsibility.

She was mad, scared and grieving; she felt deceived and discouraged and believed she would never trust another man. For a few years after the divorce, Nina kept busy to get over her hurt. This helped her to successfully build her business. However, when she started to date again, it seemed she invariably attracted men who took advantage of her. She got the feeling they took what they wanted and gave back very little.

When Nina came to see me, she was upset, confused and filled with despair. That day she discovered she had paid thousands of dollars to a mechanic who had been taking advantage of her. What's more, her date the night before had been a disaster. She had invited her boyfriend to come to her house for her birthday dinner. He didn't bring her a gift, a card, a flower or even a bottle of wine. When she made a comment on his inability to give, he put her down by telling her, "You're not as giving as you think you are."

Nina fears that she will never find a partner again. Because of her age, she believes she doesn't have any choice but to accept men whom she calls "losers." Nina is fifty. Though she keeps in shape, she thinks she looks older. She's been considering a facelift. Her belief is that men want only young, sexy, attractive women and that she no longer measures up. This leaves her feeling hopeless. No matter what she does or how hard she tries, she will never win.

■

Ann and Barbra are sisters. Barbra is the youngest of the four daughters. Ann has always been the studious, intellectual one. She got good grades in school and was always very responsible. She also excelled in sports. Both her parents have successful careers. Ann got their attention by being better and smarter.

Their two older sisters are both married to successful men. They are housewives and mothers. Ann feels superior to them and doesn't feel that the rewards of being a housewife would ever be enough for her. After graduate school, she worked her way up to became the head of an advertising company. Ann's focus is on business, and that is where she gets her rewards. It has afforded her the opportunity to buy her own home and drive an expensive car. Ann is attractive and wears expensive clothes: beautiful suits, silk shirts and Italian shoes.

Barbra is naturally blond and beautiful. She has a fantastic body and full breasts, and she dresses to show her body off. When Ann and Barbra go out together, Barbra gets a lot of attention from men. She enjoys this attention and usually forgets about being with Ann. Sometimes she leaves with one of the men. Ann feels she cannot compete with Barbra. When Barbra is around, none of the men seems to notice Ann. Rejected, Ann is resentful and jealous of her sister. She criticizes herself; in fact, she hates herself. She feels "not enough." All her accomplishments are nothing. If she can't attract a man, she believes there must be something wrong with her.

■

Nina, Ann and Barbra are struggling to find fulfillment in their lives. Each has tried in her own way to achieve the recognition she desires. They are looking for something or someone to make them feel accepted, valued and worthwhile. All of them are stuck in a belief blueprint they have had since childhood, a system they unconsciously act on. To find fulfillment and value, they believe they have to act in certain ways and accomplish certain goals.

These are courageous women who have taken risks to grow and change. Nina walked away from a bad situation and built a new life. Ann went to graduate school and achieved a top position and recognition in a predominately male field. Even Barbra is struggling to get what she wants. But in spite of their accomplishments, they are stuck in old beliefs: the unconscious blueprint that keeps them confused about who they are, what their role in society is and how to find the fulfillment they long for. Their efforts feel empty without the rewards they so desire.

After more than twenty years of working with women in individual and group therapy, teaching and giving seminars, I have discovered that most women are dissatisfied with their lives and confused about how to bring about change. Each longs to be happy and fulfilled, but at the same time, each feels lost about how to deal with their mothers and fathers, lost in unfulfilling relationships, lost in how to parent their children and lost in unfulfilling careers and dead-end jobs. These are symptoms of a deeper underlying problem.

Long before today's women were born, before their mothers and grandmothers were born, women were silenced. They learned very early in life that their voices had no meaning because *they* had no meaning. To find meaning in their lives, they had to turn to an external authority. Women have traditionally carried the belief that they have little or no power on their own, and to have power they must find it through a man. Of course, there were women in history who did not follow these traditional beliefs, but they paid a social price. Over the centuries, these beliefs have changed very little. Change takes time. It requires an awareness of the beliefs of the society and culture that women continue to accept as ours. We must stop struggling to prove our worth and look inward to find that lost part of ourselves, and discover that the authority of who we are belongs to us.

THE PATRIARCHAL SYSTEM OF BELIEFS

We live under many belief systems. These are family systems, religious systems, social systems, cultural systems, ethnic systems and corporate systems. Each carries a belief blueprint. All have been established from the master blueprint of patriarchy, in which inheritance and power belong to the male. Religion, education, politics, economics, medicine and legislation have been dominated by patriarchy. In this system, women are seen as inferior and powerless just because they are born female. This is the core belief in women that they are *not enough.*

The fact that we live in a patriarchal system is no one's fault. It is a system that worked 5,000 years ago when the role of men as protector was established. As hunter-gatherers, men faced danger for the survival of the family and the community. Later, because of his physical strength and power, men fought in wars.

I am convinced this patriarchal blueprint is now thoroughly outdated in our contemporary world. In the patriarchal system, the male child is preferred. An acquaintance of mine who is an obstetrician remembers many deliveries of girls in which the wife apologized to her husband for not giving him a boy. Comments like "Too bad your first child wasn't a boy" and "Better luck next time" support the notion of female inferiority.

Even today, in cultures where there is overt male preference, there is a high incidence of female infanticide. Often female children are abandoned, put in orphanages, or sold as child labor. Young adolescent girls are sold into prostitution. Girls and women are seen as property and a burden in many countries where the support and care of women shifts from father to husband. In many countries, when a woman exhibits sexual behavior that "dishonors" the family, she pays with her life. These murders are called honor killings and are seen as a legitimate defense of men's honor. Throughout the world, women are physically and sexually abused, battered and raped and are often considered to have "asked for it." Many of these crimes against women are tolerated and the sentences minimal.

Men fear women's sexuality and believe it must be controlled. Some cultures condone the abuse of women from murder to clitoridectomy on the belief that women are unable to control themselves sexually. In many cultures, including ours, many men believe they own women. The fear that women's powerful, magical sexuality will take them away from their role as their caregiver and attract them to other men is threatening to many males.

I have experienced in myself and other women a great concern, compassion and sense of empathy for the suffering women have experienced throughout the world. Though we as women may be unable to change generations of cultural and social beliefs that violate women, we can change our own consciousness and stop the abuses in our own lives.

Some of us will even contribute our time, energy and money to change the world's collective consciousness.

THE LIVES OF ADOLESCENT GIRLS

A nationwide survey in 1990 by the American Association of University Women (AAUW) focused on how our education system encourages low self-esteem in adolescent girls. Throughout their lives, girls are traditionally rewarded for being quiet, demure and good, obeying the rules, pleasing others and being clean and pretty. The AAUW survey contained basic questions on how boys and girls think about themselves and their abilities. Sixty percent of elementary school-age girls and 67 percent of boys of the same age were happy with themselves. But by the time they reached high school, only 29 percent of the girls still felt that way. Nearly half of all the boys still felt happy about themselves. The biggest drop in girls' feelings about themselves occurs between grade school and junior high.

The survey also found that adolescent girls have a declining sense of themselves that inhibits their actions and abilities. Twice as many boys as girls considered their unique talents to be what they liked best about themselves. Unfortunately, twice as many girls as boys considered what they liked about themselves to be some aspect of their personal appearance. Girls experience a higher degree of self-doubt, anxiety and depression than boys and are traditionally seen as intellectually inferior.

Adolescent girls suffer from depression, disturbance about their appearance, eating disorders, stress and psychological disorders more often then boys do. Boys tend to act out their stress through delinquency and aggressive, violent acts. Girls tend to internalize their stress and blame themselves as *not enough* and inadequate. They tend to have feelings of helplessness and hopelessness and attempt to kill themselves four to five times more often than boys do.

Reports from the 1990 study indicate that girls lose ground in school beginning at adolescence. Girls are silenced in school while boys are encouraged and taken more seriously. When asked how their lives would be different if they were the opposite sex, 50 percent of the girls spoke of the advantages of being a boy, whereas only 7 percent of the boys saw any advantage in being a girl. Twenty percent gave extremely hostile comments about being a girl. One boy wrote, "I would kill myself right away."

ADAPTING IN A PATRIARCHAL WORLD

Women have learned many ways of adapting under the patriarchal system. The struggle to achieve equal rights for women began in the eighteenth century. The demand for enfranchisement of women brought forth women's suffrage—the right to vote—and inheritance rights, leading to major changes in women's rights in most countries of the world.

Though times have changed, most women today still live with the vestiges of patriarchy. A belief in women's inferiority was passed down unconsciously from our mothers, fathers, educators and society. The messages our mother gave us may not always have been verbal but were instead expressed in her actions: how she reacted to her husband, how she reacted to her boss, how she reacted to other authority figures. How women act in relationships, at work and at home, is based on her belief that she has to comply, submit, ignore her own needs and pretend to be what others want, or people-please.

◼

In their therapy session, Michelle puts her hand over her heart as she expresses her feelings of deep sadness. She tells Robert about the anger, pain and shame she feels when he watches every sweet she eats. Though she is not overweight, Robert pushes her to exercise and diet because he thinks she should look a certain way. She resents it. She feels like a child, constantly having to justify every cookie she eats. It is her body, and when he criticizes her, she feels not enough and inadequate. Michelle believes that she has to give herself up to be loved by Robert. She believes she'll be loved by a man only if she measures up and tries hard to please him. Sometimes she feels hatred for all men.

Sad memories from childhood come up for Michelle about how her father made fun of her mother for being overweight. Even though her mother felt humiliated and hurt, she said nothing and ate more. Tears well up in Michelle's eyes as she expresses empathy for her mother.

Michelle sees similar patterns in her relationship with Robert. When he reminds her of her diet, she wants to eat more. She tries to be whatever Robert wants her to be, or she rebels against him if she doesn't get his approval. In other areas of her life, when she stands up for herself and makes decisions for herself, she feels empowered. By being in an intimate relationship with Robert, she gives him power over her. But if she does her own thing, she fears losing closeness and intimacy. She can't seem to have both, and it frustrates her.

■

Our mothers and grandmothers, and their mothers before them, complied. For them to succeed in the world, it was necessary to be attached to a man for protection. In most cultures, women became submissive, like children, and were supposed to be seen but not heard. A woman feared being discarded by her husband if she no longer served his purpose, or if he found another woman who was younger and more attractive, someone who could bear his sons.

Traditionally, men and women existed in separate spheres and had clearly defined roles. A wife made herself responsible for all of her husband's needs. She cooked his meals, cleaned his house, bore and cared for his children (preferably males), often worked his land and made love when he wanted it. The man of the house had the power. These defined roles may have eliminated confusion, but they also left women feeling powerless and frustrated, living in a system in which they had no voice and no equality. In such a system, the oppressed often become the oppressors of those less powerful. The home was where women were allowed to dominate, and it was here that she could express power and control. Children often experienced physical, emotional and verbal abuse because mothers could not find an outlet for their frustration and rage.

Even today, many women are still paralyzed in their fear and suffering and quite often are unable to express their anger. They have learned helplessness and are unable to turn around the very situation they themselves have participated in creating. Many women have no idea how to make their lives work and feel they have no choice but to endure. These women feel hopeless, weary, depressed and desperate.

WOMEN AND DEPRESSION

More than seven million American women experience depression. Women have been and are twice as likely as men to be depressed. About one in four women can expect to have depression sometime in their lives.

Most of my female clients have anxiety and depression. There is a correlation with depression that has to do with women's role in society. Women are not equal to men economically, in the job market and in personal relationships, and they are often exploited and victimized. They carry with them the belief of their inadequacy that is perpetuated by the society in which they live. Even if they become empowered, society usually is not ready to accept their attempts at equality.

The feelings of inadequacy and *not enoughness* have been carried by women for generations. Women constantly receive messages about how they should act to gain acceptance in their careers and in their relationships. Men and women do not share equal standing at home, at work, in religion and in society in general. Women earn less money and more often experience sexual harassment and discrimination. In the United States, four million women a year are battered; 75 percent of the people living at or below the poverty line are women and children; and 20 percent of the homeless population are females.

Women have learned to put the needs and desires of men above their own. Due to the fear women have of asking directly for what they want, they have learned to manipulate, control, seduce and coerce. These are behaviors that children often use to get their needs met, and in turn, women have been viewed as grown children without an equal voice. If the adaptations they develop to get their needs met in a male-dominated society fail, they feel hopeless that things will ever change and withdraw into depression. Men act out their anger, whereas women usually internalize their anger and often become self-destructive and self-abusive, which leads them to stay in destructive relationships and demeaning jobs, or leads them into prostitution or drug and alcohol addiction. More women than men have eating disorders.

LEILA'S STORY

In Leila's native country, women are treated poorly. Leila did not want that kind of life for herself. When she was twenty years old, she and a cousin came to the United States to visit an aunt in New York. It was wonderful. Leila explored Manhattan and took in all the shops and Broadway shows. It seemed so perfect. She when to California, and the people there seemed so free and relaxed, and the women dressed however they wanted. It was then that she decided she would find a way to move to America.

Leila was slim, beautiful and exotic looking, with dark eyes and lovely dark hair. In California she met George. He was attractive and was attracted to her. She knew very little about him other than that he was a first-generation American. She liked him and found herself dreaming of a wonderful future with him, getting married and maybe living in California.

When she returned to her native country, she missed George. She thought about him every day. They began to correspond regularly. It was through their letters that they got to know each other. He told her the American women he met were selfish and he preferred a foreign woman like her. Two years later in a romantic love letter, he asked Leila to marry him. Her parents forbade it. George sent Leila an airline ticket, and she left without saying good-bye to anyone.

Today, Leila is forty-three years old and still lovely. She has been married to George for eighteen years. Unfortunately, she has created the same marriage that she would have had in her native country. George acts as if he owns her. She is afraid of disobeying him and feels obligated to take care of his needs, the needs of their son and of George's father, who has moved in with them. They come first. George gets angry when he comes home from work and food is not on the table. He gets angry if she isn't up every morning at six to fix his breakfast. George doesn't want her to work and thinks she should stay home and take care of her responsibilities. When Leila objects to how he treats her, he tells her, "What do I need you for if you aren't going to do these things for me?"

Leila feels tired, anxious, depressed, helpless, hopeless and stuck. Her dreams are gone; she doesn't know who she is and can't figure out what happened to that wonderful future she imaged so long ago.

■

When we can no longer tolerate our pain, it can be a turning point in our lives. So it was for Leila. Her physician referred her to me. In our first session, Leila felt everything was George's fault. He took advantage of her. He used her like a slave. He made promises he didn't keep. He was selfish and inconsiderate. He intimidated her, and she was afraid to speak up and afraid of his anger. Leila feared that George meant what he said that her only value was in serving him. She was filled with blame and doubts about herself. During our session, her body was racked by deep, wailing sobs.

Leila felt desperate and hopeless. There was nowhere to go. She really had never reconciled with her parents back home. When she told them she was unhappy, they told her she was being punished for disobeying them and for disobeying her husband. She couldn't go back to her native country. She had no money of her own, and her parents refused to help her. George gave her a weekly allowance. If she asked for more money, she had to explain what it was for. Leila needed George's approval for whatever she bought. Ironically, he had approved and offered to pay for her therapy because the doctor said that *she* had a problem.

First, I suggested that Leila start keeping a journal of her feelings, thoughts, self-talk, judgments and false beliefs. What she discovered was that she had re-created the same circumstances she had left behind, using the blueprint of herself as a woman and a wife.

The following are some of Leila's false beliefs from her notebook entries:

I need someone to take care of me financially.

I don't know how to survive. I am inferior and not good enough to do anything.

I'm not smart enough or educated enough to make it on my own.

I need to be married to be OK. Without a husband I have
no worth.

I have to do what George, his dad and our son want me to
do. It is my obligation.

If I don't do what they want, they will be upset and angry
with me.

It's not OK to upset others.

Others' needs are more important than my own. It is selfish
to think of myself first.

I have to please others to get their approval.

Other people are right, and I am wrong.

George knows what is best for me.

I have to put my family's needs first no matter how difficult
it is for me.

It's not OK to be upset and angry.

I have responsibilities to my family, and it's not OK to complain.

It is OK for the men in the family to judge me, and I must do
what I am told.

I have to prove myself before I can get what I want and need.

It's not OK to ask for what I want. George will get mad at me.

I should be grateful for what I have.

Doing what others want is the only way to be liked.

I should overlook how George treats me. He works hard for
the family.

If I don't do what George wants, it would be terrible.

I am a failure; if George left me, no one else would ever want me.

Next, I had Leila review each belief and rewrite it in a positive, affir-
mative way. *It's not OK to ask for what I want* became *It's OK for me to
ask for what I want. I deserve to be heard and validated, and if George
gets angry it is about him. We explored all of the fears around her "what*

ifs": What if George got angry? What if he decided to leave me? What if I started listening to my own needs and put them first? What if I admitted to myself and George how upset and angry I am about our situation? What if I asked George to come into therapy with me to work on our issues?

In time, Leila began to recognize that her self-talk reinforced her feelings of depression and anxiety. And she recognized that all the "what if" scenarios created a fear that made her feel inadequate, uncomfortable and insecure. Real fear is what we feel in the presence of an immediate danger that threatens our survival. Unwarranted or imaginary fear is based on anxiety and past memory. Leila's anxiety caused her to feel fear when there was no real danger.

Leila imagined negative results to all her "what ifs," and she exaggerated the possibility that something terrible would happen. She discovered that it wasn't the event that caused her fears, it was her reaction to the event, the self-talk, the judgments and the interpretations based on false beliefs. Reactions are always cover-ups. We choose how we react. Some of our choices are conscious, others are unconscious. The unconscious choices come from our beliefs about the event. This is what creates our reality.

Encouragingly, Leila made some major changes in her life. She regained the courage and empowerment she had as a young girl to face her fears. And George was willing to come into therapy with her. He had been unaware of Leila's reactions to him and was willing to make some changes himself. George began to see how they had both created their relationship. He recognized that his expectations in marriage were based on his blueprint, which was based on his parents' marriage. George and Leila love each other and are willing to explore the false beliefs that have kept them in an unhappy relationship.

BLAMING OTHERS

One of the most common complaints I hear from my female clients is blame. They believe that someone, somewhere, has stolen their right to happiness and fulfillment. They blame their boyfriends, husbands, brothers and fathers. If these men have violated them in any way, they are convinced that all men are the same. Many women have developed an entire belief system around men: *Men by nature are aggressive and violent. They can be physically and sexually abusive, and you have to be afraid of them. Men start wars. Men don't understand women at all. We have to cater to their every whim or they will find someone else. Men are unfaithful, and you can't trust them because they lie and cheat. If they want you, they want other women, too. They are deceitful and covert. You can't depend on them. They are totally insensitive, selfish and self-centered. Men play games and can't commit to a relationship. In fact, most men aren't capable of intimacy. All they want is to have their needs taken care of, someone to pick up after them, serve them and have sex with them whenever they want it. Most of them have dirty minds, and all they think about is sex. They enjoy getting off on sexy magazines and pornography. Women are just sex objects to them.*

These negative messages were passed down from our mothers and our peers, and we believed they were true. We believed our mothers knew the truth. It might have been her *experience,* but it wasn't *the truth.* If her husband was unfaithful to her, if he lied and tried to deceive her, she developed a belief that all men were like that. If she was abused by her father and her husband and was afraid of them, she would project those negative messages onto all men.

We blame our mothers for not breaking free of the system they lived in, and we blame them for conditioning us to conform to the belief in our inferiority and the superiority of men. In our belief system, established in childhood, there is a chain of command: The man (father) is at the top and has absolute power. Mother is second in command, and adolescent and older boys are next. Girls are last. Until boys reach adolescence, Mother is in charge of them (however, some mothers maintain their authority over their sons even into adulthood). These beliefs—unconsciously accepted in childhood—about men and our relationship to them became a part of our belief blueprint. What we believe is what we attract. We project our limiting beliefs onto men's behavior and judge them as truth from our blueprint. There is a part of us, however, that wants to heal these false beliefs. We bring experiences into our life that will reveal our limited and false perceptions. If we continue to live as if these beliefs are true and blame others for our problems, we will continue to suffer. Our feelings of unhappiness and dissatisfaction are only pieces of information that tell us that we are refusing to listen to ourselves.

I ask every client of mine who feels *not enough* and blames others, past or present, for her suffering to look at what she is doing to keep herself in situations that bring about these feelings. Feelings come from our false beliefs and the messages we tell ourselves about the circumstances in which we find ourselves. To change our lives, we must look diligently at what we are telling ourselves based on the belief blueprint we have chosen to accept as truth. To change our situations in life, we must make different choices about what we want to believe.

BREAKING BARRIERS: CHALLENGING THE SYSTEM

Throughout the centuries, women have defied a system that sees them as powerless. Courageous women have fought for the right to vote, for equal pay, for job security and for positions of authority, and have fought against sexual abuse and harassment. The militant feminist movement of the 1970s was a rebellion against a male-dominated society.

Today many women have a new false belief that to be enough, a woman must gain power by competing with men for high positions, acquiring material wealth, driving luxury cars, not relying on an external authority to give them permission to do what they want, aggressively pursuing sex, even having babies and raising them without a husband or father. It is time for women to set their own standards for excellence and achievement without competing for power, and to recognize their own unlimited potential.

WOMEN'S SEXUALITY

There is an attitude about women's sexuality that still exists, even in Western culture. If men have sex with many women, it is a sign of masculinity. But for women, it is a different story. If a woman has sex with many men, she is considered promiscuous and a whore. Many false beliefs shroud women's sexuality, such as the madonna/whore complex. This attitude creates confusion in women who are trying to understand their own female sexual power. In our patriarchal system, women are objectified, diminished and infantalized by labels like *babe, chick* and *doll.* Women are often referred to as "girls" no matter how old they are. *Bitch* and *cunt* are also commonly heard. There are no words that mean the same thing in the English language for men.

Women are confused about their own sexuality, their feelings and their sexual curiosities. What brings them into womanhood and supposedly sexual maturity is the loss of virginity. In school, girls are taught the mechanics of sexuality and birth control. Culturally, socially and religiously, they are given messages about sexual rights and wrongs. Most young women have no concrete understanding about their own sexuality, however. They learn about their sexuality through their limited experiences and the shared experiences of other young women. Usually their first sexual experience is with a teenage boy who is equally confused about sex.

Traditionally, our sexual roles were clearly spelled out. We had a belief blueprint of how women should behave sexually and what they could do in and out of marriage. It was established what was proper and what was improper. There were good women who repressed their sexuality, and there were prostitutes. Today there is a loss of social norms, and women are searching for the rules about their sexual behavior.

A question I often hear from my clients is, "When do I have sex with someone I am dating? On the first date, on the third date?" If a woman has sex too soon, the man will think she is a slut. If she waits too long, she will be judged as a prude. Either way, the possibility of losing the relationship because of making the wrong sexual decision can create insecurity. When they are in a relationship, women often use sexuality as a reward for favors and withhold it to punish their partner. This only adds to the confusion. Women want and need security in a relationship before they become involved sexually. Women want love, commitment, intimacy, exclusivity and monogamy in order to have sex. I believe it is a basic instinct that women have for the protection of themselves and their offspring.

Like Barbra, who was mentioned earlier in this chapter, women with low self-esteem take sexual risks that leave them vulnerable because they believe their sexuality is what will get them a man. If a man finds Barbra sexually attractive, it must mean she is *enough*. But when she experiences sexual intimacy with someone with whom she hasn't established a relationship, she is left feeling used and devastated when the man never calls again. Because of low self-esteem, women will often have sex with a man even if she doesn't want it. She allows men to decide her sexuality. She gives her power away to a man.

In understanding sexuality, it is important to respect and honor ourselves. Our bodies belong to us. We need to listen to ourselves and our sexual and emotional needs and never have intercourse until we feel safe, sensually aware and ready. If we trust ourselves, we will know what is right for us and when. We must value our sexuality, and the decisions we make must come from a place of empowerment and self-knowledge.

In her book *Promiscuities: The Secret Struggle Toward Womanhood*, Naomi Wolf suggests the need for girls to experience a rite of passage into womanhood. The initiation would be performed by older women when a girl turns thirteen. In a safe community with older women and other girls, the thirteen-year-old would commit to an ethic that might include committing never to do anything one does not fully consent to do; never to use sex to get something (love, status, money) that one should seek in other ways; never to have sex without consciousness; never to use drugs or alcohol to mask one's sexual intentions and responsibility; never to degrade or violate one's own sexuality or tolerate others' degrading or violating it; and to practice saying what one wants; to practice saying what one doesn't want; and to seek consciously, with every means at one's disposal, to avoid having to undergo an abortion or to bring into the world a child one is not ready to parent.

WHAT WOMEN NEED AND WANT

We all get confused about our needs as human beings—men as well as women—and we all get confused about the difference between what we need and what we want. I have found that most women believe they need a man in their life to be OK. They believe that without a man they are nothing, and they fear being alone.

Finding a man is a driving force that creates competition between women. To get what we want, we believe we must prove our worth and "be sexy." This driving need to attract a man is evident everywhere in the commercialism of the Western world. Ads entice us to attract a man by telling us how to color our hair and use makeup, how to care for our bodies, how to dress, where to live and all the "in" places to go. In every paper are ads for finding the perfect mate. This commercialism reinforces our belief of our not enoughness. We keep buying products to live up to some sort of consumer standard that we can never reach. To deliver the "goods," the goal is to buy more and not to accept ourselves as we are.

The driving force for perfection to attract a man comes from the belief in women's imperfection. The media and fashion world constantly bombard women with the message "If you don't look this way, you are not acceptable." Women undergo plastic surgery, nose jobs, facelifts, breast implants and liposuction. In spite of these surgical changes, many women continue to hate themselves and feel imperfect, hopeless and not enough. They aren't making these changes for themselves; rather, they are for someone else's approval. A friend of mine went through a painful surgical replacement of twenty-year-old silicone breast implants. When I asked why she had it done in the first place, she said, "Because I didn't feel enough the way I was. I thought I would attract a man if I had breasts."

According to an article on body image in *Psychology Today,* 56 percent of the women surveyed said they were dissatisfied with their overall appearance. Drastic measures for weight control include cigarette smoking, vomiting, abuse of laxatives and taking diuretics or diet pills. Fifteen percent of women said they would sacrifice more than five years of their lives to achieve their perfect weight. The same survey, done in 1972, showed that only 25 percent of women were dissatisfied. A belief in body perfection to overcome feelings of worthlessness and to get a man is damaging to women's health. And ultimately, it never changes our poor self-image or our lack of self-worth.

Love, relationships and marriage are dominant themes in novels, films, magazines, TV shows, music and workshops. Notice the latest self-help books. Most of them are written for women about how to be with men. Look at women's magazine covers. More often than not, feature articles are about relationships. In one month, June 1997, the headlines in women's magazines included:

"Bitchin' Brides and Ideal Husbands"

"How to Make a Man Give More in Bed"

"The Fixup: Who Can Find You the Ideal Man?"

"23 Ways to Drive Him Wild in Bed"

"The No.1 Relationship Mistake that Smart Women Make"

"How Couples Can Keep It Together: Couple Diplomacy"

"How Not to Say What's on Your Mind"

"How Much Intimacy Can Your Relationship Take?"

Not only do we believe we need a man to feel fulfilled, as women we often believe we need children to make us whole. A single actress who adopted a baby says she realized that she would find rapturous love only through being a mother. Being a mother is a wonderful experience for many women, but it is not the source of our love. It does not fulfill the longing that we carry as human beings. In a class I taught for women in the 1970s, I found most of the women had grown children to whom they had devoted their lives. They had husbands they supported through school and in developing their careers. After their husbands achieved their goals, many of them dumped their wives for younger women. At that point, these women were lost and felt desperate; they believed their purpose in life was finished, and they had no idea who they were.

It is easy to get needs and wants confused. Need implies that we can't exist without something. We need water, food and oxygen. A plant needs water. A car needs gas. I also believe we need to love and be loved. Helpless babies die from neglect because their needs aren't met, including being touched and loved by their caregivers. We don't need a glass of wine. We can survive without one. We don't need a new dress and a pair of matching shoes. We don't need a brand-new car. We don't need a man in our lives to make us happy. We may want one, but we don't need one. We may want a baby, but we don't need one. Wants are different than needs. Often the anxiety we feel is the confusion we have about our needs and wants. It is OK to want a healthy relationship with a partner. It is OK to want mutual respect and honesty. It is OK to want a man in our lives. It is OK to want a child. But we don't need one to make us worthwhile, nor do we need a man to remove our false beliefs about ourselves that we are not enough.

The belief that we need a man is so powerful that it terrifies some women to be without one. They try diligently to find a man or the fear of being alone keeps them in abusive relationships. To have an intimate relationship with someone else, we must first have one with ourselves. We must love and believe in ourselves. It is then that we will attract love into our life.

MAKING WOMEN'S VOICES HEARD

In ongoing studies at Harvard University, Wellesley College's Stone Center and other research centers, psychologists are beginning to understand the different voice of women. Women's experience, the research contends, is interconnected and relational, and women's self-development occurs in the context of relationships. The long-accepted theories of human development by Sigmund Freud and his followers saw emotional growth as a search for autonomy. Freud viewed anyone who deviated from his viewpoint as emotionally dependent, immature and mentally ill. This model for human development was based on the study of males. Freud diagnosed women as emotionally unstable and hysterical if they didn't fit into his male model for human development. I believe his sexual theories and his theory of "penis envy" are based on the patriarchal system of the inferiority of women and are his personal fears projected onto women from his own misogyny and sense of deprivation.

The new theories on women's development are based on connectedness in relationship to others. Carol Gilligan, who oversaw Harvard's Project on the Psychology of Women and the Development of Girls, says, women have a "different voice." The difference, researches contend, is the interrelationship with others. What they are discovering is that women's psychological balance is dependent on human connectedness and the ability to make and sustain relationships. Relationships govern every aspect of a woman's life. Women will use conversation to connect and develop relationships; women tend to see people as inter-dependent and inter-connected; women share and care about others in a nurturing way; women function best in context.

A major obstacle in pursuing change for women remains, however. For change to happen in women's lives there must be a change in consciousness. Until now, women's differences have been viewed in the context of a patriarchy.

A wonderful story was told to me by a dear friend that was told to her by another woman friend. In Africa, the women of the village would walk a mile to the river and back every day to retrieve water. The women would carry heavy vessels on their heads to transport the water. One day, the Peace Corps came to this village. The first thing the workers did was to dig a well to relieve the women's burden of carrying heavy vessels over such a long distance. Everyone rejoiced. But soon the women ignored the well and began once more to walk the mile to the river. The fulfillment of their connectedness with one other is what the women needed and missed.

EXERCISE

Refer to chapter 1 to find your core belief blueprint, and review the messages and beliefs that came from society, your parents, your peers, your culture and your religion.

TAKING STOCK OF YOUR MESSAGES AND BELIEFS

Complete the following with the beliefs and messages that formed your blueprint. Your awareness of where they came from is an opportunity to change them. Only you are responsible for continuing these beliefs. The power of change is in the present.

Messages Received from My Mother About:

Her mother:

_____

_____

Women in general:

_____

_____

Herself:

_____

_____

Women's bodies:

_____

_____

Her body:

_____

_____

Women's sexuality:

_____

_____

Menstruation:

_____

_____

PMS:

_____

_____

Menopause:

_____

_____

Women's emotions:

_____

_____

Wife's role:

_____

_____

Mother's role:

_____

_____

Daughter's role:

_____

_____

Me as a woman:

_____

_____

Messages Received from My Father About:

His mother:

_____

_____

_____

Women in general:

_____

_____

Your mother:

_____

_____

Women's bodies:

_____

_____

Menstruation, PMS, menopause:

_____

_____

Women's sexuality:

_____

_____

Women's emotions:

_____

_____

Wife's role:

_____

_____

Mother's role:

_____

_____

Daughter's role:

_____

_____

Me as a woman:

_____

_____

Messages Received from Society, Culture and Religion About:

Women:

_____

_____

_____

Women's bodies:

_____

_____

Women's sexuality:

_____

_____

Women's emotions:

_____

_____

Wife's role:

_____

_____

Mother's role:

_____

_____

Daughter's role:

_____

_____

Messages Received from Siblings and Peers About:

Women:

_____

_____

_____

Women's bodies:

_____

_____

Women's emotions:

_____

_____

Women's sexuality:

_____

_____

Wife's role:

_____

_____

Mother's role:

_____

_____

Daughter's role:

_____

_____

What I Believe About:

Women:

_____

_____

_____

Women's bodies:

_____

_____

Women's emotions:

_____

_____

Women's sexuality:

_____

_____

Wife's role:

_____

_____

Mother's role:

_____

_____

Daughter's role:

_____

_____

Decisions

From the messages and beliefs I received from my childhood about women, I made these decisions about women:

_____

_____

The results of my decision:

_____

_____

New beliefs and decisions I choose to make about women:

_____

_____

We can change limiting beliefs about women by changing behavior. What changes in behavior do you need to make? (review chapter 2):

_____

_____

_____

_____

Chapter 4

MEN AND BELIEFS

Ben is a successful banker. He is of retirement age, but he likes his job, and working keeps his mind off his current problems. It was his job that kept him focused after his first wife died. They had been married forty years and had two sons. The loss was devastating for him, but he never showed it. Ben had bought a lovely home in a prestigious old neighborhood when their boys were young, and his wife had created a beautiful, well-run household environment for him and the children.

The year after his first wife's death, Ben met Mary, a stockbroker. Their paths had crossed years before, but they had never really connected. When they met, Mary was getting a divorce. Though she was twenty years younger than Ben, they were able to comfort each other in their loneliness. Ben was a problem solver, and he helped Mary get through her divorce. For Ben, it felt good to be needed. In time, the relationship developed, and a year later they were married.

What Ben never allowed himself to see earlier in his relationship with Mary soon became overwhelming. He had hoped Mary would keep a home for him like his first wife had, but she wasn't interested in taking care of or managing the household responsibilities. She felt he could afford to hire someone to do that. Instead, Mary was interested in her own career. Many times she'd work late, and Ben would come home to an empty house and no dinner on the table. When Mary finally did come home, she was tired and wanted to watch TV and go to bed. He was beginning to feel more alone than ever.

On weekends, Mary's teenage children would hang out at the house. They swam in the pool and brought their friends over to party. Mary fixed meals for them, played games with them and enjoyed their company. Ben liked her kids and didn't mind spending some time with them. He sometimes took them out to dinner during the week. But it seemed to Ben that he was always on the outside looking in. He wanted time with Mary, but she was always too busy. If he asked her to spend more time with him, she told him he was being selfish and to stop complaining.

In therapy, Ben talked about his feelings of frustration and hurt. At the same time, he said: "I can see she wants to be with her kids, and maybe I shouldn't say anything." He felt shame at showing his feelings. "Maybe I am selfish," he said. But underneath were deep feelings of sadness and hurt. Ben remembered his childhood in England after his mother died. He was eight years old and was sent to a boarding school. He'd never been away from home, and he was scared and grieving for his mother. He recalled sharing his fears with his uncle while his uncle was buttoning up his vest. With each button he told young Ben, "Keep a stiff upper lip. Learn to be tough. Don't ever show your feelings. You are a man, and if you shut off your feelings, you can get through anything." Nearly sixty years later, Ben still carries his uncle's beliefs. To Ben, expressing feelings is a sign of weakness. He believes his feelings of anger, sadness and hurt are weak and unimportant.

■

Ben is not unlike many men. He grew up in a time when men were taught by other men to be tough under any circumstances, especially those under which one felt the most vulnerable. As the patriarch, the head of the household, Ben was diligent in his duties. He never failed to be a good provider and protector for his family. Now he was with a woman who also saw herself as a provider, and Ben was very confused about his role with her. The patriarchal rules he had been living out, either consciously or unconsciously, were being challenged.

The core beliefs of many men are different from the core beliefs of many women, even if they grow up in the same family. At birth, the mere announcement that "it's a boy" has a different ring to it than "it's a girl" and starts the whole process of false beliefs. Before the umbilical cord is cut, the boy is often perceived as following in his father's footsteps or in the family tradition. Even circumcision is part of the message: "Pain is something you are going to have to learn to endure, so here's a taste of it." Perhaps the trauma of circumcision is the beginning of men's disassociation from pain.

PATRIARCHY AND MALES

Boys born into a strong patriarchal family have more defined expectations that are translated by the child into beliefs about himself. For example, the expectation to "make something of yourself" is great. When these expectations are incongruent with the boy's talents or physical capacity, the belief is that he has let down his father, his family, his culture and in some cases, his country. The pressure is to succeed, sometimes at all costs. Deceit, fraud, broken marriages and broken lives are often the result.

Although men's roles in society today are not as clearly defined as they were forty or fifty years ago, the belief systems of previous generations still influence men's behavior and create confusion because they are not compatible with the times. This is especially true in those countries where many different cultures have come together, such as the United States, England and throughout Western Europe. Similar confusion has risen in Eastern Europe ever since the fall of the Iron Curtain. Men are having a difficult time making life decisions. They are seeing that life is not as narrowly defined as they were taught to believe, but they are having difficulty defining their lives on an individual basis. Because the old patriarchal beliefs are becoming more obsolete, men often perceive that there must be something wrong with them or that they are *not enough*.

There needs to be a paradigm shift in consciousness that allows men to look at the beliefs in their life that have no practical application. There must be a willingness to change: a willingness to take responsibility and tune into one's own inner authority, and a release of the beliefs that are not in alignment with one's own destiny or talents. This takes courage, especially if these beliefs are sacrosanct, framed in religion or believed to be the will of God. Chaos often results when revered beliefs are abandoned and a new or different worldview is created. Families often feel threatened by radical changes of a member of the family, especially if that member is Dad, the breadwinner, the patriarch. When a man starts to take a look at his life and the belief system that propagated it as irrelevant or absurd, the whole family can feel threatened because the status quo—their very foundation—is being disrupted. Even friends, extended family, acquaintances and business associates can be affected. Men who question their lives in such a way are perceived as emotionally disturbed or narcissistic. Often it is simply chalked up as a "midlife crisis." In many cases, divorce or loss of business or career is the result. The support systems to help a man find himself can be found in men's groups, but these are difficult to find and are generally viewed with suspicion and cynicism.

SHATTERING THE MYTHS

The belief that manhood is achieved by joining the military, by becoming CEO of a major corporation, by winning the Heisman trophy or by emulating the Marlboro Man is totally false. We have seen firsthand the tragic results of these beliefs: the dehumanizing pictures that have come out of war-torn Bosnia; the demythologization of O. J. Simpson during his criminal trial and the Watergate scandal and subsequent resignation of President Richard M. Nixon.

Through the medium of television, which makes news instantly available, we have seen disturbing scenes of war, one after another, from all parts of the world. Most of the destruction we see was perpetrated by men. How did these men arrive at such a state of insensitivity as to be able to slaughter other human beings with bombs, rifles, even bayonets?

Some of the people who were slaughtered were longtime neighbors. Others were mothers and children. What happened in the development of the consciousness of these men that would allow them to murder so casually? Based on the work I've done with men, it seems to me that many of them grow up believing it is necessary to be tough, hard and sometimes cruel in order to be a man. To be sensitive and gentle is to be a girl, and that is an emasculating thought for some men. Being called a girl is probably the worst insult an adolescent male can receive. How many times have we heard the taunt: "You throw like a girl" on a high school baseball field?

By examining men's beliefs about manhood, we may shed some light on this phenomenon. One very powerful belief that permeates our society is that of being the breadwinner. Today, however, it is more than just being the breadwinner; it is also providing and maintaining a lifestyle. The concept of "Too tired to keep running, too scared to stop" becomes part of the breadwinner's daily life. His mantra becomes "push, push, push." The head of the house cannot rest. He cannot get sick. Showing feelings of vulnerability is shameful. A patriarch becomes trapped in a role based not only on the beliefs he inherited and is loyal to, but also on the beliefs of his family, relatives, culture and society.

Statistics show that for every wife who goes to the store for a loaf of bread and doesn't come back, there are two hundred husbands who leave and never return. This shocking dichotomy reflects the pressure that our belief systems create. Ralph's story is one example.

■

Ralph had been working eighty hours a week for ten years. At the age of thirty-two, he told his wife that he was burned out. The previous year, his father-in-law died of a heart attack at the age of fifty-nine, and six months later his own father died of cancer, also at age fifty-nine. Ralph didn't think he would even make it to thirty-nine if he didn't stop. He had seen both his father and his father-in-law working at jobs they weren't happy with. They didn't feel appreciated by their wives or children because they often came home too tired to interact with the family. No more the lover, the companion, the best friend, the mentor, they were now just working machines. Both these men believed strongly in the work ethic, and that left little room for any other form of human development. This was the belief that Ralph was also locked into.

One day it occurred to Ralph that his life was totally absurd, that he was just a working machine and had lost his humanness. He no longer saw himself as a person but as someone who provided a lifestyle that he didn't even have time to enjoy himself. What's more, Ralph also realized that nothing he had done in his life since he was a toddler had been of his own volition. His life had never been his; his time had never been his. It was an astounding epiphany, so astounding that he couldn't go on any longer. He told his wife that he was taking the next year off to find himself. He arranged for her to be taken care of financially, then he took his trail bike, his backpack, twenty dollars and his dog and took off.

His first night out on the road, Ralph felt confused, plagued with doubt and so vulnerable and lonely that he cried himself to sleep. As he continued on his journey, though, he found an inner strength he didn't know he had. He had met many men like himself on the road. Some had been CEOs, others had been successful in their careers to one degree or another, but all felt too scared to stop and take a look at their lives. Ralph's wife filed for divorce before the year was up. He felt liberated not because she divorced him but because he had changed the limiting beliefs about himself. He is now a holistic health professional, a career he had thought about for years but had not acted on—until he tapped into the potential within him.

Like women, men get locked into beliefs about the roles they must play in life. If you are a husband, then you have to do all the "husband" things that you learned growing up with your family. The role is perceived as a belief system with very little input from the individual and is further enforced by the extended family, the culture and the religion.

The story of Ralph is an example of how alone a man can be in making radical life decisions. It wasn't until the late 1960s that Ralph began to notice that the way he was living his life was absurd. Many New Age books sent him questioning. That led him to books on Eastern philosophy that in turn led him into opening up to a more universal approach to his own life. Such a radical change in a worldview and implementing that worldview does not come without pain, or difficulty and, of course, consequences.

It takes a lot of courage for Ralph and other men like him to leave behind all the beliefs that are not in alignment with their new vision. Some men wind up on the street, emotionally and psychologically broken, for lack of family and social support. Some men retreat to the mountains and congregate with other men who have also "dropped out." Some men join Eastern religious sects or set off for India on a pilgrimage. Others become emotionally unstable and paranoid and join paramilitary groups to take their pain and rage out on the government. Still others, finding the new path too difficult, return to the previous lifestyle with a new wife (often the same age as their children or younger), a new business or a new career. Some even go to the extreme right, becoming "born again" and adopting a narrow, conservative worldview in order to maintain a sense of security.

"MEN DON'T CRY": THE ROLES MALES PLAY

I have often heard from male clients how they were told as young boys— six and seven years of age and younger—that men don't cry. They felt constant pressure to "be a man." Getting Dad's approval meant holding back the tears. This belief about manhood was also supported by the women in the family. Boys must learn to be tough and stifle feelings of pain, both physical and emotional. By the time a boy is ten, the unspoken message among his peers is that crying is for sissies. This message is often unspoken but is communicated psychically. After the Mission Viejo, California, team lost the 1997 Little League World Series, the front-page picture in the local newspaper showed a member of the team in tears. An acquaintance of mine thought it was despicable that the picture was published. She believed it would be a source of shame for that particular player now and in the future. Some women as well as men are socialized into thinking that expressing emotions is taboo for men and boys.

There is so much shame over crying that my male clients will often apologize to me for shedding a tear. Sometimes, when they feel safe enough, a floodgate of tears is released. Shame is the controlling emotion that boys learn from their fathers, other men and sometimes women. In some cultures, shame will lead men to commit suicide rather than face his family or his superiors. Again, the false belief of not measuring up, that we are basically inadequate, permeates our consciousness.

For men, enduring pain is something to be proud of. It is manly, especially if the pain is perpetrated by another man. Boxing, football, pro wrestling and other sports in which hurting your opponent is part of the game are played predominantly by men.

It is interesting that the word *endure* in French means, essentially, "to make hard." Perhaps, when one endures enough he becomes hard and eventually has difficulty feeling because the armor he has built up is almost impenetrable. The sensitive, soft child learns to become the insensitive, hard teenager and thus becomes better equipped for all of the roles society expects of him. Let's examine some of those roles.

THE SOLDIER. If we are to send our sons to war and have them endure the hardships that war demands, then perhaps, unconsciously, we start preparing them for it early in life. By the time they are seventeen, if they haven't developed enough discipline and toughness, they can always join the Marines and learn how to "become a man." Some kind of collective consciousness proclaims that in order to be a man, you have to have your humanity stripped away. Once we dehumanize you, once we strip away all of the abilities that you were born with that enable you to feel, then you have achieved manhood. Once you have learned to maim and kill and risk being maimed and killed, then manhood becomes a title you deserve.

Can a society that feels a need for a strong defense allow its soldiers to experience their feminine energy? Can these soldiers be truly dependable warriors without a tough armor? Can compassion, empathy, vulnerability and gentleness find a place on the battlefield? Can a soldier look into the eyes of the enemy, see his soul and not feel compassion? Does the belief of a General Patton or a General Eisenhower as the archetypal man continue to stand up in the face of the recent dismissals of top-ranking U.S. military officers for sexually harassing or allowing the sexual harassment of female soldiers? These female soldiers were treated no differently than other men have been treated. Even the cruel and dehumanizing way many rookie officers are hazed is finally being seen as void of many virtues. This should wake up some of us to the failures of our concepts of manhood.

THE MARLBORO MAN. We don't have to go the way of the Soldier to see men who have "endured" and become hard and insensitive. The stereotypical Marlboro Man is one who has stoically endured physical hardships in his work. He is seen also as a man's man. The familiar image of the cattle-driving, rough-and-ready cowboy and his many derivatives are deeply ingrained in Western culture. The Saturday afternoon Western matinees of the forties and early fifties personified the belief that men had to be heroes to the helpless and the weak. Actors such as John Wayne, Gene Autry and Gary Cooper, and characters like Hopalong Cassidy and the Lone Ranger portrayed men as loners (or sometimes with a male sidekick) with only a horse for a companion. What messages did young, impressionable boys get about manhood from these movies? That men are in charge, women are to be protected and the enemy is to be conquered.

THE JOCK. Today the Western has been replaced by Monday Night Football. The cowboy has been replaced by the Jock, whose identity is found in his muscular strength and macho presence. The model of manhood today for young boys is very similar to that of the Soldier and the Jock: a man who prefers to hang out with other men in a clublike atmosphere that excludes women. Being tough and treating each other harshly is acceptable behavior. On television I saw a football player carried off the field with a concussion or other type of injury, and when the replay was shown, I heard the announcer say, "It was a clean hit." When a boxer is knocked unconscious and possibly brain damaged, we accept it as "just what men do." We have made the Jock our hero. When Muhammad Ali was selected to light the torch at the 1996 Summer Olympics in Atlanta, he was perceived as a hero. And what was the condition of that hero? He had been reduced to a cripple from the beatings he took in the boxing ring. This was the hero whom the nations held up to the world, someone who had literally been so badly beaten that he had difficulty functioning. And we applaud that.

THE PLAYBOY. From one end of the spectrum, we move to the other: the Playboy. The Playboy sees his manhood honed and validated through his conquests of women rather than through military accomplishments, athletic feats or the ability to brand a steer. Bob's role as the Playboy put a strain on his marriage.

Bob is tall and handsome, with a quick smile. He's the kind of guy everyone likes. The thoughtful things he does endear him to his colleagues. Bob has a lot of friends he hangs out with. His hobby is racing cars.

Bob is also thoughtful with Sally, his wife. He brings her flowers, mushy cards and takes her to surprise dinners and the theater. Though Sally has a successful career that requires a lot of traveling, they spend as much time together as possible. They are an attractive couple. He's tall and dark, and she is medium height, with blond, curly hair, blue eyes and a very pretty face. Thanks to both their successful careers, they can afford to own a large home, drive nice cars and take expensive vacations.

Because they are in the same business, they often go to the same functions. Sally tends to be businesslike and reserved on these occasions. When she searches for Bob, though, she usually finds him flirting with another woman. This makes her feel uncomfortable and embarrassed. Sometimes he tells her to go home by herself and he'll find a ride later. Naturally, it has been the source of conflict for them. They decided it would cause less conflict if they took two cars. Bob feels relieved when

Sally leaves the party or function without him. He stays as long as he wants and sometimes doesn't come home until dawn.

Bob has had affairs in their ten years of marriage. He is always sorry he has hurt Sally, and somehow they remain together. But she feels she can never trust him. He thinks she is overreacting, jealous and controlling. Bob's mother was very controlling when he was a child. She always wanted to know where his dad was going and when he'd be home. His parents fought a lot. It seemed his mother was always mad at his father about something. She bossed him around and told him what to do. Invariably his dad would yell "Get off my back," and walk out the door.

When Bob and his brothers were young, Bob began to develop a system of beliefs about women. His dad gave him the message that women were difficult, hysterical and bitchy. "Women are full of it. Don't listen to them. All they do is complain. You can never satisfy them. I bust my balls, and it still isn't enough for her," his father would tell him.

Though Bob was very attached to and protective of his mother, he could see her same controlling, bossy behavior with him and his brothers. He began to believe that his dad was right: "You just have to accept that is how women are." It wasn't until Bob was in high school that he discovered his dad was a womanizer. By the time he graduated from college, his parents were divorced.

■

Bob's belief in his manhood has to do with his appeal to women. His worth as a man has to do with the attention he gets from women. He isn't yet "tired of running," but he is definitely "too scared to stop." You see, he can't stop chasing women because he thinks he'll stop getting the attention he believes he needs to feel whole, to feel enough. His belief in the importance of attracting women is perpetuated by his core belief of inadequacy, imperfection and not enoughness.

The Playboy's attraction to women doesn't come from an inherent integration of his masculinity but from having observed what women will respond to, starting with his mother. He is more comfortable in the presence of women than the Marlboro Man because he knows exactly what they want and is willing to give it to them. The Playboy never allows the women he's with to touch the feminine aspects of his psyche at all. Objectifying women is his main preoccupation. With the Playboy, there is no acknowledgment of his identity with the female but rather a need to control and satisfy women. This male role is not new to our society or to our culture. Probably since the beginning of the human race, men have been flaunting their seductive, testosterone-driven behaviors like the metaphorical peacock. It always works, and women continue to be seduced.

What does a man do to seduce women? He uses charm, which is learned at an early age. I have often observed little boys charm and seduce their mothers. Mothers often dress up their "little man" as little men. Often the choice of clothes and hairstyles is to please Mother, not the son. From their mothers, boys are taught what it takes to please and manipulate women.

Next comes behavior. Boys learn early on that some women are pleased, even impressed, when a man opens the door for them or picks up the tab or orders for them in a restaurant. Again, most boys learn these "gentlemanly" behaviors not from other men but from their mothers. Even learning how to say the "right thing" such as complimenting a women on her clothes or hair or any aspect of her physical appearance is usually learned from Mother. If seducing Mother is OK, then it must be OK to seduce or flirt with someone even if you are married, because after all that is what a woman likes to hear and what a real man does.

We don't have to look too far for playboy role models. They exist in every walk of life, from presidents to kings to sports figures and celebrities, from Uncle Albert to the next-door neighbor.

THE RIGHT IMAGE: WEALTH AND POWER

If you look through most magazine racks, you will see articles on everything from how to create and maintain a CEO image to how to create the perfect body. Many men "buy" into a belief system about appropriate dress codes that are determined by the fashion industry. To be enough, to be acceptable, they have to conform to these codes.

The "good enough" belief system causes us to believe, "If I follow all the rules, I will be properly rewarded. If I follow the direction and beliefs of my parents, I will be successful as a man, especially if I emulate the successful men in the family. If I am true to the dictates of my church or religion, I will please God. If I follow the dictates of my government and sacrifice my life, they will honor and maybe even take care of me. If I follow the rules of society, I will be approved of and rewarded. If I go to the right schools and take the right courses, I will be acceptable and pursued by big business. If I find the right woman, get married, and have a family, I will have succeeded as a person. And, of course, if I consume what advertising is feeding me, I am guaranteed happiness. Then, maybe, I will be enough."

Becoming the CEO of a large company and accumulating wealth and material items are often part of a man's belief that manhood has been achieved. I have had men of extreme wealth come to my office in a total state of despair because they have achieved the pinnacle of business and wealth, yet their lives, according to them, are "empty." In our sessions, they become little boys, defeated and weak. All of their achievements have left them unfulfilled and often at the expense of broken marriages and children who are totally alienated from them. The impulse to accumulate wealth is derived from competitive posturing with other men. Oftentimes these men had fathers who were absent either physically or emotionally, and as boys they learned about manhood either from their mothers, who were often contemptuous of men, or from a male teacher or coach. Some of these men went to an all-boys high school and then to an all-male college or into the military. Ironically, these men eventually came to a female therapist with whom they could feel safe, validated and nurtured, something most of my male clients were ashamed to admit they needed. It never occurred to them that they could get nurturing from another man. That concept brought up their hidden fears of homosexuality because somehow they equated closeness and nurturing with sex and penetration.

INTEGRATING THE FEMININE

A man with a false sense of his own masculinity has no room for a woman or for integrating his own femininity into his life. He will never allow a woman to get too close to him, and he will keep his inner feminine self at a safe distance. By keeping his feminine side at a safe distance, he will never embrace the sensitive part of himself or the mysteries of nature. For the Marlboro Man, life will always be rigid and concrete. A man who clings to his rigid, one-sided masculinity will never experience softness, warmth and gentleness. He might perceive these attributes as weaknesses rather than as virtues. In turn, he will want a woman to feel and think like a man and allow herself to be abused, just as he allows himself to be abused as proof of his manhood. Without the development of his feminine side, a man is emotionally poverty-stricken. He becomes a cardboard figure. He becomes the composite of overcompetitiveness, foolhardiness and a macho personality.

In spite of the fact that past generations of men grew up believing that being gentle and tender was shameful, today we occasionally see examples, sometimes even in the sports world, of grown men breaking down and crying. Sometimes the tears come from winning or losing a close contest. I recall one particular situation in 1992 in which football player Dennis Byrd of the New York Jets had been rendered a quadriplegic because of injuries sustained in a game. When his teammates were asked to comment, some of them literally sobbed. These men did not identify hardness and manhood as synonymous.

The program "A Gathering of Men," hosted by Bill Moyers and shown on PBS in 1980, covered the work that Robert Bly was doing with large groups of men in helping them look at their core wounds, which came from beliefs about themselves that were damaging and shameful. The visible shedding of grief was part of the process and was often accompanied by sobbing. It was only in a safe environment, however, that the men were able to process their grief. Many men believe that to cry in front of women is a sign of weakness, and this display of vulnerability invites shame.

In a men's group led by my husband, who is a spiritual counselor, none of the men felt that they had arrived at manhood. These men ranged in age from late thirties to early sixties. All of them still felt like boys and believed that they were alone with their feelings. They believed that all other men were "men" except themselves. They believed that if they did what society, their culture and their upbringing prescribed, they would achieve manhood.

The grief that men have has to do with a loss of self, not a loss of manhood or family or career. The fundamental loss of one's connection with his wholeness is at the core of their distress. Sometimes the grief has to do with the loss of one's own feeling of manhood and the possibility that it is too late to recover it. Until a man can recover his wholeness, any attempt on his part to move into manhood can only bring about disappointment. Manhood is inherent within the context of a man's wholeness, just as the fruit of the tree is inherent within the seed itself. Nothing more needs to be added.

A belief in one's own manhood cannot come from fulfilling external criteria. It must come from having reached deep enough into one's own psyche, where manhood already exists. Manhood is not a social status. It is a realization that comes from the soul. It is a presence felt at the deepest level. It is a state of being that no one can strip away because it has always been there. It only has to be revealed to oneself. Once a man has discovered this state of being, he has found something he can truly anchor his belief in. He has discovered something no one can strip him of except himself. The only way that he can lose his manhood again is if he abandons himself.

MEN AND RELATIONSHIPS

Men who come to see me for help in their relationships often tell me that they don't feel comfortable with intimacy. They say it is not a priority as a source of personal and emotional satisfaction. Many of my male clients fear getting closer to a woman because they believe a woman wants to control them and smother them. These beliefs are picked up subtly as young boys from either their dads or other adult males. The "leash" or "shackle" is often mentioned in conjunction with committed relationships. Sometimes it is castration anxiety ("She's got me by the balls"), a belief that certainly puts a definite damper on intimacy. When a boy hears this kind of attitude from men, he develops a fear of women. And when he sees the "shackle" attitude in movies and on television and hears the jokes about marriage by male stand-up comics ("Take my wife . . . please!"), it is no wonder that a fear of intimacy develops.

In many parts of the world, men see women as being beneath them in status and in some cases as less than human. Women are the child-bearers and in the service of men. In traditionally patriarchal countries, men believe they have supreme, undisputed and God-given authority over women. Here in the United States, these beliefs have become quite blurred and highly challenged by men as well as by women.

According to Michael Gurian in his book *Mothers, Sons and Lovers,* if a man did not have appropriate initiation into manhood, he is usually stuck in adolescence on the relationship barometer. The relationships that men have with women are often very similar to the relationships they have or had with their mothers. Men will project their attitudes toward women onto their partners and will react in much the same way as they reacted to their mothers. They will fear their partners the same way they feared their mothers. If Mom was a shaming person, they will fear being shamed by their partner. If Mom withdrew her love when Junior did not please her, they will fear abandonment if they don't please their wives. If they were afraid to stand up for themselves with Mom, they will fear standing up for themselves with women and usually will be passive-aggressive in their relationships.

Some men attended male-only high schools or grew up in farming or ranching communities where hypermasculine roles were encouraged and clearly defined. Often these men develop strong bonds with their peers, which are often the envy of their mates. It must be noted, however, that these relationships are characterized by competitive posturing and one-upmanship. These kinds of relationships leave little ground for developing mutual respect. I am always amazed how easy it is for my husband to strike up conversations with male strangers over a particular sporting event. I have seen this phenomenon in almost every country we have visited together.

OWNING YOUR INNER AUTHORITY

On the flip side, a number of men have little difficulty relating to both their feminine and masculine sides, whether it is in their relationships or by valuing their feminine aspects: nurturing, creativity, vulnerability and gentleness. Their ability to integrate the masculine and feminine into their lives makes it possible for them to empathize with women. For these men, vulnerability is not a threatening feeling. They have found their inner authority.

I'm always deeply touched when I see a strong bond between father and son. On one cross-country flight, I happened to sit next to a man and his thirteen-year-old son. I saw the son take his father's hand in his and place it next to his own cheek, caress the hand and kiss it. When I mentioned what I had observed, the father told me that he and his son were good friends and were never afraid of showing affection to each other. During the course of our conversation, I found out that the father was an accomplished musician and was deeply spiritual. When a son can openly hug and kiss his father, I know that their relationship is healthy. Unfortunately, they are the exception. It seems that fathers in our society have related to their children as an afterthought. Fathers often express feelings of inadequacy when it comes to relating to their kids and to kids in general. The expression often is, "I don't know what to do with them."

The authority that a man feels when he is in touch with his manhood does not come from the external world. It is not something that can be taken away from him. Once a man has grounded himself in his inner authority, his God-given authority, no one can take that away.

Let me be clear. I'm not talking about an external authority such as a knowledge of science, or a job or religion, or anything of the outside world. I'm not talking about an authority that comes from acquiring the position of a CEO or from having reached the military rank of a four-star general. I'm not talking about the authority that comes from having been elected president or from ascending to the throne after the death of a king. I'm talking about a man's authority of himself, free of judgment, criticism, opinion, or interpretation. This authority is a gut feeling, not the result of a logical conclusion. It is not necessarily rational, but it is always wise. It is always intuitive. It always knows.

This authority cannot be taught. It can only be discovered. That is why a man rigid in his own identity cannot allow himself to delve into his psyche because he believes he already has achieved manhood. After all, he has his horse, his cattle, his range and his fellow cowboys. If the Marlboro Man were to admit to himself that he was dissatisfied with his feelings of manhood, it would mean that he has lived a lie all those years, that he has been pretending to be a man, and this admission would be a threat to his fellow cowboys.

Here's an example of how tapping into your inner authority can yield positive results. When my husband was out one day with his six-year-old son, the boy wanted to go to an arcade. It had been agreed upon previously that the arcade on this particular day was off-limits. My husband kept reminding his son of the agreement, but the strong-willed boy continued to nag him about going to the arcade. My husband was actually quite impressed by his son's persistent behavior and marveled at his lack of fear; it was not something he would have pushed with his own father for fear of being put down or shamed. Baffled as to how to deal with the situation in a kind and loving way, my husband went deep into himself, to that place where his inner authority existed, and asked for help. They stopped walking, and he bent down to his son's eye level and said, "Son, look into my eyes. We are not going to the arcade. Continue looking into my eyes. Now repeat what I said."

His son said, "We are not going to the arcade."

My husband went on, "I don't want to talk about this any further. Now, repeat what I said and keep looking at me."

"You don't want to talk about this any further."

"That's right. Do you get it?"

"Yes."

"Do I have to say anything more about it?"

"No."

The two of them continued walking, and about half a block farther his son turned to him and said, "Dad, let's do that again. That feels really good."

What transpired above could fill volumes. What my husband's son learned was more basic and fundamental than any lecture about authority or manhood. What he got was a practical experience of both. A part of him resonated with his father's feelings of authority, and because it came from a close male role model, he associated it with his own feelings of manhood. I'm not saying that achieving manhood takes place overnight. What needs to happen for boys to germinate and reach full realization is a constant dose of personal authority from another male.

In talking to my husband about the experience, he explained that while he was having the verbal exchange about the arcade, his critical self-talk surfaced and judged him for being too authoritarian. It suggested a more lenient way of dealing with it. All of my husband's negative issues about authority—based on his memories of his father—used to surface when it came to disciplining his son. Prior to owning his authority as a father, my husband used to deal with his son either in an extremely lenient manner where boundaries were nonexistent or by losing patience and treating him in a harsh manner. His belief in his own authority is now based on a deeply felt experience.

MAKING MEN'S VOICES HEARD

Our program of old beliefs does not lose its power instantaneously. It loses its power over a period of time as we proceed to give power to another set of beliefs that comes from wisdom and personal experience rather than from fear or a need to be accepted. Inner authority can never be compromised by an outside authority.

All of the help that men need to find their voice and grow into their own manhood is available. Mentors are available. An old adage says, "You don't find the teacher. The teacher finds you when you're ready." A man's desire to find his own manhood must first come from the realization that his beliefs about manhood up until now may be false or unacceptable or don't work at all. He must then be willing to open himself up to unlearn in order to learn. Just as a full cup can no longer hold anymore, a man must first be willing to empty his cup of false beliefs. There is a certain courage that comes from this intention, and a certain relief as all of the false security he has held on to his whole life is released.

The whole process involves cutting away the branches of the tree that do not bear fruit. These branches only waste energy. To learn about his manhood, a man must become totally humble. He must be willing to go to his inner heart—not the heart created by his mind, but the heart that has been there since the beginning of his life. It is in his heart that he will find all the answers. His heart will know what he needs to do and will show him how to behave as a man. His heart will give him the courage he needs. He must be willing to set clear boundaries for himself and for others.

When a man finally realizes that his life is absurd, he can examine it and realize that he has been totally naive and has been lied to by well-meaning but misguided people. He must wake up to the fact that death is inevitable and that a man's acknowledgment of his own presence, his own authority, can only be found by going to the source deep inside him.

All the information that tells us how to be all we can be lies inside of us. It is in nature's design. What tells a mango tree to bear fruit is contained within its seed. We don't have to tell a sheep how to be a sheep or a salmon how to be a salmon or a collie how to be a collie. Even within the animal kingdom, uniqueness is apparent. How did we as human beings get so far off track and believe that we had to teach people how to be themselves? All we need to do is give proper guidance, protection and support and move to the beat of our own drum in order for our children to become themselves and develop their inherent gifts.

The core pattern and blueprint of our being has always been there. We just need to push aside the limiting beliefs about ourselves to reveal our truth. This way of being is our truth.

EXERCISE

Refer to chapter 1 to find your core belief blueprint, and review the messages and beliefs that came from society, your parents, your peers, your culture and your religion.

TAKING STOCK OF YOUR MESSAGES AND BELIEFS

Complete the following with the beliefs and messages that formed your blueprint. Your awareness of where they came from is an opportunity to change them. Only you are responsible for continuing these beliefs. The power of change is in the present.

Messages Received from My Father About:

His father:

_____

_____

Himself as a father:

_____

_____

Himself as a man:

_____

_____

Men in general:

_____

_____

His body:

_____

_____

Men's bodies:

_____

_____

Men's emotions:

_____

_____

Men's sexuality:

_____

_____

Men's role as head of household:

_____

_____

Men's role in business:

_____

_____

Husband's role:

_____

_____

Father's role:

_____

_____

Son's role:

_____

_____

Me as a man:

_____

_____

Messages Received from My Mother About:

Her father:

_____

_____

Men in general:

_____

_____

My father:

_____

_____

Men's bodies:

_____

_____

Men's emotions:

_____

_____

Men's sexuality:

_____

_____

Men's role as head of household:

_____

_____

Men's role in business:

_____

_____

Husband's role:

_____

_____

Father's role:

_____

_____

Son's role:

_____

_____

Me as a man:

_____

_____

Messages Received from Society, Culture and Religion About:

Men:

_____

_____

Men's bodies:

_____

_____

Men's emotions:

_____

_____

Men's sexuality:

_____

_____

Men's role as head of household:

_____

_____

Men's role in business:

_____

_____

Husband's role:

_____

_____

Father's role:

_____

_____

Son's role:

_____

_____

Messages Received from Siblings and Peers About:

Men:

_____

_____

Their bodies:

_____

_____

Men's bodies:

_____

_____

Men's emotions:

_____

_____

Men's sexuality:

_____

_____

Men's role as head of household:

_____

_____

Men's role in business:

_____

_____

Husband's role:

_____

_____

Father's role:

_____

_____

Son's role:

_____

_____

What I Believe About:

Men:

_____

_____

Men's bodies:

_____

_____

Men's emotions:

_____

_____

Men's sexuality:

_____

_____

Men's role as head of household:

_____

_____

Men's role in business:

_____

_____

Husband's role:

_____

_____

Father's role:

_____

_____

Son's role:

_____

_____

Decisions

From the messages and beliefs about men that I received from my childhood, I made these decisions about men:

_____

_____

_____

The results of my decision:

_____

_____

_____

New beliefs and decisions I choose to make about men:

_____

_____

_____

_____

_____

We can change limiting beliefs about men by changing behavior. What changes in behavior do you need to make? (review chapter 2):

_____

_____

_____

_____

_____

_____

_____

Chapter 5

BELIEFS ABOUT RELATIONSHIPS

The day Sandi and Andrew were married was the most exciting day of their lives. They couldn't believe how lucky they were to have found each other. For as long as she could remember, Sandi had dreamed about getting married. Never had she been so in love. After a string of unsuccessful relationships, Sandi felt that this time she had found the right man. She had done a lot of her own growth work, had been in individual and group therapy and she had read many self-help books. Now she believed she had found the right partner and was ready to make this relationship work. She felt so alive as she anticipated a life of happiness. This is what I've wanted all my life, she thought.

Sandi was thirty-eight, and Andrew was forty-five. After Andrew had met Sandi, he thought about her constantly. This was his third marriage, but he felt he had found the right partner and was willing once again to take the risk. He loved her more than any other woman he had been with. Sandi was different from the others. He had so much fun with her. She was beautiful and funny, and she laughed at all his jokes. And their lovemaking was passionate. Sandi assured him that they would work out all their challenges, including his two former wives and his two grown sons.

Each saw something special in the other. Andrew was a successful attorney, and Sandi saw in him a partner who would be strong and dependable, someone who would always care for her. Sandi worked as a trainer with a cosmetics company, and Andrew saw in her a partner who not only was beautiful and fun, but who also seemed to be successful and independent. He, too, felt he had found someone who would love him forever.

The marriage was off to a great start. What Sandi loved best about Andrew was his strength. He knew what he wanted and how to get it. He took command at the best restaurants. He made suggestions for what she might like to eat and knew the right wines to order. He even ordered for her. Sandi felt so taken care of. He bought her fine jewelry and expensive clothes. He had marvelous taste. At his urging, Sandi worked out regularly and kept her body in shape. Her trim figure pleased him. He seemed totally interested in her. Sandi had never gotten so much attention. At home, Andrew liked things done a certain way, and because Sandi appreciated all the love and attention she got from him, she tried hard to please him by doing what he wanted. She also excelled at her job and was rewarded financially for it. But away from work, she had to push herself to get things done and often procrastinated.

Andrew, in turn, loved Sandi's strength. Her intelligence and ability to speak in front of large groups impressed him. She seemed very successful, yet he didn't feel competitive with her. Whenever they went out, she turned the reins over to him. He liked being married to a strong woman who was comfortable letting him take control. He felt she was a real prize. But Sandi didn't seem to have the same interest he had in keeping the house in order. At times he would have to remind her of how he wanted things done.

Within two years the relationship had changed. Their marriage was falling apart, and Sandi and Andrew didn't know what had happened. It had started out so well and felt so right. They both had such high hopes of getting everything they dreamed of. Each blamed the other, and both believed the marriage had been a mistake. They felt they couldn't continue the relationship the way it was going, but they didn't know how to change it.

■

By the time Sandi and Andrew came to me for counseling, they were feeling desperate, hopeless and helpless. In our sessions, we proceeded to dig deep into their respective childhoods—where their limiting beliefs were created and incorporated—and produced a core belief blueprint for each of them. From there, they were able to discover themselves as individuals and then work mutually to save their relationship.

First, we focused on Sandi's story. Sandi was a child of an unavailable father and an anxious, fearful mother. Her brother, who was two years older, was seriously ill throughout his childhood. Sandi's father, a workaholic, was rarely home, which left her mother worried and feeling overwhelmed most of the time. She began to project her fears onto Sandi. She was afraid to let her swim in the pool, she was afraid she might fall off her bike and she was even afraid to let Sandi walk a block to a friend's house. Consequently, Sandi became fearful and anxious like her mother.

Most of the time, Sandi endeavored to be a good girl and please her mother to alleviate her mother's fears. Sometimes, though, Sandi rebelled and acted out; she even had temper tantrums. Sandi hated being controlled, but at the same time her mother's control gave her a sense of security. Even though she resented it, Sandi was dependent on her mother. Even throughout high school, her mother told her what to wear and what to do, whom she could see and whom she couldn't. Mother continuously reminded her that she made sacrifices to buy her things, but the things she bought for Sandi were always her mother's choice, not Sandi's.

The pattern of people pleasing, rebelling and giving in followed Sandi throughout her life. Sandi was caught between her obligations and her own desires. Her decisions were often based on what other people wanted. She had difficulty making decisions for herself.

Whereas Sandi gave in to control, Andrew took control. Andrew's father was successful and provided well for the family, but he had a drinking problem. When he was sober he was a nice guy, but when he was drunk he was mean, critical, judgmental and verbally abusive. It left Andrew feeling fearful, powerless, anxious and hypervigilant, never knowing from day to day how his father would act. What Andrew did when his father was drunk and abusive was to withdraw and hide. His anxiety lessened when he took control of the situation at home by becoming the caregiver. The oldest of three boys, Andrew felt the need to protect his mother. He was there to help her in ways his dad couldn't and took over adult responsibilities at a young age. He discovered he felt better when he was needed. To cover his feelings of anxiety and insecurity, he developed a great sense of humor.

Sandi and Andrew are a perfect match. When they first met, they fell blindly, madly in love, but eventually, as their emotional clarity returned, they saw things about each other that had eluded them before. In the beginning, Sandi felt safe when Andrew controlled her every move, and she loved all the things he gave her and did for her. She felt dependent on him even though deep down she didn't like being dependent. Some part of her felt she needed to be controlled to feel safe and to be OK.

Now, however, she can't ignore her rebellious feelings. She acts out by not doing what Andrew asks of her, or she does things she knows he doesn't like. Sometimes she throws temper tantrums, as she did with her mother, so he will stop telling her what to do. She criticizes him and is verbally abusive as both her mother and Andrew's father were. It is a pattern she feels she can't control.

When Sandi yells at him, Andrew's anxiety increases, and he becomes five years old again and afraid of his father. His defense mechanisms come into play, and he finds himself controlling more and bossing her more. He became possessive of Sandi. In time her rebelling and yelling drives him away, and he withdraws. Ironically, when he does, that is when Sandi feels the neediest and is overwhelmed with fear very much like her mother's when Sandi's father wasn't there. Trapped in an unconscious nightmare, Sandi and Andrew function as children and relate to each other as they did with their parents. They have never matured emotionally into adulthood and developed their own power and authority. Instead, they give their power away to each other. As part of their therapy, we charted their adaptive reactions to each other (see figure 5 below).

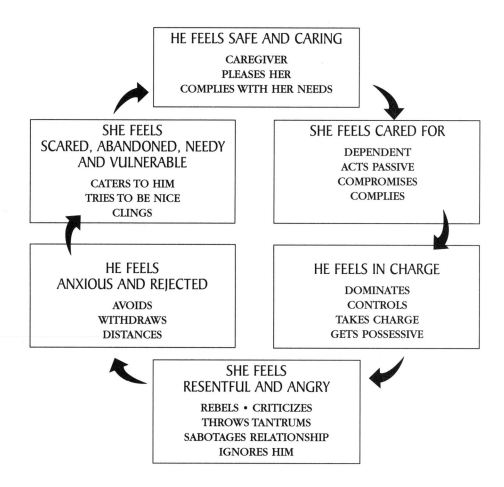

RELATIONSHIPS: THE OBJECT OF OUR DISCONTENT?

Relationship problems are what bring most of my clients in for counseling: Either they have a relationship and are unhappy, or they don't have a relationship and are unhappy.

Why do we seek love, relationships and marriage? I think wanting a relationship is a natural impulse. A relationship starts out as an unconscious attraction to someone. It feels familiar. We believe it will offer us a chance to have the love, romance and security we long for. As reported in the February 15, 1993, issue of *Time* magazine, anthropologists William Jankowiak of the University of Nevada at Las Vegas and Edward Fisher of Tulane University found evidence of romantic love in at least 147 of the 166 cultures they studied. Says Jankowiak, "It is a universal phenomenon, a panhuman characteristic that stretches across cultures."

Our impulse to love and be loved is often distorted by the belief blueprint of the culture and society in which we live. We may feel we need a partner for various reasons. The blueprints may be different, but the basic impulse is the same. It is important that we look not only at the impulse that attracts us to a mate and the process of relating, but also at the underlying, unconscious beliefs that are the foundation for that process. By doing so, we can find the answers to some of the "whys" of marriage and relationships and discover our own limiting beliefs.

THE ROLES THEY ARE A-CHANGIN'

Marriage is a social institution with its own blueprint. Into this blueprint we incorporate our own personal core belief blueprint. Marriage has pre-scribed stages: the courtship, the engagement, the ceremony with its ritualistic customs and symbols, and the maturing relationship that may lead to procreation and the nurturing of children. In almost all societies, husbands and wives divide economic activities and domestic work between them according to tradition.

Historically, especially in working-class families, partners are and were chosen from the same cultural, ethnic and religious community. They had the same or similar blueprints with similar expectations. The mar-riage was a partnership formed around mutual responsibilities. The wife took care of all domestic chores and had the responsibility of raising the children, and the husband provided for the family. In rural farming com-munities, relationships were developed around the division of labor for economic reasons. The children often continued the tradition and mar-ried partners with qualities similar to those of their parents to sustain the farm. Here, the blueprint for marriage changed very little. There was no time or even concern for much emotional intimacy with one's partner. Often women shared emotional intimacy with other women while they shared their labors. The blueprints of men in these communities traditionally never allowed for emotional intimacy, even with other men.

Many parts of the world continue the same traditional, homogeneous relationships. In some cultures, however, the roles differ. Women have responsible outside jobs in addition to their domestic challenges of caring for the home, their children and their husbands. Even though this practice is becoming more and more common in Western culture, many American couples are still caught in old traditional roles, albeit with growing confusion about the changing blueprint.

Among many cultures and societies, marriages were and are still arranged for economic, social and political reasons. Africa, China, India and the Middle East traditionally practice arranged marriages. In Western culture, arranged marriages are more subtle: Catholics are expected to marry Catholics, Jews are expected to marry Jews, Christians are expected marry Christians. In aristocracy, marital relationships were and are political. Partners are picked to create an alliance between groups and countries for political and economic reasons. The partners they choose require the respect of the populace. Though the masses see royal marriages as something out of a fairy tale, these marriages are often arranged, and there is usually little or no emotional intimacy between the partners. Among the wealthy, marital roles are less defined. Partners usually find each other in the same socioeconomic circle of acquaintances, or if they marry outside of the circle, they expect the partner to accommodate to their blueprint. They can afford to hire others to perform the more traditional duties of housekeeping and such.

In arranged marriages, the bride and groom expect less emotionally from each other because their roles are based on practical expectations. In societies where one chooses his or her marital partner, more is demanded. Until now, there has never been a time in history when there have been greater expectations—and greater confusion—about relationships and marriage, especially in Western cultures. We are shifting from familiar, homogeneous environments to places with multiethnic, social, cultural and religious differences. There are increasing opportunities for intermingling and intermarriage between different religions, cultures and races. With every difference comes a different blueprint, thus creating more choices, more conflict and more confusion.

We believe marriage will bring us the love, fulfillment and happiness we desire. Within each of us is a longing to return to that state of bliss we felt when we first came into the world. That state of bliss gradually ended as we became socialized. The longing to return, however, never stops. Under the onslaught of parental, social, cultural and religious demands, we lose touch with our blissful and joyous self. Soon we begin to see ourselves as *not enough* and begin the long search to *be enough*. One of the ways to be enough is to find someone who will give us the love we want and need. We believe relationships and marriage will give us that peaceful, secure place that can increase our self-worth.

THE RULES OF ATTRACTION

In our society, a strong social blueprint dictates that being married is better than being single. Being without a partner has a negative stigma attached to it. Even today in some large corporations, being married is essential for moving up the corporate ladder because it is perceived as showing stability. Unmarried clients of mine who are successful in many areas of their life often feel unfulfilled. No matter what they achieve, they never feel *enough* and think what is missing is a relationship. They have an overwhelming fear that they may never find love and that they will be alone for the rest of their lives. The feelings that there must be something drastically wrong with them triggers feelings of shame.

The intense drive to find a mate, and the fear of never finding one, colors our behavior. In many cultures there are rituals for attracting and courting a desirable partner. In Africa, there are both arranged marriages and marriages of the heart. To attract a partner of the heart, young men and women adorn themselves with face paint, fancy costumes and headdresses with beads and feathers. Women in the highlands of Chiapas, Mexico, wear beautiful handmade shawls to show their weaving skills to potential husbands.

Love and romance is what brings two people together to begin the ritual of courtship and marriage. Of all of the thousands of people we encounter, why is the unconscious selection process limited to a very few? What is so significant about the one that we attract and are attracted to? Harville Hendrix, Ph.D., author of *Getting the Love You Want,* says, "It appears that each one of us is compulsively searching for a mate with a very particular set of positive and negative personality traits."

Lovers feel overwhelmed by romance, and in truth, they are. Our brain releases endorphins that make us feel giddy and euphoric. Our skin flushes, our palms sweat, our hearts beat faster and we become short of breath. We feel fearless and temporarily happy, joyous and fulfilled. Because we believe the source of this joy comes from the partner we attract, we pursue, seduce, display certain behaviors, seductively adorn ourselves and hide anything we believe about ourselves that is unattractive.

The feelings of euphoria and bliss can be triggered whenever we see, hear or smell the one we love. We can "get high" looking at a picture of them, talking about them or even just thinking about them. I refer to this as the "in-love" phase. The endorphins that create this high are phenylethylamine (PEA), norepinephrine and oxytocin. The high generally lasts from six months to two years and then begins to wear off. I think there is a correlation between our first feelings of bliss as infants when we felt one with the world and the re-experience of bliss when we fall in love. During that period of life, from about six months to two years of age, we are infatuated with Mother, and life is wonderful. Watch a baby's gaze of love as it looks fondly at Mommy, Daddy, the family dog or a favorite toy; it is bliss. The period of bliss in relationships is how nature brings us together for procreation. It lasts long enough for bonding to happen and begins to wear off as the partners differentiate, just as a child begins to individuate as she or he is socialized into the world.

THE LOVE/RELATIONSHIP BLUEPRINT

Scientists can measure the physiological changes that happen when we fall in love, but they don't know what triggers these emotions. We appear blinded by overwhelming feelings of attraction as we have a momentary reconnection to our once blissful state. In our feelings lies the promise that anything can happen. Our hopefulness is born of our projections onto the other person that lacks real knowledge of that person. But we remain happily optimistic.

We carry in each of us a *love/relationship blueprint.* Recorded from infancy, this blueprint carries everything that is upsetting or joyous, that is exciting and enticing, that feels good or bad about relationships. It also carries our beliefs, our decisions, our early relationships and our childhood wounds.

To find someone whose love/relationship blueprint matches ours, we consider the partner's looks, her eyes, the color of his hair, his build, her personality, how he walks and talks, how she laughs, the jokes she tells, his moods, how she behaves, how he touches us or doesn't touch us. Even though this person may be a relative stranger to us, the match is sufficient to trigger our emotions. The current partner may not be like the last one. Like genetic combinations, each partner carries a variety of positive and negative characteristics that fit our blueprint. The positive characteristics remind us of our father's smile, our mother's touch, our brother's jokes, our sister's hair, our best friend's laugh, our first teacher's kindness, our priest or rabbi's wisdom. The negative characteristics remind us of our mother's silent withdrawal, our father's controlling behavior, our brother's sarcasm and our sister's incessant teasing. Our love/relationship blueprint carries all these positive and negative traits.

OUR SYSTEM OF SELF-CORRECTION

The unconscious selection of a partner is not done at random. We each have a self-correcting system that attracts the perfect partner so that we can grow. Even though that partner may be a source of pain for us, denying us what we want most, she or he really is the perfect partner to help us learn to stretch, grow and heal. Our psyche, that part in us that knows how to heal us physically as well as emotionally, brings us to these experiences so that we can return to our wholeness. Desire and attraction is a paradox that carries unconscious hidden truths. The longing to be fulfilled through a loving relationship and marriage is the same longing that drives us to succeed and accumulate material possessions. Being in a relationship, we believe, will heal our basic feelings of inadequacy and not enoughness and fulfill our desire for wholeness, contentment and joy. The more successful our partner scores on our blueprint "test," the more we believe we will receive greater fulfillment and heighten our feelings of self-esteem.

Relationships and marriage are an opportunity to learn about ourselves and others so that growth can happen. Our relationships are never separate from the rest of our lives; they are about our lives. They are not outside of the system in which we live, nor are they a manifestation of the system. They are the system in process, the system that comes from our multitude of beliefs. Some of these false beliefs derive from fairy tales we read that always end with "and they lived happily ever after." Relationships take work; they don't just happen. When we commit to a relationship or marriage, it is like matriculating in a school for learning and growth. Our partner is the exact teacher we need to learn about ourselves. Being in a relationship with a partner who is equally willing to grow and change provides an opportunity to break our old dysfunctional patterns. This is the key to a healthy relationship and also provides an opportunity for mutual growth.

WHEN THE IN-LOVE PHASE WEARS OFF

During the PEA or in-love phase, we see only positives about our beloved. We project our dreams and hopes onto the other. Even negative characteristics are attractive. If, for example, we repressed or never developed our emotional side, we are unconsciously attracted to a partner who shows emotion. It is the lost or missing part of us that we find attractive in others. When the in-love phase wears off, however, it can be a source of conflict as we now try to repress our partner in the same way we repress ourselves: "You're too emotional." "Think things through before you get so upset." "You don't see me getting upset over small things." "There must be something wrong with you." When the PEA wears off and we are no longer emotionally blind, we begin to see negatives about our partner that annoy us. Either we believe we made a mistake, or we think our partner has somehow changed. This is when the power struggle starts. We recognize the differences in our blueprints and try to change her to convince her to see things the way we do. In turn, our partner tries to change us to fit his blueprint. We trigger each other's reactions, and they cover up our blueprints (see chapter 2).

When Sandi left the in-love phase, she discovered that the wonderful caregiving traits she saw in Andrew now felt more like controlling traits. Previously she responded to his taking charge with love and affection, feeling protected by him. As the in-love veil lifted, she began to feel angered and annoyed by his dominance. Andrew's behavior now triggered her old belief blueprint.

When the PEA is gone and the romantic phase is over, the power struggle begins. We think that we have made a mistake and that divorce is the answer. Because we believe that the failure of the relationship/marriage is in the partner we have selected, we look for a new partner to fulfill our dream. Having become addicted to the experience of falling in love and the high it brings us, we believe finding another partner will return us to that euphoric state. I call this the *revolving-door romance*. We leave one partner to find another and repeat the same pattern. What we don't resolve we will re-create.

The high divorce rate is the result of our collective the blueprints, which are filled with unrealistic expectations. Statistically, American marriages fare worse than marriages in other countries. In the United States, more than half of all first marriages end in divorce, and second marriages fail 60 percent of the time. Most of us enter marriage hoping we won't become one of these statistics. If the marriage runs aground, and if we don't choose divorce or separation, we find ourselves living parallel lives with an emotional separation. The symptoms of emotional separation are many: affairs, alcohol, drugs and overwork, or preoccupation with the children, church, volunteer work and even spiritual pursuits. These symptoms help to block out our discomfort and emotional pain. Many of them can bring us financial rewards, such as working overtime, or the praise and attention that seems to be missing in our relationship. Relationships can be disappointing, confusing and overwhelming, so we look elsewhere for emotional intimacy and growth. Each of us copes with unhappy relationships in our own way by applying the adaptive survival skills we learned in childhood. We work harder, give more, attack, withdraw, submit or control.

JEFF AND KAREN'S STORY

Jeff and Karen met in a psychiatrist's office. They were seeing different doctors who shared the same waiting room. They often happened to have the same appointment times and invariably would end up talking before and after their sessions. Karen was seeking help for the dark periods of depression she'd had since childhood. Jeff was being treated for free-floating anxiety. As they shared with each other their emotional pain, their relationship grew. Something about each of them felt familiar to the other.

One day Jeff asked Karen out to lunch, and both had a wonderful time. Their relationship soon moved into the wild, crazy, falling-in-love stage. They were hot for each other. Both felt an emotional high that was better than they had ever experienced before. She was happier, he was more open and both soon felt well enough to stop therapy. Six months later Jeff and Karen decided to get married.

Two years passed. The high was gone. Their hot sexual relationship had begun to diminish. Jeff shut down and communicated less and less with his wife. Karen sank progressively deeper into her old depression and despair. The more depressed and unhappy she was, the more anxious Jeff was. He felt unable to meet her needs no matter what he did. Consequently, he got more involved with his career, where he felt in control and was rewarded for his efforts. Though he spent long hours away from Karen, he was generous to a fault. He provided her with whatever material items she needed. But what he gave her was never enough; she needed to spend more time with him. Karen felt isolated, empty, lonely and at times in total despair. Her old suicidal thoughts resurfaced. Jeff and Karen had each triggered the other's blueprint.

Let's examine Jeff and Karen's unconscious reactions and how they triggered each other's blueprint. Jeff is a fixer. It is a natural trait in men. He likes to solve problems. In time, Jeff realized he couldn't fix Karen's depression. No matter what he did, nothing seemed to work. He felt anxious, and work seemed to alleviate these feelings. The problems he solved at work always brought positive rewards. Jeff became a workaholic and believed he could afford to buy Karen whatever she needed to be happy. Work, for him, was a major exit to avoiding intimacy. That exit eventually led to an intimate relationship with his secretary. Jeff spent more hours with her then he did with his wife, and a romance blossomed.

Once again, the answers lie in childhood. Jeff's mother was depressed after his father died. He remembered the quietness in the house and his mother's long silences. It filled him with anxiety. It seemed no matter what he did, he couldn't bring her out of it. He did all the things a young boy of six could do to help her. The sadness that permeated the household lasted for years and began to affect every area of his life. He had mixed feelings: the desire to stay away from home as much as possible to avoid his mother, and guilt because he was not there to "rescue" her. He was torn between the two. He had deep feelings of inadequacy and failure.

Karen resented Jeff's long hours away from home. She felt abandoned, as she did when she was a child. Her family was very wealthy. Her father was a physician and worked late into the evening. By the time he came home, Karen was asleep, and when Karen got up in the mornings, he had already left. Karen remembered some mornings when they ate breakfast together, and she cherished those memories. Her mother was involved in charities, which also took her away from home. She was always too busy to spend time with Karen, and Karen sensed her mother's impatience whenever she was with her. She loved the feel of her mother's clothes—silks and velvets—and the smell of her perfume, and she felt sad whenever she hugged her mother good-bye.

Karen was raised primarily by a nanny who always seemed busy and interacted with Karen by scolding her. As a child, Karen had all the material possessions she could want: beautiful clothes, toys, regular trips to Disneyland and the zoo. She went to the best schools and had the best doctors. But she was lonely and sad. She felt there must be something wrong with her because she could not get the attention she wanted and needed. She developed a deep and shameful belief about not being enough and made a decision early in life that no one could ever love her just for herself.

Because of her family's wealth, Karen didn't have to work. Like her mother, she tried to fill her loneliness with charities, but she found them boring. An only child, Karen had difficulty making friends. As an adult, she isolated herself and self-imposed a re-creation of her childhood. She saw the best doctors and took all the antidepressants they gave her. The one drink with lunch turned into several drinks. She developed a drinking problem and would tell herself, "Tomorrow I'll quit." On the Internet, Karen discovered how pleasurable it was to connect with people she never had to face. She could say whatever she wanted without fear of abandonment. These were strangers. In time she began to have on-line romances. This was her exit to avoiding intimacy with Jeff.

REDISCOVERING INTIMACY AND HEALING COMMUNICATION

To experience real intimacy, we must be willing to see our partner as different from ourselves and be willing to accept these differences. When others are different from ourselves, we often feel discomfort and emotional pain, and so we hang out with people who are as close to our belief blueprint as possible. If we are around others who have a different blueprint, we make every effort to convince them to believe and experience as we do. Many times couples sacrifice their individual differences for fear they will be abandoned. This is called *symbiosis*.

In my practice, I usually see couples that are undifferentiated, where one of the partners insists that the other see and do things the way that partner does. There is a *wrong way* and there is *my way,* which is the *right way,* the partner feels. These couples have great difficulty resolving their conflict. One of the partners will submit and lose himself or herself, or both will engage in a constant power struggle.

Many years ago, while visiting my sister, I gazed out her kitchen window to see two baby birds leave the nest and fly to the telephone wire just below the tree. They clung to the wire and leaned on each other in fear. It was several minutes before they had the courage to separate and fly away. In relationships, we tend to lean and cling to each other out of fear. We must learn to see relationships as an experience that can lead to our own individual wholeness, but it means standing side by side *in support* of each other, not *dependent* on each other.

As noted in previous chapters, men and women are different. A man and a woman in the same relationship may each be experiencing a totally different relationship from the other, based on their individual beliefs. Our blueprint is based on our combination of gender, cultural, social, ethnic and religious differences. It is in accepting these differences and learning to tolerate our discomforts with these differences that intimacy can happen. In couples that are differentiated, there is growth, intimacy and passion. They are able to work through conflict much more easily than couples that are *symbiotic, or undifferentiated.*

Relationships are about emotional intimacy. Often people mistake emotional intimacy for sexual intimacy. Couples can be together and have great sex for years, yet never experience intimacy. What, then, is intimacy? It is being able to reveal ourselves entirely to another human being and know we will be embraced and accepted as we are. By letting go of the false self we have developed, we can be accepted and loved. It is exposing ourselves emotionally and allowing ourselves to be vulnerable with another.

To share totally who we are with another takes absolute trust. Trust means different things: dependability, honesty, fidelity and loyalty. Trust is essential to have emotional safety in a relationship. It enables us to express our deepest feelings, our fears and hopes, our dreams and desires, knowing our partner will respect and handle them with loving care and will not judge us, condemn us or try to fix us. When we have developed trust and emotional safety, intimacy can happen. It is in our commitment to experience real intimacy with another human being that our lives can be transformed. Marriage and intimate relationships are a pathway to wholeness.

Honest communication with another is difficult, especially in intimacy. It reopens our old childhood wounds, but it also creates an opportunity to heal these wounds. Harville Hendrix says, "Relationships are an opportunity to complete childhood." It is also an opportunity to become aware of the limiting beliefs that distort our perception of current experiences. Our partner can become part of our healing process. (See the end of this chapter for an exercise on developing effective communication skills.)

Two clients of mine, Sherri and Michael, have been married for two years. They have been seeing me since before they were married. In their sessions, they are caring and supportive, even when they are in conflict and feel angry and upset. They have learned how to communicate with each other and have grown to accept each other's differences. Keeping each other safe allows them to share their vulnerabilities and have real emotional intimacy.

In one session, Sherri related how she feels unappreciated for all the work she has been doing in preparation for moving into their new home. There are carpenters, roofers, plumbers, electricians, painters and tile installers to deal with daily. Sherri spends long hours at the new house, and when Michael comes home she tells him how much work she has done and how exhausted she is. He doesn't respond, and it leaves her feeling angry and unappreciated and hurt. She feels Michael doesn't hear her or acknowledge her efforts. Sherri recognizes, though, that her frustration and anger is about her. In the session, she asks Michael if he will listen to her not only so that he can understand her anger, but also so that she can understand what it is in her that pushes her to prove herself. Michael agrees and takes a moment to put aside his own judgments and interpretations in order to listen with interest, curiosity and respect. Then lets her know he is ready to hear her. The following is an excerpt from their dialogue.

> SHERRI: *I know this is about me. My reasons are about me. I feel self-destructive and angry. I tell you how tired I am, and you don't respond to me, and I hope in some way you'll say, "I see how tired you are, and I want you to take some time off; in fact, I insist you take some time off!"*

> MICHAEL: *What I hear you saying is what you'd like from me is to acknowledge how tired you are and insist you take some time off. Is that right?*

> SHERRI: *That's right. The reason I don't tell you I am going to take time off is I feel too guilty and that you'll be pissed off and get angry, and you have a right to be pissed off because this was the deal we made. You would go to work every day and weekends, and I am suppose to work on the house every day. I took the semester off to do this. When I get into that mood that I have to do what others want me to do or they'll get mad at me, I feel seven years old again or younger. I'm afraid of being forced to do something or they'll stop loving me. (Cries.) I feel sadness. I have to perform to be loved. I'm not of any value. I feel ashamed that I feel like this.*

> MICHAEL: *You feel shame because you feel like you have to perform to be loved.*

> SHERRI: *The shame is there must be something very wrong with me that I'm not just loved, something wrong with me because I don't feel I am worthy of love. I've based all my decisions on that I am not enough. It's how I interact with everyone. I'm overly angry, overly pleasant, or I lie for no good reason. I am afraid.*

> JOYCE: *What if you realized it was never the truth about you, that you aren't enough?*

> SHERRI: *If I knew it isn't the truth about me and that it never was, I would be filled with absolute rage and fucking sadness. It makes*

me sick, like my heart is broken. I have spent my life committed to making up for the part of me that is lacking and trying to be better.

MICHAEL: *You make sense to me that you are enraged about the theft and violation for being told you weren't OK and lovable and—*

SHERRI: *(Interrupts) —that I am overwhelmed that my whole life is a lie. That is pretty hard to take at one time. It's hard to convince myself that I am of value.*

MICHAEL: *It must be overwhelming for you to feel your whole life is a lie and to feel you must convince yourself you are of value.*

JOYCE: *Michael, does it make sense how this affects your relationship?*

MICHAEL: *(To Sherri) I can see how this has affected your daily life. I can see you need to perform to be valued, and if you didn't perform you wouldn't be loved. I can see you believe that if you stop performing, I'll stop loving you. (With deep empathy) What a horrible way to live.*

(Sherri begins to sob deeply.)

JOYCE: *She doesn't even value herself enough to give herself permission to rest and needs you to give it to her.*

SHERRI: *I am so embarrassed. I've spent my life cheating so no one knows the truth about me. It's out now. (Sighs heavily.) I feel enlightened, I feel free. It wasn't so bad. But now it is over.*

(Michael holds her in his tender, loving gaze.)

SHERRI: *What I need to know is that you love me, who I am and not what I do. I don't even know who I am. I always thought I am what I do.*

MICHAEL: *You need me to love you as you are and not what you do. What do you need from me to help you heal this? What can I do to let you know I love you as you are and support you in loving yourself?*

SHERRI: *I need you to love me and to accept me in all those deep places, and to be committed to go there with me so I won't feel so alone, to let me know you value me and encourage me to value myself.*

MICHAEL: *I am committed to go there with you, to accept you as you are. I want to be there with you and for you. I want to be there because I love you and value you as you are.*

(They reach out to each other in a loving embrace.)

Throughout their dialogue, note that Michael does not give Sherri solutions or try to "fix" her. He stays there for her, making it safe for her to explore her fears and sadness. He validates and empathizes with her without judging or criticizing. The following exercises will guide you and your partner in discovering the source of your beliefs about relationships and improving your communication skills.

EXERCISES

MESSAGES AND BELIEFS THAT FORM YOUR LOVE/RELATIONSHIP BLUEPRINT

Messages Received from Your Mother About:

Relationships:

_____

_____

Marriage:

_____

_____

Her marriage:

_____

_____

Husband's role:

_____

_____

Wife's role:

_____

_____

Her role as a wife:

_____

_____

Sex:

_____

_____

Intimacy:

_____

_____

Love:

_____

_____

Divorce:

_____

_____

Not being married:

_____

_____

Messages Received from Your Father About:

Relationships:

_____

_____

Marriage:

_____

_____

His marriage:

_____

_____

Wife's role:

_____

_____

His wife:

_____

_____

Husband's role:

_____

_____

His role as husband:

_____

_____

Sex:

_____

_____

Intimacy:

_____

_____

Love:

_____

_____

Divorce:

_____

_____

Not being married:

_____

_____

Messages Received from Society, Culture and Religion About:

Marriage:

_____

_____

Husband's role:

_____

_____

Wife's role:

_____

_____

Sex:

_____

_____

Intimacy:

_____

_____

Love:

_____

_____

Divorce:

_____

_____

Not being married:

_____

_____

Messages Received from Siblings and Peers About:

Marriage:

_____

_____

Husband's role:

_____

_____

Wife's role:

_____

_____

Sex:

_____

_____

Intimacy:

_____

_____

Love:

_____

_____

Divorce:

_____

_____

Not being married:

_____

_____

Messages I Believe About:

Relationships:

_____

_____

Marriage:

_____

_____

Husband's role:

_____

_____

Wife's role:

_____

_____

My partner in a relationship or marriage:

_____

_____

Myself in a relationship or marriage:

_____

_____

Sex:

_____

_____

Intimacy:

_____

_____

Love:

_____

_____

Divorce:

_____

_____

Not being married:

_____

_____

From the messages I received in childhood, I made the following
decisions about relationships and marriage:

_____

_____

_____

The results of my decision:

_____

_____

_____

_____

How I would like to change those beliefs and decisions to a new
decision that feels right for me:

_____

_____

_____

_____

Behavior changes I need to make following my new decisions about
relationships (see the exercise "How to Change Beliefs and
Decisions" in chapter 2):

_____

_____

_____

_____

_____

_____

COMMUNICATING EFFECTIVELY

Communicating with a partner with whom we share true intimacy can
help us learn not only about our partner, but also about ourselves and

the blueprint that is covered up by our reactions. Most of us live unconsciously, unaware of why we react the way we do. Being able to relate honestly with our partner is a way to become conscious. It is an opportunity to shift from being reactive to being intentional. It is an opportunity to change our beliefs and change our lives.

■ Steps to Examining Your Reactions

Review the "Reactions Are Cover-ups" chart in chapter 2.

1. Write down the event that triggered your reactions. Example: *"She criticizes me, yells at me and blames me."*

2. Write down your feelings that are triggered by the event. Identifying feelings will help you untangle them. Some feelings layer others. Anger usually covers up feelings of hurt, frustration and fear. Feelings are always summarized in one word. "Feeling that" or " feeling like" are thoughts. The following "feeling words" may identify what you are experiencing:

Anger • Rage • Hurt • Sadness • Fear • Disappointment • Worry
• Irritation • Frustration • Blame • Loneliness • Shame
• Guilt • Anxiety • Depression

Circle the feelings that are OK, and underline the ones that are not OK.

3. Write down your self-talk, thoughts, judgments and interpretations, which trigger your feelings. Examples of self-talk: *"What a bitch." "I really hate her." "I wish she'd get off my back." "She is so inconsiderate and insensitive." "All she thinks about is herself." "Why doesn't she look at her own problems." "What can I say or do to get back at her?" "She really doesn't care about me; if she did, she wouldn't treat me this way." "I feel like getting as far away from her as possible. Why do I stay?" "Maybe she's right and I deserve to be criticized." "At the same time, I'm scared she might leave me." "Maybe I'll never find someone who is considerate and kind." "What's wrong with me?"*

4. Write down your beliefs and decisions about the event. Examples: *"The world is a scary place." "There is something wrong with me." "I have to prove myself to be loved." "I'm not important enough." "I can't trust anyone but myself." "No one will ever love me." "I'll never get what I want, to be accepted." "All women are bitches."*

5. What are the messages from your parents, society, culture, religion, siblings and peers about this event or your interpretations of this event? *Remember, messages are spoken and implied.* Write them down. Example: Father may have told you all women are controlling and bitchy. Or, while you were growing up, the guys told you, "Women are a ball and chain." "Women are a trap."

6. Write down what these feelings remind you of. What were your *childhood experiences* that were similar? What events in the past supported your beliefs and decisions? Maybe someone in your past acted the same way. What does the present event remind you of? Example: *"Mother always blamed me, criticized me and yelled at me. I was afraid of her and felt anxious and hypervigilant."*

7. Notice how you adapt and write it down. These are the protective defenses you learned in childhood. Example: *Submit, Attack, Hide, Withdraw, People-please, Control, Act emotional, Overeat, Yell, Criticize, Blame.*

COMMUNICATING

■ The Sender

1. Before you start, get clear using the above seven steps. Become aware of your automatic reactions and your beliefs to make sense of them for yourself.

Reminder: Confronting others may be a new experience for you and may bring up anxiety and fear. After getting clear what you wish to communicate, sit quietly and focus on your intention.

This is a good time to meditate for about ten minutes to get centered. If during the process you feel anxious or fearful, report it to your partner and stop for a few minutes to regroup.

2. When you are clear, ask your partner for an appointment so you can share what happened and express your feelings, interpretations, beliefs and early experiences. Appointments are a way to keep ourselves and our partner safe.

3. Express clearly your feelings, thoughts, interpretations, judgments, beliefs and decisions without blaming your partner. This is difficult but not impossible to do. Blaming keeps you from knowing yourself and recognizing the belief blueprint you carry. Present events are a catalyst for the past and are opportunities to discover limiting beliefs about yourself, your partner and your world. Remember: *This is your problem.*

How to send:

WHEN YOU: *Trigger-Event (Example: criticize me and raise your voice)*

I FEEL: *Feelings are one word. (Example: angry, blamed, scared, hurt) "Feeling that" or "feeling like" are thoughts. (Example: like you don't care about me)*

MY INTERPRETATION: *Self-talk, interpretations, judgments (Example: You don't care, I'm bad or wrong, You're a mean person)*

MY BELIEFS AND DECISIONS: *Share beliefs, decisions, messages from others.*

REMINDS ME OF: *Childhood experiences (Example: How my mother treated me as a child)*

WHAT I DO: *How you adapted as a child and still adapt. (Example: I withdraw to avoid you)*

■ The Receiver

1. LISTEN AND REPEAT. Repeat back to your partner as accurately as possible. If you feel overwhelmed by too much information, ask your partner to repeat in smaller segments. Check to see if

what you have repeated is accurate. Ask, "Did I get it right?" and ask your partner, "Tell me more about that." Refrain from defending yourself. Know that what your partner is telling you is about them. You are a catalyst that triggers their past stuff. It is 90 percent them and 10 percent you. Be curious about your partner and accept your differences. You do not have to agree with your partner's interpretations or beliefs. Your partner has his or her own feelings, thoughts, family history, personality and experiences.

REMINDER: *Listening is not easy. Take a few minutes to get quiet and centered. If you meditate, take ten minutes before you start. It is important to put all your interpretations and judgments aside. Listen as if you are listening to a story or a song for the first time. You'll hear your partner differently than ever before. Listen to understand your partner's point of view. Ask questions until you do understand. Learning to listen takes practice and perseverance. If you fail, take a break and try it again.*

2. *Validate what you understand.* Share what makes sense to you from your partner's point of view. Move away from your own judgments and interpretations.

3. *Express empathy for what it must be like to be your partner.* Put yourself in his or her shoes. Imagine what it must be like for the other person, and share what you imagine.

Communicating with what Harville Hendrix calls the dialogical process is the foundation of my work in Imago Relationship Therapy. In addition, I have explored the unconscious beliefs that limit our perceptions and ability to communicate with others.

The greatest gift we can give each other is to share honest emotions, thoughts, beliefs, decisions, and past experiences and to listen, validate and empathize with each other. By sharing honestly and creating safety for each other, we will be able to support each other's growth and change old, limiting beliefs.

Chapter 6

JOURNEY TO THE PAST:
Patterns from Childhood

It is in childhood that we develop the beliefs that control and limit our lives. To be good parents and to raise our children to be self-reliant, with high self-esteem and resiliency, we must first understand our own childhood and the parenting we received. By developing the ability to "see objectively," we can look back on our lives as well as forward. It is as if we are standing on a high peak and can see where we have been and where we are going. From this objective, we can observe how our parents were raised and what happened in their lives, their society, their culture and their religion that formed the belief blueprint they then passed down to us. Subsequently, we can look at the events, experiences and messages in our own lives that helped to create our limiting beliefs. In the previous chapters, we saw how these limiting beliefs have affected us and those close to us. Exploring our past enables us to become aware of what we need to do to change our future and the future of our children.

OUR INNER CHILD

Most of my clients are still struggling with their own unfinished childhoods and their unresolved issues involving their parents. Essentially, they are still functioning as children in adult bodies, living with old out-moded ideas and limiting beliefs. They have not developed emotionally. Our parents had difficulty raising us because each of them was also grappling with an inner child from the past. Often, we were raised by parents who were wounded, ignorant, insecure, frightened and emotionally immature.

We never outgrow our inner child. It contains our playful, joyful part, but it also contains an immature, traumatized part. During our development, if we were repressed or wounded by our parents, or if there was trauma, we stopped growing emotionally. That emotionally undeveloped inner child still lies within most of us. Even though we grew physically, that inner child continues to function in our adult bodies. In fact, it usually ends up running our lives. As children, if we believed there was something to be afraid of, then we will still feel that fear as adults when anything resembling the cause of that feeling appears.

In order to change what we believed at four years old, we must re-evaluate our beliefs to see if they still apply, confront those that no longer serve our best interest and stop the internalized, critical parent inside us. How we treat our inner child is how we were treated as children by those around us. We internalized our parents' attitudes and judgments because they offered us a sense of stability and security in a world that felt insecure and at times chaotic. At the end of this chapter are exercises to discover the self-limiting beliefs we still adhere to as adults. Once we have explored these beliefs, we can become clearer about our intentions, strengthen our relationships, empower ourselves and find our inner strengths and self-worth. From this journey, we can become good parents to ourselves, our children and our children's children.

We can start by asking ourselves, Where do our beliefs come from? As we discussed in other chapters, our beliefs came not only from parents, but also from relatives, siblings, friends, teachers, church or synagogue, society, authority figures, the "heroes" in our lives and the commercial world. We accepted these messages and believed they were the truth because we trusted the authority of the messenger. Whereas some of these sources gave us wonderful, positive beliefs, other left us with beliefs that crippled our lives and filled us with doubt, fear, stress and emotional pain.

Our first response is to be angry and blame our parents. The answer to healing the past, however, is to avoid blame. Most parents mean well, even though they may lack parenting skills and are probably emotionally immature. We must remember that they also carried limiting beliefs and wounds from their childhoods. If they had known better, they would have done better. Blaming others only keeps us rooted in the problem and bound to repeating the same old patterns.

Often, when my clients confront what they have believed to be true about themselves based on messages received from parents, religion and society, they feel rage. I suggest they allow themselves to validate their anger. If necessary, I tell them to yell, holler, scream, beat a tennis racket on the bed, write out their feelings in a journal or do whatever is necessary to relieve the anger. Underlying these feelings of rage is usually sadness and grief over the lost part of ourselves that never had a chance to grow and develop. Once the anger and rage is past and we allow ourselves to grieve, we can begin to take responsibility for changing the beliefs that we have continued to perpetuate for so long.

What happened to that small, perfect child who was filled with clarity, joy and bliss? That bliss was gradually covered over by messages from others of what we "should be" and "ought to be." As we developed in our parents' environment, we gradually stopped trusting our inner wisdom, which holds the authority for our lives. We gave our authority for who we are and what our needs are over to others because we were helpless and our lives depended on them for survival and security.

Our inner wisdom was and still is within us, directing our lives at all ages. It is the source that tells us who we are in relationship to our world, and it is where we find our inner reference and true authority. As infants we cried when we were hungry, cold or wet, when we were angry, lonely or in pain. This was how we communicated with our world. If our parents gave us messages from their beliefs that our expressions were not acceptable and that there was something wrong with us, we no longer trusted ourselves and stopped communicating.

Within each of us is a magnificent perfection that will always be there. We each have the potential to reach that perfection. Whether we are able to express that potential, though, depends on our environment. If our perfection is recognized and the environment supports us, there is room for growth. But if our environment is stifling or filled with chaos, and we are reminded of our imperfections and lack, the potential within us is aborted, lies dormant and can possibly die.

THE FAMILY SYSTEM

The family system carries beliefs that are passed down from generation to generation. There are different types of family structures depending on the culture, the society and the religion in which we are raised. By the age of two, each child unconsciously absorbs the blueprint of his or her family system. And it can take a lifetime to sort out what fits and what doesn't in order to get underneath these beliefs, to understand who we really are.

Like any system, the family is made up of several parts that come together to achieve a desired goal. In the 1960s, psychologists regarded the family as a system that struggled to maintain homeostasis. Theorists saw the family structure as an undifferentiated ego mass, meaning that the same belief blueprint is absorbed by all members to keep the family functioning as a single, cohesive unit.

To put up a good front for others, families often view themselves in a consistent, particular way: "We are a perfectly happy family," they tell themselves. "Everyone in our family is happy. We never say a cross word. We never argue. Fighting isn't allowed. No one ever gets angry. We are never negative. Everything is perfect. We all love and are kind to each other."

Similarly, the status family associates only with people at a certain socioeconomic level: They act and talk like those of upper-class standing, make the best grades, become class president, go to prestigious schools, hold high-paying jobs. This is their game. If any member thinks or feels differently than other family members and doesn't follow the family pattern, that person will be punished or ostracized. They fear having feelings that differ from the rest of the family's of what is acceptable to feel and what is not.

There are two basic family systems: open and closed. The difference lies in their reaction to change. The open system provides options and choices in resolving issues and is flexible with its rules. The parents share equal power, and their role is to inspire and encourage uniqueness and difference. Individual emotions and needs are taken into consideration. The parents model behavior, yet have the ability to be arbitrary. In this type of family, members are allowed to fully express their feelings, and open communication is encouraged and validated. Each member is valued, and there is room for self-growth.

The closed system is rigid and based on law and order that operates through physical and emotional force. Power is usually held by a tyrant who determines the rules and provokes compliance or resistance in others. The father or the mother can be the dominant authority. The goal of the parents is to indoctrinate and influence using the tools of fear and coercion. A closed system operates on a set of beliefs and rules that are usually out of date, incongruent with the circumstances and unchanging. Rigid rules for behaving, thinking and feeling are enforced, and any diverse thoughts and feelings are forbidden. In this system, there is no room for self-growth, and dependence on external authority is encouraged.

A third system, the permissive family, is the most dysfunctional. This family system is severely disturbed. In this family, there are no clear-cut authority figures. The parents reject the children in favor of their own wants and fantasies. Often, individual members have emotional or addiction problems, and these affect the entire unit. Usually there is a role reversal, with children taking on the parenting or caregiving role and parents assuming the part of the immature child. The family is in a constant state of confusion and chaos, and everybody does whatever he or she wants. Members of this family alternately avoid and collude with one another. The emotional disturbance is passed down to the children, leaving no room for healthy growth. This is what happened in David's family.

David was raised during the 1960s, a time of free drugs and free love. His parents worked as massage therapists. Sessions with clients often turned into orgies. Both of his parents experimented with drugs and sex, and strangers wandered in and out of their home at all hours.

In David's family, no one was really in charge. No one cared when David and his brothers went to bed or where they were. No one cared if their schoolwork was done. From a young age, David took on the responsibility of fixing breakfast, lunch and dinner for himself and his two younger brothers. He made the effort to help his brothers and parent them, but there was no one for him to turn to. David felt abandoned. He was failing in school and had bad feelings about himself.

Now, as an adult, David has a deep sense of inadequacy, a shame that leaves him feeling inferior. His core belief is that he is not enough, and no matter what he does, he'll never be enough. David struggles with depression and alcohol addiction. He works hard, but he is convinced he is good only at menial jobs. Though he is kind and caring, he has difficulty in relationships: He becomes needy and latches on to a care-giver, or assumes the role of caregiver and seeks out someone needy. David tends to be promiscuous and sabotages any relationships that have potential. David's emotionally bereft childhood has left him with distorted beliefs that keep him from leading a healthy, productive life. He keeps hoping and waiting for something or someone to change his life. He doesn't believe he has the tools to change it himself. David is trapped in old beliefs and feels overwhelmed in his inability to change them.

■

Individual family systems can include any aspect or combination of the above three styles. They can be authoritarian with strict rules of "shoulds and oughts" and still have aspects similar to those of the permissive family. In studies of family systems where there was consistency, as in the closed or open family, less delinquent behavior was found in the children. Where there was inconsistency, as in the permissive family, there was increased delinquency and pathology was observed in the children.

The family system we grow up in affects our lives and determines our belief blueprint. Until we reevaluate that system when it comes to raising our own children, we will tend to either re-create it or go to the opposite extreme. If our parents were too strict, we will either repeat their behavior or go to the other extreme and become too permissive. Our parents' messages and beliefs established our beliefs about family, relationships, being a woman or a man, the role of husband or wife, the role of father or mother. It established our beliefs about the rules for interacting: who makes the rules, who keeps them, who is the authority and who we should fear. We were taught what is acceptable and what is not, what we should do and what is forbidden. Before we were seven years old, we began to develop beliefs, ideas and feelings about ourselves, which I call *self-worth*. All of this is unconsciously reflected in our belief blueprint.

FAMILY DYNAMICS: WHO IS THE REAL PATIENT?

Each person plays a role in the system, and each has an impact on the whole system. Where there is a disturbance in one part, other members will make up for it to create homeostasis. Where there are repressed emotions in one member, other members will carry and express the repressed feelings. When I treat families, there is usually an identified patient, the person in the family who is labeled "sick" or "disturbed." But the real patient is the family as a unit. In working with families in conflict, I often find that one of the children turns out to be the identified patient. She acts out what the parents are repressing and not resolving. Like Patty and Tim in the story that follows, the child is locked into the system and is the symptom bearer and the focus of an emotionally disturbed relationship.

■

Patty is angry all the time at Tim. No matter what he does, she is enraged. If he is late, she is upset. If they don't have enough sex, she is angry. If he does something without telling her, she goes ballistic. If he makes promises and is unable to keep them, she is furious. Whenever she is not yelling at him, she is sniping at him with criticisms and sarcastic remarks.

When Patty and Tim came to see me, they were separated. Though they love each other, they can't live together. In fact, they can't even be together for any length of time. Trying to make their relationship work is overwhelming, but they are afraid to give up. Every time they go out to dinner hoping to reconcile, it turns into a horrible argument. For days they stay away from each other. Patty soon longs to have Tim back, and she feels anxiety without him. And without Patty, Tim slides gradually into a deep state of depression.

In our therapy work, it became evident that Patty carries Tim's anger. Tim is a passive man and unsure of himself when it comes to relationships. In business, he is successful. In relationships, however, he always feels inferior and fears making the wrong decision. Even in sex, he fears his performance won't measure up—and to Patty, it usually doesn't. Tim's mother was a rageaholic. She was always angry at his father, who ignored and avoided her. His mother took out her anger on everyone in the household, more so on Tim than on his sister. Her messages to him were: "You are stupid and dumb. You never do anything right. You are totally inadequate. When will you ever learn?" As a result, he learned to be as invisible as possible and never step into her path. He learned to never share his feelings or emotions for fear of her wrathful criticisms. Tim was afraid of his own anger and soon repressed those feelings. He spent his childhood in fear and depression. Tim was the scapegoat and the symptom bearer of his parents' disturbed relationship.

Patty's mother is an intellectual, a college professor. An only child, Patty was eight years old when her father left her mother for another woman. Though her mother was upset, she expressed it in the same manner she dealt with all her problems: She coolly and calmly rationalized it. She saw her husband as a loser and said that they were better off without him. All are men losers, she would say. Her mother refused to talk about her feelings and instead analyzed and intellectualized everything.

When Patty came to her mother with her own problems, her mother always provided solutions that came from her impersonal, distant analysis. There was no real emotional connection. Patty felt dismissed and invalidated. If Patty wanted to talk about her feelings of missing her father, her mother immediately changed the subject. Even when she had temper tantrums, her mother coolly ignored her. Mother's message was: "It's not OK to have feelings. Just ignore them." Patty remembers feeling anxious and angry all her life. She carried the rage and sadness her mother refused to deal with. She, too, was the symptom bearer. And now she carries Tim's anger. Thus, when he isn't around, her feelings have no direction and she feels extremely anxious.

All families have patterns of relating that began during the parents' courtship and that crystallized as the family grew. We carry these patterns into our adult relationships, especially in issues surrounding intimacy. Often members in a family are typecast by other members: "Dad has all the answers. Mother is scatterbrained. Sally is just like Mother. John is the smart one. James is the slow one. Ann is so clumsy she'll never be a dancer. Father is the philosopher—don't expect him to fix things. Mom is the practical one. Bobby is like his dad, always losing things." Labels and typecasting limit us. But if the family is open to change and family members can freely interact, patterns and rigid roles will not be established. If at one time we were slow in our development and other members in the family continue to see us as slow, we begin to believe this is the truth. Family beliefs and judgments become patterns that unconsciously limit us for the rest of our lives.

When the entire family views one of its members as the problem, that member becomes the scapegoat. The scapegoat unites the family. The other members can stop hating each other or dealing with their own conflicts if they can hate one of the members instead. In societies and nations around the world, scapegoating is often used to direct hate towards blacks, Jews, women, gays and the poor. What we hate and judge in others reflects our unconscious and unresolved beliefs that bring up our own self-hatred. If a couple can't vent their rage on each other, they will take it out on one of the children. In time, that child will act in the way that has been proscribed. This is the scapegoat-child.

In a family where one of the children resembles the hated partner or a hated relative of one of the parents (sister, father, brother or mother), the unresolved anger will be displaced on that child. If a wife judges her husband as incompetent, she will see the same qualities in her son and express to him what she feels she can't say to her husband. She will berate the child and remind that him he is lazy and good for nothing. Or if being an athlete is what Dad wants, and the son is an artist, that child will be verbally abused because he doesn't live up to the father's expectations. If looks or size is important in a family, the child who is too fat or too tall will be the brunt of family jokes and abuse. In time, the child believes these messages because his parents are the authority, and no one in the family tells him any different. Outside the family dynamics, children in school who are different, smaller, weaker, taller, fatter, defenseless or sickly often become the scapegoat.

Unresolved conflict can lead families to sabotage each other. The wife who is dieting to lose weight can be tempted by her husband with sweets used unconsciously to get back at her for not supporting him in his ventures. The mother who resents her daughter will be consistently late for her daughter's school programs or will be too busy to attend at all. A mother who is jealous of her teenage daughter will make comments that put her down: "Your hair is too long. That color isn't good on you. You're getting too fat." In this way, family members can destroy each other's self-esteem and establish in each child a belief blueprint that she is worthless, inadequate and not enough.

In addition to the role each members plays, the situations each family experiences help form the belief system. The experience of conception, gestation and birth is a part of the atmosphere in which children develop. Research has now shown that from the sixth month of gestation, the fetus is affected by the mother's habits, especially if the mother smokes, drinks or uses drugs. The child's development is affected by her stress, anxieties and fears as well. Studies funded by the National Institute of Mental Health found that newborn babies of mothers who suffered from depression during pregnancy and after the baby's birth showed physical symptoms of depression. Most alarming is the similarity of brain-wave patterns between the infants and their depressed mothers.

Many unpleasant circumstances surrounding the family have an affect on children's lives: unemployment, poverty, illness, death and family conflict. The number of children in the family and the gender of each child also have an impact. I have a woman friend whose father wanted a boy. The name they selected was Paul. When a girl arrived, they named her Paula. Paula feels like she never measured up to her parents' expectations and thinks she has somehow disappointed them. There are many children born to mothers who for one reason or another are alone, whose husbands are away or sick, or have divorced them or deserted the family. Many of these mothers give up or abandon their children. If the child isn't wanted, he will unconsciously know that.

The family is where we learn if our world is safe or dangerous, educated or ignorant, abundant or impoverished, trustworthy or untrustworthy, positive or negative, or if we can take from it or give to it. Families sometimes have great difficulties and depend on fantasies to create the illusion of stability. The fantasy may be the secrets we hold about one member. If Mom or Dad is an alcoholic, the story that is told is that they are tired, have the flu or have a heart condition. The family collaborates with this story. If Dad is having an affair, the family covers up whatever they know to protect Mom. No one talks about it. Where there is physical or sexual abuse, there is silent collusion to deny the problem. Children always know the truth, even if it is not verbalized. If they are expected to compromise their integrity and honesty, they will grow up confused about their own truth.

SETTING BOUNDARIES

The dictionary meaning of *boundary* is "something (a line, point) that indicates or fixes a limit or extent; a border." Often boundaries are unclear and become enmeshed with other people's boundaries. We don't know our own boundaries, and we don't know other people's boundaries.

We are not born with boundaries. We learn about them in our families. One night I was at a restaurant and observed two young mothers with their children. After finishing her glass of water, one mother then drank her young son's water without asking him. He was very upset and asked her not to do that. The mother reacted with anger and loudly scolded the boy for being selfish.

Boundaries are taught to us by our parents. Some families have no sense of boundaries, while others have rigid boundaries. Because infants have no boundaries, they are at the mercy of their caregivers. If any of us has weak boundaries, we will absorb others' feelings like a sponge. When my clients explore feelings that don't make sense to them, they often discover that they have picked up the feelings of someone else, or they are still carrying feelings that were absorbed in childhood.

In an open family system, members respect each other's thoughts, ideas and space. They don't invade each other's territory. There is room for healthy growth, with a solid sense of individual selves. The members are able to think for themselves, have their own feelings, ideas and beliefs, and are given the freedom to express them. Boundaries set by parents in open family systems are age-appropriate, flexible and non-invasive. Given limits and consequences, children will grow to develop internal boundaries that will help them to relate to their world with courage and competence. As ant parent knows, children constantly test the boundaries between themselves and others. To offer stability and security, parents must create "fences" that expand as the child grows. To help children develop their own boundaries when they are very young, parents can reasonably limit their choices and options. This will help youngsters to gradually discover their own wants and needs and develop their own self-awareness and ability to make decisions. If parents respect their child's boundaries, the child will, in turn, learn to respect those of others.

David's family had no boundaries. He was physically and emotionally neglected. His parents were caught up in their own habits with no concern for their children. They set no boundaries because they had no boundaries in themselves. Children in families with weak or nonexistent boundaries create unhealthy beliefs about themselves and their world. They believe the world is not a safe place, and they learn not to depend on others for emotional support. These children have low self-esteem, shame, feelings of worthlessness and a strong belief of not being enough. They are unable to develop a healthy sense of self and lack the direction and internal boundaries to find themselves.

Boundaries are often crossed when the parents themselves have not grown up. If they have unresolved issues in their own development, parents will interact with their children as if they are their children's siblings, causing confusion and insecurity. By the time the children are in grade school, they have often become their parents' confidants and listen to intimate adult problems when they should be playing games on their own level; for example, a mother who dresses just like her daughter and even exchanges clothes with her, just like girlfriends, or a father who hangs out with his son, drinking, smoking pot and flirting with teenage girls.

In authoritative families, children must accept and obey the parents' rules and beliefs. Controlling parents invade boundaries and believe it is their right to do so. Parents inflict their thoughts, ideas and beliefs with no regard. As helpless and insecure children, we allow our boundaries to be crossed because we are unaware of our own thoughts and beliefs. Often children are pressured to do what the parents want because of the parents' unfulfilled dreams. Parents may push their kids into certain activities because it is the "in" thing. They enroll children into Little League, soccer, swimming, dancing and music because it is what they think the child should do, even if the child has no interest. Children need to develop their own interests and desires at their own rate. If parents push their ideas and expectations on children, the children will grow up not knowing what they want and have difficulty making choices for themselves.

Families can be held together by a "common enemy." If, as children, we received strong beliefs that are prejudiced against people who are of a different belief, race, religion or socioeconomic level, we accept these prejudices because of our lack of knowledge. This common enemy can be Christians, Jews, non-Catholics, blacks and people with less money or lower status. Families make jokes about others who look or act differently: a fat person, a homeless person or someone who does things in a different way. These disturbing beliefs become part of our blueprint and are the source of hate.

If we are told often enough that we are bad and stupid, in time we believe it. We soon learn not to trust ourselves or our feelings and are unable to develop a sense of our own self-worth. Usually we harbor a prevailing, unexpressed fear of making mistakes and failing, or deep feelings of anger that often turn into depression and despair. I have had many adult clients who, like Mark in the following story, are still controlled by their parents, afraid to disagree with them, afraid to make decisions that are different than theirs. They continue to allow their mothers and fathers to interfere in their marriages, the raising of their children and how they manage their home, their career and their spiritual lives.

Mark is warm and friendly but fears relationships and intimacy. He puts up a wall to keep people out and himself safe. He has been married and divorced three times, Whenever he gets into a relationship, he becomes totally enmeshed and does everything his spouse wants. In the process, he loses himself. As each marriage ended, he vowed he would never get involved with another woman again. Now he finds himself attracted to Lynn, his new assistant. They have started dating. A part of him wants a relationship, but what he wants he also fears, bringing up feelings of confusion.

When Mark is not involved in a relationship, life goes smoothly. But the moment he gets involved, he starts to feel crazy. In our session, I ask him what he feels. He says he feels anxious, fearful, confused, smothered and trapped. I ask him about his self-talk, the things he tells himself about this new relationship with Lynn. "I tell myself I must keep her at a distance because she will expect me to do what she wants," he replies. "I have to give up my freedom and who I am to have her love. And if I don't give up myself. I will lose the good feelings and happiness I feel with her. I can't call her too much, I can't let her know I am really that interested in her. I have to play it cautious and maintain control."

As we explored Mark's self-talk and all the fears it brings up in him, I ask him what it reminds him of. He remembers his childhood. An only child, Mark was very attached to his mother, who showered him with love and attention. He was "her little boy," and she wanted to show him off. She bragged to everyone how cute he was and chattered on and on about all the cute things he said and did. If he behaved like the perfect child, she would be admired by all her friends. Consequently, Mark feared not being perfect for her and did everything he could to please her. His reward was his mother's undivided attention and love. He went everywhere with her—shopping, to the movies, to church, out to dinner. She asked his opinion about what she should wear and how she looked. Mark's father was a salesman and was often out of town for long periods of time. Whenever his parents were together, they acted like strangers. As Mark grew older, his mother confided in him all her worries and concerns. He became the kind of mate she had always dreamed of having.

Mother totally involved herself in Mark's life. She told him how to dress and how to act. She even did his homework so he would never fail. She directed him into drama and theater because it was her interest. Even in college, she called him every day and had him send his clothes home for her to wash and iron. When he dated, Mother decided who was right for him. And Mark listened to her. He felt love and hate for his mother at the same time. Her invasiveness left him feeling trapped, smothered and helpless around her.

Only after Mark finished college did he begin to individuate from Mother. She tried to hold onto him by reminding him how lonely and unhappy she was without him. After he married his first wife, Mother tried to interfere with his relationship. She would tell his wife what to do and how to handle her son and, later, their children. It created great conflict. Mark felt torn between his mother and his wife. He tried to please both of them as they vied for his attention. Again, he felt confused, lost, helpless and hopeless.

Though Mark withdraws and ends relationships with wives and girlfriends that seem to be too much like his relationship with his mother, he simply re-creates the same people-pleasing situation in another rela-tionship. Mark doesn't want to continue with this craziness, but he doesn't know how to stop.

■

If we have rigid boundaries, we put up walls to keep others out. We fear intimacy and closeness. We reveal little about ourselves and are careful in our interactions with others. The messages we give to others are: "Stay away from me. Don't come too close." We keep others away by intellec-tualizing, analyzing, distancing and withdrawing.

If our boundaries are too lax or nonexistent, however, we often engage in inappropriate behavior and actions. On a personal level, we talk inti-mately with strangers, allow others to speak or act for us and direct our lives, are afraid to say no, accept things we don't want, allow others to invade our space and believe we hold all the answers. In relationships, we give to get, fall in love and have sex on impulse, are sexual for our partner and not for ourselves, strive to please others and believe our part-ner should instinctively know all our needs. And on a more serious level, the lack of boundaries can lead to self-abuse through food, drugs or alco-hol, or by allowing someone else to abuse us physically, verbally or sexually.

A CHILD'S DEVELOPMENT: THE FIRST SIX YEARS

In order to reach our inner child, recover that feeling of bliss and per-haps strengthen our boundaries in life or set up new ones, we must first understand what occurs in the early years of a child's development.

Many families are started by parents who are not mature themselves and don't have the knowledge and skills necessary to raise a child. Most parents want their children to have a life as good as or better than they had. Often parents want their children to accomplish what they accom-plished or what they wanted to accomplish. I believe most parents have the best intention in raising their children. And, if they knew better, they would do better.

Researchers have looked for the difference between heredity and environment in the development of children. Heredity provides the raw material, and environment molds the child's life. What makes the difference in the uniqueness of each child are the experiences they learn before they are three years old. A child's personality is developed in the first year of life. Babies who feel loved and cared for are more likely to grow up with self-confidence and self-esteem.

The first six years are the most important. These years lay the foundation for our personality. It is during these years that we develop our belief blueprint. Each level of development builds on the previous one. Sometimes we get stuck and stop growing emotionally at one level because of traumatic events and experiences during that period. This will become a core problem that is woven into our beliefs and will be the source of difficulty and conflict for us in many areas of our lives.

If a newborn experiences a relatively stress-free gestation period and birth, it will be in a natural state of bliss, joy and contentment. That state of bliss, however, will be disrupted as the child begins to experience the insecurity of a new environment. There is a rupture in the child's peace and connectedness with itself. In a state of total helplessness, the child must depend on others to establish its survival and security. It is a period of getting and receiving. The child gradually begins to develop a level of security and trust in her caregivers and in her world. During this period, the infant falls in love with her primary caregivers and forms necessary attachments as she moves from the secure womb into an unfamiliar and insecure place.

Attachment and bonding fulfill a basic need for security and remain with us throughout our life. If our security and survival are threatened at this stage, we develop a fear of abandonment, and as adults we will have dependency and trust issues. We develop emotional ties that influence our resiliency, our survival skills, our accomplishments and whom we attract and marry.

At the next stage of development, we began to explore our world. The level of insecurity rises as we leave our mother. If the earlier stage of attachment was developed, we can began to separate emotionally from our caregivers. At this stage we learn to hold on and let go, moving from attachment to a willingness to become detached. One moment the child rebels and wants to distance himself from the parent, and the next moment he may cling tightly to the parent, seeking love and reassurance. To be secure at this level, the child internalizes Mother and Father and accepts their beliefs, establishing an image of himself and an image of his parents. If the child feels secure, he will develop a self separate from his caregivers. This process is called *individuation.*

Through each stage of growth, we develop our own identity and sense of competence. This pattern of growth will continue through the rest of our lives. If parents are overprotective and controlling because of their own fears, like Mark's mother, the child feels smothered and has difficulty individuating. It is a rather fine line: In order for a child to become *independent,* he must be able to *depend* on the healthy parenting skills of his caregivers. From there, he can go on to develop healthy, interdependent relationships in adulthood.

THE SIGNIFICANCE OF BIRTH ORDER

Children from the same family are born into different atmospheres and each will develop a different belief blueprint. The first child is born into a different atmosphere than the last child. Each child will become part of the family system and play a particular role in the family dynamics.

The first child is the testing ground for first-time parents and can set the blueprint for the siblings who follow. In studies done on birth order, firstborn children usually carry more expectations than the other children—or the *only* expectations if she is an only child. Firstborns carry most strongly the family's beliefs and tend to obey external authority and be other-oriented, following rules and regulations to the letter. Their belief blueprint more closely resembles that of their parents. Words that usually describe a first child are *responsible, critical, judgmental, conformist, competitive, a leader, conservative* and *independent.* They tend to be caregivers. According to John Bradshaw, author of *The Family,* the first child will make decisions and hold values consistent with or in exact opposition to the father. They experience the *not enough* syndrome and look to external authority to validate their self-worth.

By the time the second child is born, parents are a little more relaxed. The second child will be more attached to the mother and react for or against her values. This child will often act out the unconscious emotional needs of the family, especially of the mother. A male child will strive to be what the mother wants. A female child will act out the mother's hidden fantasies and desires. If the second child is the middle child, they are often the most diplomatic because they are able to relate to both older and younger siblings.

The youngest child is usually pampered by the parents and the older siblings. They are usually creative and fun-loving. Depending on the family circumstances, they tend to be less fearful and are inclined to take more risks than the older children. They are often manipulators and learn to inspire others to give them special care and attention. The youngest child tends to be dependent because he has learned to be helpless and relies on others to meet his needs. Often into adulthood, the youngest will continue to be manipulative and act in childish ways to get his needs met. If parents are overly indulgent with an only child, she will have many of the qualities of a youngest child.

Siblings have a profound effect on each other in developing beliefs. How siblings relate depends on the family dynamics. Competitive families usually value differences. In families where similarities are valued, differences will decrease. Often older siblings become surrogate parents, especially in homes where both parents work or the mother is unable to give the necessary attention to the younger children.

Our belief system incorporates our interactions with our brothers and sisters. Infants form attachments with older siblings during the first year of life. From our siblings, we can experience the emotional dynamics of relating: competition, rivalry, jealousy, conflict, negotiating, problem solving, loving, empathy, teamwork, and just getting along. We also learn adaptation skills from them: fighting physically or verbally, running away, acting covertly, submitting and giving up, or withdrawing. In general, children raised with other children have better relationship skills. They learn to share and problem-solve with peers. It has been found that children raised with siblings and or with other children have higher IQs.

Besides siblings, a child's social skills are developed through relationships with other individuals during these primary years. Grandparents, aunts, uncles, cousins, nannies, baby-sitters, friends of our parents and teachers all play an integral part in a child's development. These relationships help to create a supportive community for children to develop beliefs about themselves and the world.

PARENTING IN THE 1990S

To become a good parent to our children, we must start by being a good parent to ourselves. Most of us don't know how. When our inner child is depressed, sad or hurt we do everything we can to avoid our feelings. We criticize and judge ourselves for having the feelings we have or blame others for our discomfort. Our feelings are telling us a truth that we need to listen to. Feelings don't come out of a void. They are ways to get our attention. What we need to do is listen, validate our feelings and comfort ourselves.

Parenting is learned. Even parents who treat their children harshly and give them negative messages really want the best for them. Their behavior was based on fear and ignorance and came from limiting beliefs. To understand our parents' behavior, we need to look at their thoughts, judgments and decisions based on their beliefs. Those beliefs came from the society they lived in and the beliefs of their parents. To heal our past, we must move from blame to self-discovery.

Today we are striving for equality and rights for everyone: men, women and children. We are striving for equality in all races and religions. By offering children equality and rights, they develop self-esteem and can contribute to society as healthy adults. Parents are children's role models. Children learn not only from what parents tell them, but also from how their parents behave. If parents play submissive roles and lose their self-worth in the process, their children will follow their example. If youngsters learn from their parents a role model of tyrannical, authoritative control, they will grow up believing that to survive, either they must control others or they must give up their inner authority to a controlling external authority.

Children do not develop self-reliance and responsibility in homes that are too strict or too permissive. In an atmosphere of shame and blame, children will learn that they can't trust others or trust themselves, and they shame and blame others in the same way. Children do not create negative feelings about themselves by themselves. These feelings come from their home lives. Often parents manipulate and encourage their children to succeed out of their own hidden agenda for their youngsters to measure up to their expectations. Many times a child will not be at the same developmental level, physically or academically, as other children, and the parents will see the child as inadequate and not enough. They fear that it is a bad reflection on them as parents. The child will be given conditional love as a reward for behavior that meets the parents' needs, and as a result, these children will not grow emotionally.

Jane Nelson, author of *Positive Discipline,* based on the theories of Adlerian psychology, provides a set of basic concepts that offer a wealth of knowledge in understanding our children's behavior. According to Nelson, a child needs to feel significant in her family and have a sense of belonging. Children make decisions about themselves and how to behave based on how they see themselves in relationship to others and how they think others perceive them. They want to be liked, accepted and given attention, but in trying to achieve this goal, they often act out in obnoxious ways because they do not know any better. Misbehavior is based on a false belief of how to get recognition and a sense of belonging. The child is confused about how to get what she wants. A misbehaving child is a discouraged child.

Every child needs to be listened to and validated. If children can grow up in an atmosphere of mutual respect, shared responsibility, equality, validation and kindness, they will learn self-reliance, responsibility and respect for themselves and others.

Child rearing in the 1990s probably holds more stress for families than ever before. Today in most families, both parents work. Between juggling careers and business meetings with children's schedules, home-work and after-school activities, parents live on the edge of exhaustion. Baby-sitters and child care workers cannot give children what they need from their parents. Children need not only quality time, but quantity time they can depend on, time that is filled with honest, relaxed, loving, mutually respectful connections.

Our children come through us, and they bring with them their own blueprint, their own potential. We are here to nurture that potential, to create a fertile soil for those natural seeds to grow. Long before they became your children, these young people had their own agenda. Each child has his path already within him before he is born.

FAMILY MEETINGS

I suggest to the families I work with to hold weekly family meetings. The decisions that are made in these meetings are the consensus of all members. Each member can place problems for group solutions on the agenda. During the meeting, each person has a chance to talk while others listen. A talking stick can be passed around to each member who wishes to be heard. (For more information on how to mirror, validate and empathize, see the section on healing communication and the exercises in chapter 5.) This will teach children to have respect for each other.

But meetings are just one way to open the lines of communication; planning a family outing or vacation is an excellent opportunity to establish responsibilities and strengthen the family unit at the same time.

A fun and educational game involves switching family roles. One of the children can be Mother, one can be Dad and the parents can play the children. Again, use the communication skills in chapter 5. Dialogue with each other in the new roles. Once into the game, each member will feel the role she or he is playing and get a sense of what it is like to be the other person.

EXERCISES

At the core of each of us are our own unique gifts that life itself has given us. These gifts are buried under the limiting beliefs that we carry around with us. Our truth lies under it all and will be revealed to us as we let go and shed these beliefs.

To find yourself, you must first look at the beliefs you have accepted from your parents, your family of origin, your family's structure and style, your siblings and other people in your life. This awareness will give you clues to the limiting beliefs that make up your blueprint, enabling you to move from blame to self-discovery.

WHAT BELIEFS DO YOU CARRY?

Review the exercises in chapter 1 on your Not Enough Messages. Remember where you got these messages and write down names, places and situations from your childhood. Which members in your family had the same beliefs? Did your childhood friends have the same beliefs?

The Not Enough Messages were passed down to you from your parents. They came from the experiences and the people in their childhood. Not Enough Beliefs are multigenerational. To understand our own belief blueprint we need to look at our parents' belief blueprint. You may want to create a core belief blueprint for your mother and father.

■ Explore your mother's life to discover the beliefs and decisions that she accepted as truths in her life. Before you start this process sit quietly and bring your attention inside. Breath deeply as you remember your mother. See her face, hear her voice, smell her, feel her presence. Then in your journal write a paragraph about your mother: Who is she? Where did she get her beliefs and how have they affected her life?

When you have completed this, return to your silence and see her as a little girl in the family she was raised. What was her mother like? How was her father? What kind of a home did they have: open, closed or permissive? Were they religious? What was their financial situations? What were the experiences she had that developed her beliefs and formed her decisions?

Now write in your journal several periods, no more than twelve, about her life from birth to the present. Write them in the first person. Start the first phase with "I was born" . . . and then . . . and then. Continue with a paragraph for each phase of her life. The phases or periods may be from infancy to grade school years, high school, and so on through her life. Remember the stories you have heard from her or others or even what you imagine. Write about her illnesses, health, womanhood, her friends, her relationship with her parents and siblings, work, her loves, marriage or marriages, her children, the crossroads in her life, her religion or spiritual faith, the deaths is her life, disappointments, joys and sorrows. For each phase of her life write what beliefs and decisions began to develop. Remember to write this in the first person. By doing this you will feel her essence and her journey in life.

■ Now, repeat the same about your father. Explore your father's life to discover the beliefs and decisions that he accepted as truths in his life. Before you start this process sit quietly and bring your attention inside. Breath deeply as you remember your father. See his face, hear his voice, smell him, feel his presence. Then in your journal write a paragraph about your father: Who is he? Where did he get his beliefs and how have they affected his life?

When you have completed this, return to your silence and see your father as a little boy in the family he was raised. What was his mother like? How was his father? What kind of a home did they have: open, closed or permissive? Were they religious? What was their financial condition? What were the experiences he had that developed his beliefs and formed his decisions?

Now write in your journal several periods, no more than twelve, about his life from birth to the present. Write them in the first person. Start the first phase with "I was born" . . . and then . . . and then. Continue with a paragraph for each phase of his life. The phases or periods may be from infancy to grade school years, high school, and so on through his life. Remember the stories you have heard from him or others or even what you imagine. Write about his illness, his health, his manhood, friends, relationship with his parents and siblings, work, his loves, marriage or marriages, children, the crossroads in his life, his religion or spiritual quest, his disappointments, joys and sorrows. For each phase of his life write what beliefs and decisions began to develop. Remember to write this in the first person. By doing this you will feel his essence and journey in life.

To understand another person we must walk in their shoes and see their perspective, beliefs and decisions that formed their reality. From this perspective they can make sense to us even if we don't agree or accept the same beliefs. And from looking at others' lives from this perspective we can have empathy for them instead of judgement.

■ How did your mother and father adapt to their Not Enough beliefs? What sub-personalities did they develop? Have you adapted in a similar way? How have their adaptations affected your life? Example: *When my mother's controlling and criticizing sub-personality was there, I felt fear and withdrew.* Use your journal to discover more about the beliefs, decisions and adaptations that have been passed down to you. Remember you do not have to accept anyone else's beliefs and decisions. Once brought to conscious awareness, beliefs, decisions and adaptations are choices. Change your beliefs, change your life.

■ Now, list all the people in your life who gave you positive messages that became the foundation for positive beliefs about yourself and your world. Who validated you? Who encouraged you? Who believed in you? Write in your journal what they did to encourage you and how you felt. Explore how their recognition and support has affected your life. Write them a letter of appreciation.

QUESTIONS FOR SELF-DISCOVERY:

1. What family system did you grow up in: open, closed or permissive?

2. Who was in charge? Who set the rules?

3. What are your beliefs about family? About children?

4. What was your family game? Were you the High Aachievers, the Superior Family, the Religious Family, Do-gooders, the Worriers, the Status Seekers, the Happy Family, the Whiners, the Secret Keepers, the Pretenders, the Know-It-Alls, the Perfectionists, the Loyal-at-All-Costs Family?

5. What belief patterns did you get from your family?

6. Which of these beliefs still have authority over your thoughts and decisions? Which ones did you discard, and what beliefs have you replaced them with?

ROADBLOCKS TO LISTENING:

Read the following roadblocks in conjunction with the communication skills covered in chapter 5. Which of the following did you experience as you grew up? Who treated you this way?

1. Ordering, Commanding, Directing: *"Stop complaining." "Go back in there and do what I tell you to do."*

2. Moralizing, Preaching, Lecturing: *"You shouldn't act that way." "Good girls don't get angry." "Always respect your elders." "Boys are tough." "When I was your age . . ."*

3. Criticizing, Judging, Blaming: *"You never do anything right." "You're stupid." "You're old enough to know better." "When will you learn?"*

4. Threatening, Admonishing: *"If you do that again, you'll be sorry." "Don't you ever raise your voice to me." "You do it my way."*

5. Advising, Giving solutions: *"If I were you I would." "If you do it my way, you'll get it right." "You haven't had all the experience that I have, so you can't figure it out."*

6. Withdrawing, Distracting: *"Let's change the subject and talk about something more pleasant." "I am too busy to listen to your problems."*

7. Shaming, Ridiculing, Guilting: *"You should be ashamed of yourself." "You always think about yourself and never do what I want." "You're _____ years old and you act like that?" "Stop being so childish." "Grow up!"*

8. Analyzing, Interpreting: *"I think you did that deliberately to hurt me." "You can never get along with people because you think you know it all."*

9. Interrogating, Questioning: *"Where did you get those ideas?" "Who were you talking to, and what did they say?" "What do you mean by that?"*

10. Sympathizing: *"I used to feel that way when I was your age." "Nobody will ever understand you like I do." "Too bad. Isn't life awful?" "Aw, you poor thing."*

The above responses carry hidden messages that children come to believe are true about them:

"I am not capable of knowing what is best for myself."

"Someone else knows more about me than I do."

"I have to be different than what I am to be accepted by you."

"I have to do things your way, or you will punish me."

"I am not able to solve problems for myself."

"I must not be trustworthy."

"I am not very smart, maybe stupid, because I don't figure things out the same as you do."

"I must not be very important because you don't take me seriously."

"My feelings aren't important because you don't seem to have time for me."

"There is something about me that I should be ashamed of."

"I must be bad."

"I am not enough just the way I am."

Chapter 7

HEALTH AND HEALING:
The Mind-Body Connection

Raul was born in Argentina. His father was a high-ranking diplomat, and the family lived a comfortable life. In school, Raul was well behaved and an excellent student. It was expected of him. His father rewarded him with approval and praise. The family was highly respected, and it was important for Raul to continue gaining respect.

When Raul was six years old, his father was assassinated. He remembers that day very clearly. When he came home from school that rainy afternoon, he felt something was terribly wrong. As he approached his father's car in the driveway, he saw his entire family standing around it. His mother was distraught and was crying and wailing. Raul bolted toward the car. "Stay away, stay away," everyone begged him. What he saw threw him into shock. His father's bloody body lay in the backseat of their limousine. A doctor was trying frantically to save his life, but it was too late. Raul's father, whom he loved, was dead.

The young boy's heart began to pound rapidly, and he had trouble breathing. Though he was covered with sweat, his little hands were very, very cold. He began to tremble with fear as the servants rushed him into the house. The scene was imprinted so vividly in his mind that he would never forget it. Fear, grief, anguish and confusion filled the days that followed, and the days grew into years.

By the time Raul was ten, he began suffering from fatigue and had pain all over his body. He was diagnosed with arthritis. When he was twelve years old, the arthritis had crippled him, and his knees had fused. By his eighteenth birthday, he had a hip replaced. The following year his other hip was replaced.

In spite of his physical difficulties, Raul came to America to finish his college education. He earned a master's degree in business. Throughout college he was a high achiever and excelled. But the stress increased the pain and discomfort of his disease. In his third year of school, his spine fused from the arthritis.

Today Raul is thirty-eight years old. He is successful in business but suffers greatly with limited movement and pain. Raul has a strong survival personality. He is controlling and dominates his environment because he does not want to be dependent on others. The fear of not measuring up to his own expectations pushes him to excel. He stubbornly refuses to acknowledge his personal difficulties. Within him, however, is an ongoing battle between his willingness to fight and his deep frustration at his inability to fight. He refuses to stop or rest when his body needs it. In fact, he abuses his body with his denial. This increases the pain and crippling of his body.

Raul avoids intimacy because he fears being vulnerable. Limited by his illness, he unconsciously controls every aspect of his life. He has rigid opinions and is not open to the ideas or opinions of others. What's more, many of his beliefs are negative, and Raul doubts that there is any healing possibility for his arthritis other than traditional medicine. Raul has had surgery and relies on prescribed drugs. Though he is determined to keep going, he lives in fear of failure. He feels great rage that he has been attacked by this disease, but he refuses to see his participation in either the disease or the healing.

Most of us take good health for granted. We pay little attention to our bodies until we experience physical or emotional pain or have symptoms that signal *dis-ease*. Dis-ease is the lack of ease in our bodies, brought on by imbalances in our lives. Eventually, it can lead to *disease,* which is a pathological condition of a body part, organ or system that creates iden-tifiable symptoms. When we have pain or symptoms, we usually feel surprise, anxiety, fear, frustration and helplessness because we believe an intruder has invaded our lives. Our view of illness is that of an accident, an annoyance or an interruption. We begin to look outside of ourselves for something that caused our illness, and we believe someone else knows what is wrong with us and can fix us.

The World Health Organization defines *health* as more then the absence of disease. Health is a state of perfect physical, mental and social well-being. To this I would add spiritual well-being. It is in that state of harmony that we experience a vibrancy, joy and zest for life. Wellness and good health is about the quality of our lives. Our health is in an ever-changing process that constitutes many levels of our being. Because perfect health, joy and contentment is our natural state, our body strives, often against great odds, to heal and bring us back to a state of wellness and wholeness.

Our health system is made up of several parts that work together to achieve a desired goal. In the body's system, the desired goal is to thrive, not just survive. It is made up of other systems that constitute the men-tal, emotional, physical and spiritual. Each system interacts with the others to maintain homeostasis. Illness is the breakdown of the body's inability to maintain that homeostasis. Where there is a breakdown of one part, other parts are affected. Emotional distress can cause physical dis-ease, and physical distress can cause emotional dis-ease. Our mind, body and spirit are one and cannot be treated separately.

Every thought and feeling we have is translated into a chemical mes-senger that affects every cell in our body. It is the mind-body connection. That instant reaction creates physical changes that are positive or neg-ative. Our thoughts contain powerful energy. How that energy is used—to destroy or to enhance—is under our control. To change our thoughts, we must first find and change the limiting beliefs behind our thoughts. In his book, *Love, Medicine and Miracles*, Bernie Siegel, M.D., writes, "The unexplained cures and survivals I have witnessed have con-vinced me that the state of mind changes the state of the body and that there are no incurable diseases, only incurable people. Those who are able to love and hope, have peace of mind and faith send their bodies a 'live' message, while those who are constantly depressed, fearful, despairing and in conflict and do nothing about it give their bodies a 'die' message."

In earlier centuries disease was seen as an invasion of malevolent external forces. This view regarded us as helpless victims. The "germ theory" was developed by Louis Pasteur, a French chemist and bacteriologist, in the late 1800s. He believed external agents caused disease. By the time Pasteur died, however, his views had changed, and he felt our internal causes were more decisive than the influence of germs. The work of Hans Selye on stress recognized external stress as the cause of illness. In actuality, though, it is our *reaction* to the stress in our lives that causes illness. Unfortunately, Selye's external cause-and-effect view of dis-ease is still prevalent in the medical community. Symptoms are removed with surgery or masked by drugs, and thoughts, emotions, beliefs and life strategies are not explored or dealt with.

Today, however, many doctors have a holistic approach to wellness and look for the causes of dis-ease from every aspect of life. The word *holistic* comes from the Greek word *holos,* meaning the entirety or completeness of a thing. Holistic practitioners do not treat symptoms; they treat the whole person.

HOW WE ADAPT: TWO STYLES OF RESPONDING

Research over the last decade has shown that 85 percent of our medical problems are related to stress. Our physiological reactions to stress are a natural, involuntary response to the danger or threats to our survival. Those who live in a constant responsive state of threat, real or imagined, however, will automatically and continually stimulate the body's alert response. Others who have learned to function in a nonresponsive survival mode trigger other natural physiological responses. The stresses in our life are catalysts that trigger a learned response that differ for all of us. There are people who respond as *high reactors,* and there are people who respond as *low reactors*. These reactions are determined by the way we have learned to adapt to life-threatening experiences.

Some of our reactions are genetic, and others come from our fetal experience. Observe newborn babies in the hospital nursery and notice the differences. Some babies are placid, whereas others are red-faced with frustration. The differences in our adaptive patterns, however, depend on our childhood development and experiences. Our adaptations are reactions to our life experiences based on our belief blueprint. It is a culturally learned reaction. They are behaviors in response to certain events. In turn, these behaviors are based on the beliefs we carry about ourselves and our world. It is not the events or stressors in our lives that create our reactions, it is how we view and perceive the events.

In childhood, we begin to develop behavior patterns that determine how we will react. The high reactor exaggerates her reaction to frustration, and the low reactor diminishes his reaction. When we experience a threat, we express our energy by expanding or contracting it. As an infant, the high reactor cries and screams and has temper tantrums to get his needs met. The infant who underreacts withdraws and diminishes her expression to protect herself. Our reactions come from a primitive part of our brain, our survival center, called the reptilian brain (see chapter 2). The function of the reptilian brain is to fight, flee, freeze or submit in the face of danger.

When we are threatened, a variety of physical changes occur with dramatic suddenness to prepare our bodies for fight or flight. For high reactors, the changes are as follows:

- Our bronchial tubes open, and our breathing becomes rapid to increase our oxygen intake.
- Our pupils dilate to let in more light and improve vision.
- Our heartbeat increases to pump blood carrying oxygen and nutrients to cells, and to clear away the toxins in our body quickly. Blood pressure rises.
- Our liver releases glucose to increase energy for survival.
- Blood flow increases to the brain to makes us mentally alert.

- Blood flows to our muscles, and our muscles tighten in preparation for action.
- Blood flow constricts in the extremities to protect our internal organs, and our hands and feet become cold.
- Adrenaline and other hormones are released into the bloodstream.
- Our body perspires to cool us off.
- Our stomach stops secreting digestive fluids, and blood flow is diverted to our muscles.
- Activity in our intestines stops.
- The hair on our bodies stands up, making us look larger.

Low reactors respond in the opposite manner by restricting energy and shutting down the body in the face of danger. To survive, they freeze or submit in threatening situations. In the animal kingdom, a lion will mobilize its energy for attack, whereas a deer will freeze in the face of danger. Their reactions are instinctual. In human beings, our reactions are escalated or decreased by our belief system, thoughts and emotions. For some, strange noises trigger immense fears; for others they go unnoticed. The difference is in our conditioning that formed our beliefs.

What is a natural physical response to threat can also become the very thing that breaks down the body. The breakdown comes from the normal physiological processes of survival and protection that have become overused and out of balance. Our autonomic nervous system, which is involuntary, is made up of two major divisions, the sympathetic system and the parasympathetic system. The sympathetic system accelerates the heart, and the parasympathetic system slows it down. The sympathetic system is immediately triggered when we are in a threatened survival situation. This is our first line of defense. The parasympathetic system slows things down so the body can rest and regroup. If we remain in a continued and prolonged state of overreaction or underreaction, it can cause damage to the body. It will compromise our immune system, which works in tandem with our entire physiological defense system and brings on illness. Raul, whose story appeared at the beginning of this chapter, is a high reactor. He lives in a constant state of threat. Some of it is real, some of it is imagined. The arousal of his sympathetic nervous system by the perception of stress causes his arthritis to flare up.

We unconsciously create a defense system by expanding or constricting our energy in the face of threat. Chinese medicine regards our bodies as in either excessive condition (expanded energy—Yang) or deficient condition (constricted energy—Yin). Where there is an imbalance of either Yin or Yang there will be dis-ease. The way to health is through the balance of these dualistic forces, which are opposite and complementary at the same time. Yang is active, Yin is passive. Yang is hot, like the sun, and Yin is cold, like the moon. Expressed energy is Yang, like boiling water that creates heat. Yin is inertia, in which no visible activity is taking place. The shift in balance from Yin to Yang continues all the time, from month to month, day to day, even moment to moment. If a man is too hot (Yang), he will drink water to cool himself off (Yin) and to create a balance in his body.

Practitioners of Eastern medicine help the patient establish a natural balance between Yin and Yang through acupuncture, herbs and lifestyle changes. The balance of Yin/Yang will lead to health and wellness. The philosophy of Western medicine has been to fix things that are broken instead of putting and keeping our bodies in balance and harmony. In the medical model, there are specialists that treat only certain parts of the body: heart specialist, kidney specialist, brain specialist. Wellness comes from the balance of the whole system.

To overreact (Yang) or underreact (Yin) is how we adapt to the stresses in our life. These are our life strategies. Dis-ease is caused by the imbalance created by our reactions in stressful situations over extended periods of time. I believe we can change dis-ease-producing experiences by changing the limiting beliefs that are the foundation for our adaptive life strategies, and by changing the unconscious choices we make. Some of us are predominately overreactive, while others are predominately underreactive. Most of us lie somewhere in between, overreacting in one area and underreacting in another. My natural tendency in work is to be a high reactor, maximizing my energy and pushing myself to excel, often at the expense of my health. In intimate relationships, I have tended to be a minimizer and withdraw in situations that I perceive as threatening. I have had to learn to balance my life by consciously looking at my adaptive patterns that work in one area and applying them to the other.

THE HIGH REACTOR

High reactors are probably what we would call type A personalities. This personality type was identified in studies done on heart patients by cardiologists Meyer Friedman and Ray Rosenman in the 1970s. The doctors looked at patterns of behavior that could predict dis-ease. They saw patients whose rage seethed just below the surface and who showed inner turmoil, fist clenching and impatience. The most significant trait of this personality type was the habitual sense of urgency, trying to accomplish too much in too little time. They had a tendency to compete or challenge other people, even in simple conversation. In the lives of these patients was a sense of pressure and urgency in their life strategies.

What are the beliefs of the high reactor? High reactors have established a *Pusher* subpersonality that constantly reminds them of what they believe they should do, ought to do, must do, have to do or are expected to do. Being a Pusher results in guilt and dissatisfaction over one's accomplishments. Pushers are the doers, the superachievers, the accomplishers and accumulators. They are the power people who dominate others and value control. To stay on top of things, they must continuously give more, do more and win at all costs—and the costs are usually relationships, peace of mind and emotional and physical health.

The thinking of the high reactor is based on a limiting core belief of being not enough with feelings of inadequacy. They have learned to adapt to this belief by striving to be more than enough and perfect. There is no room for imperfection. Highly critical of themselves and others, high reactors tend to have an "all or nothing" way of looking at their lives. If it isn't perfect, it is nothing. Their strivings create great physical and emotional demands on themselves and others around them. They must be totally in control or out of control. Either state is not healthy.

High reactors often believe they are indispensable. If they received messages during childhood that they must always be available for others, then they will think and do for others no matter what the cost to themselves. It is not uncommon for them to give more, take on additional responsibilities and put others' needs first. If any of these beliefs are yours, take them as a warning.

In our society, high reactors are greatly valued because of the lengths they go to succeed. Their high energy level and intelligence pushes them to achieve. Despite the many rewards they receive for their achievements, the feelings of not enough still exist and are often the motivator for their unhealthy behavior. It is like the proverbial carrot on a stick that keeps them running yet always remains out of reach. More often than not, in the process of proving their worth, high reactors abuse themselves and others. Even vacations are times for competition and achievement. To rest and relax only brings up feelings of guilt, shame and fear.

The world we see as a stressful place, one that requires great effort and suffering to survive, is often a carbon copy of our childhood that we have automatically and unconsciously re-created in adulthood. High reactors tend to exaggerate and view every situation as a red alert: a scratch on the car, a missed appointment, lateness, a lost item. Each event can trigger beliefs of absolute catastrophe—basically, it's the end of the world. *Awful, horrible, terrible, overwhelming, unbelievable* and *disastrous* are words high reactors often use to describe the events in their lives. Their reactions are usually above or below the emotional baseline: Everything is either a huge success or a monumental failure.

Intimacy is difficult for high reactors because it requires giving up control. They tend to have unrealistic expectations of their partner. To have intimacy, an environment of equality must exist, and the other person's opinions must be valued. Each partner must be allowed to be who he or she is. This is called differentiation. Closeness and love are exactly what high reactors need and want, but they usually don't know how to achieve it because they apply the same strategies—domination and control—to relationships that they apply to every other area of their life. High reactors have little awareness of their underlying emotions and beliefs and are unwilling to examine childhood wounds that may be affecting their present situations, until a crisis forces them to. Blame is directed at others, and people closest to the high reactor are often the target of that person's displaced frustration and anger.

Often high reactors will stay in abusive relationships or stressful jobs far longer than others, trying to fix or conquer the challenge until something in them gives out. They believe they must win and to give up is to fail. In this state of prolonged stress, the body eventually burns out and can no longer function physically, mentally or emotionally. They experience great frustration because the fear of leaving such painful situations is greater than the pain of staying. They can no longer fight but are too exhausted to run. Our bodies carry the response and manifestation of our respective lifestyles. Unfortunately, high reactors ignore the messages the body is sending them because they think they know better. Their immune system becomes fatigued from prolonged readiness and is compromised in its ability to work efficiently. A small cut or a splinter can lead to a severe infection. A cold can turn into pneumonia. The greatest risk is to the high reactor's cardiovascular system: hypertension, heart problems and high cholesterol. Other physical responses include migraines, hyperthyroid, arthritis, diabetes, ulcers and accident proneness.

THE LOW REACTOR

Low reactors have the same core beliefs as high reactors. Both believe they are not enough, and both have feelings of inadequacy, accompanied by low self-esteem and self-worth. But whereas high reactors seek self-esteem through the rewards they get for their achievements, accomplishments and accumulations, low reactors diminish their interaction with the world by giving up and believing they have no control of the outcome. They often feel helpless, hopeless and powerless.

When high reactors are burned out from prolonged internal and external stress, they become low reactors. Their adaptations no longer work, and their energy is diminished or depleted. Fatigue sets in and is soon followed by depression and despair. Feeling they no longer have control over their environment, they give up pushing themselves to succeed.

Those who are low reactors are stoic and inhibit their emotions. When their survival is threatened, they tend to withhold and preserve their energy. The beliefs they have about themselves and their world lie in a time zone that views the past the same as the present: *Things will always be the same. What's the use, I can't change things anyway. I am powerless. I have no control over what happens to me, I am just a victim. I'll make it only if someone else gives it to me, Everything will always be the same for me. I always fail and make mistakes. Life is hopeless. Everyone else can do better than I can. I can't do anything, so why bother trying?*

Fearing change and rarely taking risks, the low reactors' crucial objective is to avoid being hurt or disappointed. Often their first response is one of negativity. They believe they can't handle certain situations and give up. Being safe is the most important thing, and they avoid anything that feels like danger, often living in a vigilant state, watching and waiting for disaster. They fear making decisions or choices that could possibly lead to mistakes. To avoid all conflict, they plan almost every move ahead of time. They are essentially not involved with their lives and "freeze" their emotions.

In intensely stressful experiences, high reactors mobilize their strength to fight, whereas low reactors withdraw, remain passive and play possum so the enemy will think they are dead. Their personalities tend to be passive-aggressive. These people are often hostile and angry but suppress it. They rarely ask for what they want; in fact, they are not even sure of what they want or what their opinions are and rely on others to tell them. This shifts the responsibility from themselves to others. Their behavior, or lack of behavior, often frustrates others and sabotages relationships.

Like high reactors, low reactors have difficulty with intimacy. Low reactors often allow others to run their lives out of their belief that they are unable to do so. They have ambivalent feelings toward themselves and others, and though they want intimacy, they also fear it. Low reactors withdraw and tend to be loners. In intimacy, they are like the turtle who pulls in its head when there is a threat.

In *Keeping the Love You Find,* Harville Hendrix discusses maximizer and minimizer personality types and the complex difficulties each has in relationships: Maximizers adapt to threat by exaggerating, and minimizers adapt by diminishing. Hendrix suggests, "The earlier in life, the more primitive the [developmental] stage at which the primary wound is suffered, the greater the degree of exaggeration or diminishment." Therefore, if adaptive behaviors begin early in an infant's life, his reactions in adulthood will be more intense, one way or the other. If adaptive behaviors came at the later stages of the child's development, the degree of reaction in his adult life will be less.

Martin Seligman, Ph.D., at the University of Pennsylvania, found that patterns of helplessness are learned behaviors. Infants raised in orphanages and institutional settings who are given physical care but have minimal interaction with caregivers develop behaviors of helplessness and depression over time. They have no control over their environment and soon withdraw and ignore others. Prone to infections, most die very young. In normal families, where the child interacts with the caregiver who responds to their cries or smiles, the child develops a healthy sense of involvement and control in their lives. If the caregivers stop interacting, listening or validating the child, in time the child will stop interacting, listening and validating themselves. In homes where the message is "Don't be, don't exist," the child believes to exist is unacceptable, so they try to stop existing. Seligman contends that helplessness feeds on itself and turns to depression. It is characterized by a negative mind-set and a "giving up" on one's life.

In his work, Seligman divided people into optimists and pessimists. Though optimists often take responsibility for their part in adversity, they are more inclined to blame others. Pessimists blame themselves, even if the situation is abusive. Children who are abused often feel it is their fault. They have self-deprecating thoughts about themselves based on beliefs in their own inadequacies. These early conditionings last a lifetime unless they are reevaluated and corrected.

Low reactors tend to be pessimistic, seeing life through dark glasses and their experiences as negative. They often feel inferior, defeated, victimized, afraid and insecure and tend to be chronically anxious. A victim mentality is prevalent today that tends to let them "off the hook" and avoid responsibility. In all aspects of life, from lawsuits to crime to everyday arguments and conflicts, it seems many people point the finger at others and do not take responsibility for their own actions. Even when low reactors have achieved success and are duly complimented, they tend to minimize themselves. If they get a promotion, they believe there must have been a mistake because deep down they feel they don't really deserve it. They worry they will never measure up to the promotion and the expectations that come with it.

In low reactors, the immune system is compromised and functions like the person herself: sluggish, unsure, depressed, confused and not making an effort to defend and protect itself. Infections, colds, bronchial problems, allergies, asthma, colitis and autoimmune diseases such as multiple sclerosis and lupus are the result. Often low reactors are candidates for cell diseases such as cancer. In a twenty-five-year study documented in the 1970s, Lawrence Le Shane, Ph.D., found 76 percent of cancer patients had low-reactor patterns. Cancer cells already exist in our bodies. A healthy immune system finds these unwanted and unhealthy cells, destroys them and purges them from our body.

The immune system's job is to find and destroy invaders. Our bodies carry every kind of germ. When our defense system is weakened, germs and viruses take over. If a person feels defeated, inadequate and passive, the body works in an equally defeated, inadequate and passive way.

MAKING THE MIND-BODY CONNECTION

Remember Lora from chapters 1 and 2? In therapy, Lora's process of grieving over a friend overwhelms and confuses her at the same time. She can't make sense of it. It brings up feelings she can't understand and thus fears. I gently remind Lora that children are like sponges, absorbing the feelings (even feelings that aren't expressed) and beliefs from the people around them. I have a sense that a lot of her feelings have been historically repressed.

When Lora was seven years old, her father died after a long illness. He may have felt fear and grief about his terminal illness, and Lora probably absorbed those feelings. Lora's mother had her own feelings about her sick husband. She resented him, was afraid of his illness and feared for her survival after he was gone. When he died, she repressed her grief. As a child, Lora decided not to feel. It was how her mother had dealt with the illness and death of her husband. Mother decided never to suffer again the loss of a partner and chose never to have a relationship with a man.

Lora never allowed herself to grieve the loss of her father. In fact, whenever we talk about her father, she has very little memory of him. She says she has blocked memories from her childhood. Lora is an under-reactor. It is how she believes she must respond to life's stresses to survive. She stuffs her feelings by stuffing her body with food. She is overweight and has many health problems, including recurrent respiratory problems, bronchitis and allergies. Respiratory problems can be viewed as a repression of tears and the holding in of emotions. Now, in therapy, she feels confused when her feelings come up. To her they seem to be out of proportion to her experience

Instead of analyzing her feelings, Lora is learning to accept them. Analyzing and intellectualizing is how Lora has dealt with herself and her world. She believed it was safer to analyze than to feel. Until now, Lora has armored herself against her emotions out of the fear that she will be overwhelmed and won't be able to handle it. Gradually, she is learning to accept her feelings, free of judgment and interpretation. Every day she writes in her journal to understand that her experiences are learning opportunities. As she sees her participation in her life and her illnesses, she feels more in control and has found the ability to change her life. Her beliefs kept her in an infantile way of viewing her world. She believed others controlled her destiny, and to simply ask for what she wanted was not acceptable. Instead, she people-pleased and blocked her own feelings, emotions, needs and wants. Lora's intention now is to heal the past beliefs and behaviors that have kept her stuck.

■

I believe our health is a reflection of our lives, an expression of our history and our lifestyle. We wear our history not only on our faces, but on our bodies as well. Our health, good or bad, is never separate from the rest of our lives. It is a mirror of our thoughts, our beliefs, our life strategies and adaptations and the choices we make. Every cell in our body responds to every thought and belief we have, every word we speak.

We have a natural adaptation to situations that are stressful. For survival, our bodies' threshold rises to adapt to our stresses. But in time, these adaptations will break down our bodies if we stay in toxic relationships, keep toxic people around us, stay in toxic jobs, breath toxic air and eat foods filled with toxins. Like Lora, in crisis situations we often ignore our symptoms and choose not to feel. To mask our feelings, we gradually increase our intake of food, tobacco, alcohol and drugs. Our bodies will tolerate these toxins but not for long. To change our health, we must look at every area of our lives: We need to explore the thoughts and beliefs that allow us to continue increasing or diminishing our sense of well-being. By exploring the mind-body connection, we can learn to change our addictive and often unconscious habits and make new, healthy choices for our bodies and our lives.

BELIEFS ABOUT OUR HEALTH

We are not aware of exactly how the body performs its many involuntary functions. Those functions, however, mirror the inner data from our beliefs and ideas. Both a sick body and a healthy body perform the same functions that mirror these beliefs. If we believe we have heart trouble, or are genetically predetermined to have heart trouble, our own anxiety and consequently inner fearful messages may affect the functioning of our involuntary system that will consequently damage the heart. Our thoughts, beliefs and inner talk can help to make us sick or make us well. Health or illness are not accidental; they are a natural progression from inner thoughts and images. The nonphysical forms the physical.

Both Lora and Raul express their inner belief patterns (nonphysical) in external form (physical). Lora's body is stuffed with repressed beliefs that remind her that she has no control over her life or her eating habits. She believes she is not enough and that there isn't anything she can do to change it. She feels safer cutting off her feelings and stuffing them away because her deeper belief is that "it won't matter anyway; life will always be this way, and I will never get what I want." The inner data from her belief system create a victimized, vulnerable, sluggish, ineffective immune system. In addition, her repressed grief and tears leave her with constant respiratory problems. Raul's personality is rigid, like his body. Raul is locked into old, limiting belief patterns about his health and illness. He armors himself against intimacy and steels himself against change. He stoically accepts his illness and refuses to accept any new or unfamiliar viewpoint. His sight, and his insight, is limited by the inability to turn his head. It is stiff, frozen and immobile like his thoughts and beliefs.

How we perceive our body determines our experience of it. It is the result of our self-talk, thoughts, ideas and beliefs that we have previously held. Within one year, 98 percent of the cells in our body have been replaced. Every seven years we have in essence a completely new body. We have a new stomach lining every five days. Once a month our skin is totally replaced. Every six weeks we create a new liver. Our whole skeletal system is replaced every three months. Even our DNA changes every two months. DNA information is coded on each new cell as the old one dies. The information on each new cell contains not only memories of the function of the cell itself, but also memories that are historical. Therefore, even though each cell in our body goes through hundreds of changes, each continues to replicate past emotional and physical damage in our bodies. These memories are triggered by events that stimulate old, familiar experiences. In Lora's case, her lungs and bronchi carried a remembrance of unexpressed grief from her childhood.

Louise Hay's book, *You Can Heal Your Life,* proposes that we create our illnesses, like everything else in life, from our inner thoughts and beliefs. Our lungs, she believes, express our ability to take in and give out life. She suggests lung problems usually mean we are afraid to take in life and feel we don't have the right to live fully. Oriental medicine traditionally views our lungs as the site where we carry grief. In diagnosing dis-ease, Asian medicine takes into consideration the emotions associated with each organ: The heart's emotion is joy; the spleen holds our worries; the emotion of the liver is rage and anger; the kidneys hold our fears.

According to Hay, difficulties with our ears usually means there is something we don't want to listen to or hear. Eye problems indicate we do not want to see something or look at something in our past, present or future. Throat afflictions are about the inability to speak up for ourselves. Difficulties with our arms represent our difficulty embracing the experiences of life. Back problems are about our support system and the burdens and responsibilities we carry. Our bodies mirror our unresolved emotions, thoughts and beliefs.

Many fields of body work incorporate the awareness of the effect of emotions on the body. Ida Rolf, Wilhelm Reich, Alexander Lowen, Moshe Feldenkrais, Joseph Heller and other practitioners are concerned with how the body expresses emotions. They believe that people are expressed through their bodies, both consciously and unconsciously, and that they advertise their attitudes and beliefs in their posture and movement. For example, if a person is depressed or feels burdened, she expresses it in slumped shoulders and a bowed head. In time, the muscles and the fasciae, the connective tissues around the muscles, hold the body in that position. This is called *armoring*. Armoring will eventually change the skeletal frame and the internal organs as well. Though it is important to adjust the external physical manifestations, it is equally important to deal with the underlying emotions, thoughts and beliefs. We carry and store our emotions in our organs, in our muscles and in our movements. It is information that needs to be explored. I often encourage my patients to do body work simultaneously with therapy, combining cognitive and intuitive work with the experiential.

One client of mine, Janet, told me the work she had been doing with her chiropractor on her neck and back seemed to give her relief from pain for only about three days. I reminded her that unless she looked at the emotions, thoughts and beliefs she held in her upper back, she would continue to get only short-term relief. She discussed a program on plane crashes she had seen on TV the night before. After looking at the causes of one particular accident, investigators discovered that the nuts and bolts on only one side of the plane had been tightened. Somehow, only that one side had been inspected. Janet related this story to what I had said about her body and emotions. She understood that we must heal both. If only one side is secure and the other isn't, it can still cause a disaster.

There is no shortage of the life force in our bodies. We do not die from a gradual decrease of energy, nor do we die of old age. We die from dis-ease. Dis-ease comes from how we reacted to the stresses in our life based on our emotions, thoughts and beliefs. How we use our energy depends on our view of life.

The body naturally responds to the stresses in our lives. If we work too hard, the body tires. If we drink too much or eat too much, the body experiences symptoms. Illness serves a purpose by forcing us to rest for a while, to take care of ourselves, to give ourselves the nurturing we need, to regroup and regain our strength. The body gives us the information we need, but usually we ignore the information and look for ways to relieve symptoms. Rarely do we take responsibility for our body's symptoms and explore what is causing them. Instead, we go to our doctor or our pharmacist to get drugs. Pharmaceutical companies have developed pills to match every symptom we have. Unfortunately, we believe these companies hold the answers to our health challenges. Television and magazines bombard us with remedies to cure our bodies' ills. We believe we need drugs so we can be symptom-free.

Many doctors rely on the information and the drugs they get from the pharmaceutical companies for their patients' diagnoses. Overworked and overwhelmed by patients asking them to play God and heal them, doctors are often unaware of other methods of healing. People look to be "fixed" and turn over to a doctor the responsibility for their wellness. Doctors often treat ill patients like children, telling them what to do and what not to do. Most doctors and their patients share the same belief system in that if something is wrong, it must be fixed. Sometimes, however, illness can become a coping strategy to get the attention and nurturing that we have not created in any other way. It keeps us dependent on others to meet our needs. Our belief is that we are still helpless infants and need someone else to care for us. It puts the responsibility for our lives in someone else's hands.

Companies that advertise on TV selling health insurance, vitamins, remedies, cosmetics and products for senior citizens create images of sickly, ailing senior citizens as if this is the norm. *It is not the norm.* Age has nothing to do with dis-ease. There is the story of a man who goes to a doctor for arthritis in his left knee. The doctor tells him, "It's old age." The man replies, "My right leg is the same age. Why don't I have arthritis there?" It is easy to blame age as the cause of dis-ease and not look at our lifestyle, our reaction to stress, our emotions, thoughts and limiting beliefs and our choices. The collective belief of helplessness, hopelessness and dependency that comes with aging can be contagious. Many older people in retirement homes develop diseases *because* they are in an environment that infantilizes them, treats them as invalids, and believes they are incapable.

CHANGING OUR BELIEFS

Today wonderful changes are taking place in our view of illness and wellness. Numerous alternative healing methods are in practice: psychotherapy, support groups, acupuncture, herbs, massage, yoga, Tai Chi, homeopathy, prayer groups and many successful books on healing. These methods support our natural healing process. They are not about someone or something outside of ourselves taking responsibility for our lives. As long as we are supported in exploring what we need to do and choose to take responsibility for our illness, healing can happen. The body already knows how to heal itself; we just need to allow it to do so. The danger is that sometimes healing modalities such as traditional medicine are promoted as absolutes. Their message is that their way or their product is the *only* way to health and healing. In the treatment of dis-ease, it is important to maintain healthy skepticism and learn to trust our inner wisdom.

In each of us is a longing for wholeness, wellness, contentment, joy and bliss. Illness and dis-ease are a wake-up call that forces us to look at what has separated us from who we really are. It is crisis that brings us back to seeing our lives in a way that we have long forgotten. In the Chinese language, the characters for crisis and *opportunity* are the same. The crises in our lives are opportunities to explore the split from our natural state of wholeness. Illness reminds us of that separation.

There is nothing to fix; there is only something to be revealed. Returning to that part of ourselves will reveal the answers and meaning in our lives. We are spiritual beings on a human journey. The experiences we have on our journey are returning us to the divine that dwells in each of us. It is here that we hear the small voice that reminds us that there is a power greater than ourselves, and that it is never any farther away than our next breath. When there is a rupture from our divinity and who we truly are, it is manifested as dis-ease in many areas of our lives. Prayer can create miracles, reconnecting us to the source of our well-being and wholeness.

Many people believe all they need to do is eat right and exercise regularly to be healthy. Others believe that if they go into therapy to work through all their problems, it will lead to health. Still others believe the way to good health is through a committed spiritual or religious life. They pray continuously and believe illness is somehow related to God's disfavor. When the symptoms persist and our belief system (diet, exercise, therapy, prayer) is challenged, we blame ourselves. We believe that there must be something wrong with us and that we failed.

All of these modalities to healing—diet, exercise, working through problems and spirituality—are of equal importance in our wellness. We must choose to eat right, give up addictions that damage our body, exercise, use prayer and meditation, take time to sleep and rest, and spend quiet, introspective time for self-discovery. We must take baby steps. Change takes time and requires making the right choices moment by moment.

When I was a yound child, my father was a teacher at a rural school. By the time I started school, we had moved to the city. My parents remained friends with the people in the farming community. As I grew, I loved to go back to the farm to stay with them. I loved to get up at dawn to gather in the cows. I learned to milk a cow by the time I was eight years old. The milking stools had three legs, and if one leg was missing, without a doubt I'd fall on my butt. This story reminds me of the three legs of our health: the mind, body and spirit. Ignore one leg of our wholeness and the rest cannot support us. We need all three parts to remain well and healthy.

JACK AND PAM'S STORY

"Oh no! This is serious!" the doctor exclaimed. Jack was shocked. He had accompanied his wife, Pam, on her appointment with the dermatologist and had casually asked the doctor to look at a small, itchy mole on his back. One look at the doctor's face, and both Jack and Pam knew it was serious. The doctor removed the mole and asked the couple to come back in a week.

Life seemed to be going so well for Jack and Pam after several previous years of high-level stress. Married three years, they had just bought a fixer-upper near the beach. They had also ordered a new Ford Bronco. Jack was starting up a new business so he and Pam could spend more time together. A few months earlier, Jack had ended a demanding two-year job with a large corporation that had him commuting between Texas and Los Angeles. It was a lucrative position filled with intense stress and office politics. Everything was going wrong, and Jack began to feel overwhelmed by it all. He decided to leave the big corporation and start his own business. The years of commuting and conflict and the career transition had been stressful, but he didn't realize how stressful it was.

Jack is a high achiever and a high reactor. It is how he learned not only how to survive, but also how to succeed. As a child, he had developed a strong belief in his ability to succeed. "I can do anything I want, if I want it bad enough and if I am willing to make the necessary sacrifices," he would tell himself. This inner message carried him through any difficulty.

Throughout high school Jack maintained top grades, had lots of friends, was class president, played on the football team and played trumpet in the band. He loved music and got a music scholarship to USC. Jack worked as a professional musician for a while, but one day he decided that was not how he wanted to spend his life. He knew it would mean years on the road, playing one-night gigs in dingy bars and clubs.

Jack resolved to be a success in the corporate world. Soon, his star began to rise. He had always been a leader and a motivator. He was determined to play hard at success, and he made it. He achieved all the goals for material success. As he moved up the ladder, he did what was expected of him to fit the corporate image: He got married, had two children, belonged to the right clubs, lived in an expensive home in the right area and dressed, thought and acted like everyone else in the company. By far, he met his goals of achievement and acquirement. He traveled extensively for the corporation. As he grew in monetary and personal success, his first marriage suffered and ended in a bitter divorce. For seven years after the divorce, he played the single field until he met Pam. She was his opposite. Jack was a maximizer, Pam a minimizer.

When they returned to the doctor one week later, the news was bad. Jack had type 4 cancer and was advised to put his affairs in order, as he had only about six months to live. Pam was overwhelmed with helplessness, hopelessness and despair. "I knew it would be terrible," she said. "Let's cancel the new car." Jack's response was, "Absolutely not! We will go on as usual. No way am I going to let this happen!" With the same determination that had brought him success in his life, he would face his cancer. He mobilized his high-achiever adaptive behavior and was determined to do whatever was necessary to save his life.

The doctor referred Jack to the John Wayne Cancer Clinic in Santa

Monica, California. It was there that Jack and Pam discovered that the lymph glands on his upper right side were cancerous. The clinic thought Jack had a great attitude. Norman Cousins, the famed healing advocate and author of *Anatomy of an Illness,* was at the center and encouraged laughter as a source of healing based on his own miraculous recovery from a connective tissue disease called ankylosing spondylitis.

A week later, Jack had surgery to remove all of the lymph glands in the upper right side of his body: under his arm, his back, even under his pectoral muscle. The following day, he asked if he could go home. He didn't feel great, but he was determined to get on with his life. Even though he still had draining tubes connected to his body, the doctors agreed to let him go and showed him how to keep his medical records. He pulled on his clothes over the tubes and left the hospital. Pam drove him home, and on the way Jack asked her to stop for a brief business meeting. He had made up his mind to work as much as he was able to and to tell no one about his condition. He did not want to be influenced by anyone's fears or negativity about his cancer. He didn't want people to talk about him.

Two weeks after his surgery, his doctors let him go on a previously arranged skiing trip. Jack fell while skiing and was in pain, but he was determined to go on with his life. When he returned from his trip, the doctors were amazed at his progress and accomplishments.

How we react to illness is different for each of us. Sometimes we give up because we feel fear and helplessness; other times we use our strength to fight the dis-ease. Illness is a wake-up call for us and for those around us, too. Watching our loved ones go through painful challenges is difficult, and we must go through our own process as a result. Jack's illness brought up Pam's fears and insecurities. Her experience was different from Jack's, and her process of dealing with it was different. Pam supported and stood by Jack as he dealt with his cancer.

In crisis, we all need a support system. The greatest gift we can give our loved ones is not to rescue them but to hold up a lamp while they struggle with life's challenges and to remind them of our love. Our support is like a beacon of light that guides a ship through stormy waters.

Both Jack and Pam moved through their challenge with immense courage.

Jack committed himself to a healing program that would be overseen by doctors. He made changes in his diet, gave up smoking, alcohol and coffee and became part of a support group. He started physical therapy and practiced meditation and visualization daily. In his powerful imagery, Jack recalled the popular video game *Pac-Man* and visualized a motorcycle squad of Pac-Men with big mouths full of teeth that ate up all the unhealthy cancer cells and eliminated them. The visualization programs Jack used were established by cancer specialist O. Carl Simonton, M.D., author of *Getting Well Again,* who proposes using imagery to shift unhealthy attitudes to healthy attitudes. Simonton believes the body is capable of healing itself, and what we need is not more treatments but more control over our lives. His work involves exploring beliefs that make us sick. Whatever treatment we choose—diet, chemotherapy, radiation or surgery—must also include healthy thoughts and beliefs. We don't need to know what is wrong, we need to know how to change our lives and do healthy things. Holding positive thoughts helps to create our health and our life. Visualization is a very powerful tool in healing. We need to see ourselves as well and in vibrant health, doing what we love to do.

Jack healed and is now completely recovered. His life, however, has changed. That driving determination served him well in his healing, but now making money and accumulating material possessions no longer hold the same meaning for him. Before his illness, Jack believed he needed to prove himself, and now he no longer feels that need. This challenge has reconnected him with his wholeness. He has found something money could never buy: the preciousness of life. Through this crisis he connected with the divine spirit in himself and nature. He has learned the value of prayer. Back in high school, Jack had daily seminary classes and was interested in spirituality, never realizing that his deep spiritual longing had never left him. Jack will continue his healing and visualization program for the rest of his life. Thirteen years later, he is cancer-free and believes it will never return. His life is transformed and now holds precious meaning. "This is my soul's journey, and it doesn't end here," Jack said to me during one of our sessions. It is an inspirational statement for us all.

EXERCISES

ANSWERING THE WAKE-UP CALL

How well do you listen to the feelings (symptoms) your body is sending you to get your attention? (Example: a chronic pain in your gut) The following exercise will help you identify and explore these wake-up calls to your health.

1. What early messages does your body send you to get your attention? (Examples: fatigue, stomachache, headache, diarrhea, backache)

   _____

   _____

2. What do you think your body is trying to tell you? (Example: You're giving too much to your job, and it is creating great stress.)

   _____

   _____

3. What do you usually do when your body gives you these messages?

   _____

   _____

4. What are your beliefs about these messages?

   _____

   _____

5. What happens if you ignore these messages? Why do you ignore them?

_____

_____

6. Which messages have become chronic? (Examples: backache, cough, headache)

_____

_____

Now, write in your journal a dialogue process (see the exercises in chapter 2) to communicate with your body. In the dialogue, ask your body to help you understand the messages (symptoms) and what changes you need to make in your choices and behaviors.

ARE YOU A HIGH REACTOR OR A LOW REACTOR?

Read the following statements and check the ones that describe the way you believe, think, feel and behave.

1. I am an aggressive, go-getter type of person.
2. I am comfortable standing up for myself.
3. I feel lonely most of the time.
4. I tend to have strong ideas and opinions, and I want others to agree with me.
5. Happiness and peace of mind are more important to me than money.
6. I am stuck in an unhappy situation and feel helpless about getting out of it.
7. When I want something, I go after it no matter what the sacrifice.
8. I am comfortable with most people.
9. When someone asks me for help, I feel guilty if I refuse.
10. I have high expectations for myself and others.
11. I try to live in the present and take things as they come.
12. I am afraid to be myself around people.

13. I find it hard to slow down or take things easy and feel guilty if I do.

14. When I am tired or unwell, I rest, relax and even sleep during the day.

15. I often become ill after an emotional upset.

16. My social life revolves around networking.

17. When necessary, I don't mind working under pressure.

18. Sometimes I am overwhelmed with feelings of helplessness and hopelessness.

19. I get angry and upset when things don't go my way.

20. Sometimes I like to hang out and relax around the house alone.

21. I often think life is unfair.

22. I work hard and play hard, and my goal is always to win.

23. I like to compete, even if I don't always win.

24. I worry about what people think of me.

25. Criticism and nit-picking tend to make me furious.

26. I can accept others as they are.

27. I believe it's not OK to get upset or show that I am upset.

28. I am never totally satisfied with my accomplishments.

29. On the whole, my life seems quite full and enjoyable.

30. When I lose a friend or lover, my whole world falls apart.

31. I expect to receive praise, recognition and rewards for my accomplishments.

32. I find it hard to hold a grudge for long.

33. I believe in peace at any price, even if it causes me to suffer.

34. I tend to take charge and control situations.

35. I love to do impromptu things that are new adventures.

36. I am afraid people will not like me if I say no.

37. No matter how well things are going, my ambitions are seldom satisfied.

38. It doesn't bother me to admit I am wrong.

39. I am afraid that people talk about me behind my back.

40. I tend to demand perfection from others around me.

41. I like to meet new people.

42. I feel anxious around people who are different or who I believe are unfriendly.

43. I try to be perfect in everything I do, how I dress and how I present myself.

44. I would not work with or be in a relationship with someone who was dishonest.

45. I often feel that others are more successful than I am.

46. I hate getting sick and tend to ignore minor ailments.

47. As long as it's in fun, I don't mind being teased.

48. I am a very giving and unselfish person and put others' needs above mine.

49. I don't like to waste my time on trivialities.

50. I like friends who are amusing, agreeable and fun to be with.

51. If someone criticizes me, I get terribly upset.

52. I get back at anyone who crosses me.

53. On the whole, I have developed a "live and let live" attitude.

54. One of my faults is I try to please everyone.

55. I have a low tolerance for things that frustrate me.

56. In relationships, I am able to accept differences between myself and others.

57. I feel guilty if I disappoint anyone or let them down.

58. I believe I have to push myself and others to get what I want.

59. I am pleased when a friend scores a big success.

60. I believe I can never measure up to others.

For A, B and C below, circle the corresponding numbers of the items you checked above.

A. 1 • 4 • 7 • 10 • 13 • 16 • 19 • 22 • 25 • 28 • 31 • 34 • 37
   • 40 • 43 • 46 • 49 • 52 • 55 • 58

B. 2 • 5 • 8 • 11 • 14 • 17 • 20 • 23 • 26 • 29 • 32 • 35 • 38
 • 41 • 44 • 47 • 50 • 53 • 56 • 59

C. 3 • 6 • 9 • 12 • 15 • 18 • 21 • 24 • 27 • 30 • 33 • 36 • 39
 • 42 • 45 • 48 • 51 • 54 • 57 • 60

Now, add up how many numbers you circled in each row, and write down the totals to find your primary mode of reacting to the events in your life:

TOTALS: A. _____ B. _____ C. _____

If you have a high score in A, you are a high reactor. The higher your score, the more the likelihood of dis-ease. High reactors are candidates for heart disease, hypertension, stroke, arthritis, diabetes, ulcers, high cholesterol and hyperthyroidism and are accident-prone. To be healthy and well, you should start to change your beliefs, thoughts, emotions and choices that create the self-destructive behaviors that drive you.

If you scored high in B, you are basically adaptable and can turn crises into opportunities for growth. Your childhood conditioned you to feel secure in yourself. You have developed a sense of self-esteem that can't be easily shaken and gives you the ability to face conflict with confidence. You probably have positive beliefs about your own authority and are able to validate yourself and others. Continue making healthy choices in your life.

A high score in C shows you are a low reactor. The higher your score, the more you live in fear of being yourself. Low reactors are candidates for autoimmune diseases, allergies, respiratory problems, bronchial problems, infections, asthma, colitis, lupus and depression. To change your behavior patterns, you must let go of old, false believes of your worthlessness and replace them with the truth that you are now, and always have been, perfect just the way you are. By changing your beliefs and your choices, you can change your life.

Your second-highest score is how you react at certain times and in certain situations. If you scored highest in A and second-highest in C, look at the areas of your life in which you are a high reactor and the areas in which you are a low reactor. You may be an A at work and a C at home, or vice versa. The basic core belief for both A and C is the same: that of being not enough, worthless and inadequate. How you adapt to these core beliefs differs. Either you will try harder, or you will give up. For example, a high reactor will try harder but get no result and will then feel depressed and inadequate—in other words, behave like a low reactor. A high B score is ideal and a possible goal for you.

BRAINSTORMING

On a separate sheet of paper, write down your beliefs about health. Then do the same for illness. Finally, write down your beliefs about aging. Answer the following questions that will help you to evaluate your beliefs:

1. Are my beliefs based in fact?
2. Do they protect my life and my health?
3. What purpose do they serve?
4. What can I do to change them if they are no longer serving me?

Chapter 8

WORK AND BELIEFS

Over a twenty-five-year period, John had worked his way up to a high-paying executive position at his company. His climb up the corporate ladder did not come easy. First, his company transferred him from Cleveland to Los Angeles. A few years later, John was transferred to Japan. He and his family lived there for two years before they were shipped to Texas, then back to Los Angeles, then to Northern California. The next move was to San Diego. John went wherever his company decided he should go. The stress of constant change and the disruption of his family's stability led to the eventual breakup of his marriage.

John believed that if he was loyal to his employers, they would be loyal to him and reward him with financial security and job security. He was willing to make whatever sacrifices necessary to succeed. He assumed his wife and family would accept his career path. To John, it was the man's responsibility to succeed and lead, and the wife and family should follow.

Everywhere they moved, John's wife and three daughters had difficulty adjusting, especially in Japan, where there was a language barrier. Just as they were getting settled in and making friends, it would be time to move. Though the family came with him, John was never available for them. He spent long hours at work, and on weekends he brought work home. His company expected him to make sacrifices in exchange for rewards. He was a workaholic and expected his family to appreciate the sacrifices he was making, but in time they began to resent him.

John's father had worked for only one company in Cleveland until his retirement. He was rewarded for his efforts like a parent would reward a child for doing a good job. Like John, his dad started at a small, low-level entry position and worked his way up. John's dad was able to give his family stability and security, but this was in the 1940s and 1950s. During that time they lived in the same house, with the same neighbors. John's dad was also a workaholic and an absent father. Maintaining the home and raising the children were left to his mother. Like all of the other dads in this middle-class neighborhood, John's dad was the breadwinner. Everyone held the same beliefs and assumption that each male child in the neighborhood would probably follow in his father's footsteps.

John's grandfather came from Europe and held a strong, Protestant work ethic. His beliefs were many: Life is hard, and one must struggle to succeed. The rewards go to those who work the hardest and longest. To have pleasure is a sin. There is virtue in hard work and suffering. People who don't work hard are lazy bums. We are judged by what we do. Men have the financial responsibility for their family's needs. *These were the beliefs that accompanied the American Dream, and they were passed down from father to son to grandson.*

For John, the dream was shattered when the company he worked for downsized and let him go. At fifty-six years of age, he was too old to be hired by another company in the same position at the same salary. Though he received severance pay and had some investments and Social Security, it wasn't enough to meet his financial needs. John had remarried, had two kids in high school, and had accumulated large debts. Somehow he had lived with the false belief that things would be the same for him as they had been for his father, that his company would be loyal to him until he retired. He was devastated. He'd made major sacrifices and had given so much to his company; in fact, he had dedicated his whole adult life to it. He had followed his father's belief blueprint for success, but it was a map of another time, and things had changed.

THE PURSUIT OF HAPPINESS

Like John, many of us live with old beliefs about work. Most of us grew up in an era that promised job security and a comfortable life. We lived with the belief that if we tried hard enough, we would be rewarded for our efforts. We did what society told us we should do, and now we feel betrayed and abandoned.

When Sigmund Freud was asked, "What is the meaning of life?" he answered, "Love and work." For many, especially in our Western culture, work comes first because it is viewed as a means to get love, contentment and happiness and to find meaning in life. Many people measure their worth by what they do, not who they are. Work is the area of our lives in which we can strive to prove our worth of being enough. For many men, family and personal needs are less important than what they accomplish in their work. Often a man feels his role in a corporation or profession is far more important than his role as husband or father. His worth is measured by his status in the company and the size of his paycheck. Now that women are also entrenched in the workforce, many women have accepted the same beliefs.

Work, however, is an opportunity to find and express the true meaning of our lives. We are here to express the potential that lies dormant in all of us. Each of us has gifts that are not being expressed because they have been contaminated by limiting beliefs connected to work. We think we work to find meaning and achieve status so eventually we will be enough, but the truth is, we are already enough, and work is the expression of the passion that comes from fulfilling our potential. It is in this expression that we experience meaning and purpose to our lives.

To follow our potential takes faith, courage and trust. Like children, we look to others to show us the way, but no one knows our way except ourselves. We each have our own map, our agenda and our original blueprint. From these we choose a line of work that brings us satisfaction.

In her book *The Male Stress Syndrome,* Georgia Witkin-Lanoil, Ph.D., explains the differences in our work life. "Career, professions, and a job usually have very different meanings," she writes. A *career* is an occupation that we create. It is about our personal history. It is our vision and agenda into which we have put our energy. A person with a career could be anybody from an entrepreneur to an actor, artist, writer or disc jockey. A *profession* is an occupation that we earn. We fulfill certain academic requirements, study, train and practice in a particular field. Usually our identity is in our profession: doctor, psychologist, dentist, lawyer, teacher or professor. A *job* is an occupation to make money that supports us and our family. Usually we are working for someone else. It is our work, but it is not our life's work. Many times we hold a job while we are finding and building our career, our profession and our life's work.

Jobs that have little or no monetary rewards have little or no value in our society. Women who raise children and keep the home for the family traditionally have been valued less than women or men who work in careers with monetary rewards. The higher the position and salary, the greater the importance and worth of the person doing it. We believe that being rich and successful will compensate for our basic belief of not being enough. Our worth is measured by the things our money can buy and what we can accumulate financially or in prestige and status.

There is nothing wrong with making money, having money or the things money can buy. Many of us enjoy the game of making money and becoming good strategists. It requires intellect, competitiveness and finesse. The game itself is rewarding. But if we believe our worth lies only in what we do, how much money we make or how much we have acquired, we will exhaust ourselves in the chase. The Scriptures say, "What does it profit a man if he gains the whole world and loses his own soul?" We lose who we are if our worth is in money and prestige.

The illusion is that through money and prestige we will find the meaning of our life. This false belief can bring disillusion, burnout, illness and the breakup of families. We chase after the golden ring on the merry-go-round, the ring we believe will allow us to have what we always wanted: value and worth. We can't get off the merry-go-round because we fear someone else might get what we have been striving for and we will lose. Our life's investment has been in this game, and we fear giving up. But ultimately, we lose anyway.

Many men, especially in midlife, experience a crisis caused by a belief that by a certain age they should have accomplished certain things. Aging and death are just around the corner, bringing up fears of never being enough. These men may not have met their goal of financial success. They may feel they should be higher up in the corporate ladder, or they were never given the professional acknowledgment they had hoped for. They have sacrificed their lives to accomplish their dreams, only to discover there is no pot of gold at the end of the rainbow. Frustration, inadequacy and a loss of self-worth are the result. Or, like John, their career is aborted before they are ready for the change. They are left stranded and overwhelmed. With the loss of a lifetime career, their feelings of helplessness and hopelessness lead some men to suicide. Statistically, there is a higher rate of suicide in men than in women. In addition, men are usually more successful than women in their suicide attempts.

RETIREMENT: THE NOT-SO-GOLDEN YEARS

We live our lives as a trade-off. We'll do this now, we tell ourselves, then later we'll do what we want to do. When we have enough money, status, financial security and real estate, then we believe we can retire and do what we have always wanted to do. When the kids are grown, we'll have the kind of relationship we always wanted to have. More often than not, these are illusions. Because our focus, time and energy were handed over to someone else's agenda, we never found time to fulfill our potential or develop intimacy with our mate and family.

We retire from the daily stress of living up to the expectations of others: our company, our boss, our spouse, our family and society as a whole. Though we look forward to this time in our lives when we no longer have to live under the pressure of work, we leave behind feelings of security, not to mention treasured relationships. Retirement means separating from a familiar structure: income and status that measures our worth; co-workers that gave us camaraderie, and achievements that gave us self-esteem. Many times we are retired by our company before we are ready, and we reluctantly leave, moving to an unfamiliar place. Even though we can now enjoy the happiness we had postponed for so long, ironically we feel lost and confused, and we miss the life we had before retirement.

Work can be an escape. When retirement comes, we often discover that we will now spend our later years living in an experience we have actually been escaping from during all of our working years. We are a stranger to ourselves and to our loved ones. We find we have never created true intimacy with our spouse. We have lost the growing years of our children, and they are now adults we barely know. Many times work was an exit that helped us to avoid marital and family conflict. We were too busy and believed working hard and bringing in the money was all that was expected of us. At retirement, we face what we have not looked at during our working years and often feel like displaced persons.

In retirement, many men become depressed, with a deep sense of loss. They no longer have the same rewards they experienced while working. They can't seem to fit into their partner's world. Work was their whole life, and they had not developed other ways to express their potential. With a lack of external structure, their days seem empty. With nowhere to go and no routine to fill their days, they feel restless and lost. This sense of meaninglessness and feeling *not enough* is a common reaction to retirement, especially for men. I believe this experience can cause us to choose death as an alternative.

Retirement can be a time to renew our relationships with our spouse and family; a time for self-reflection; a time to create an opportunity to express our potential. Yet, if during our work lives we have neither connected with ourselves nor nurtured our potential, when we retire it may be too late to develop and enjoy the fruits of those loving, intimate relationships.

THE CORPORATE PHILOSOPHY

The business and corporate belief system was and still is a part of the old patriarchal system: a blueprint of a hierarchy that was established centuries ago. It is shaped like a pyramid, with the powerful at the top and the powerless masses at the bottom. If we were born into a particular class or caste, that is where we tend to stay. Even today, many cultures continue to carry the same form of hierarchy. In Western societies, however, the moneyed or privileged class at the top is no longer achieved only by inheritance. It can be gained through aggressive competition, education, intellect, creativity, skill, dedication and even lying and cheating. Until more recently, top positions were held predominantly by men. Now women can compete for top honors, and many women compete more ferociously than men.

Jeffrey, a friend of mine, has been a CEO with a large corporation for many years. While writing this book, I asked him how his individual career goals fit in with the corporation's goals. He responded by telling me that the corporate mission is to meet earning expectations for the owners, which include the shareholders and the people at the top. The ideal employee is a loyal, unquestioning individual who places the needs of the organization first, above all else. Jeffrey explained that the corporate answer to being enough is "Yes, you will be enough if you are a workaholic, are willing to do more, try harder and are willing to sacrifice your personal life." As long as an employee looks to the corporation for the answer to the question "Am I enough?" the answer will always be "Yes, if you meet our needs regardless of your own needs."

We talked about change in the corporate structure. Jeffrey said, "My belief is change will be slow." The motivation for change is a low priority because the current need for making money is number one. Helping to create and mold whole individuals is far below the current recycling program. "If an individual asks the question 'Am I enough?' of anyone other than themselves, others will always put their agenda first in response," Jeffrey added.

In the 1960s, psychologists saw the family structure as an undifferentiated mass. Like the family system, for corporations and companies to function efficiently, all members must be undifferentiated and hold the same belief blueprint from the top down. If employees don't conform to the corporate structure, they can create conflict. Those who don't conform are persuaded to see things as everyone else does, or a way is found to eliminate them. Though the corporate structure is similar to the family system, the loyalty is often not there. People are commodities that are dispensable. And many who have climbed the ladder of success have been cut off and are now "has-beens."

THE CLOSED SYSTEM

Like families, corporations have closed and open systems. More often than not, the corporate system is closed, and only more recently have open systems been introduced. In the closed system, power and control are at the top, and those who hold the power create compliance or resistance in those under them. Rigid rules are enforced by the use of promised rewards, fear, coercion and intimidation. Communication can be effected only through a chain of command. The closed system is based on a set of beliefs that are slow in changing. There are rigid rules for behaving that are determined by those in power. This system encourages a dependency on an external authority for the validation of our self-worth. It causes a rupture in our lives that separates us from our own wholeness and keeps us at a child's level, following the music of a pied piper, never our own.

Closed systems determine who belongs, what we need to do to belong, who is excluded from belonging, what we need to do to remain belonging, what constitutes no longer belonging and how to belong at the top, where the decisions are made. These are the intrinsic and often hidden rules and agendas found in every occupation, career and profession, from businesses and education to the military, religion, law, politics and medicine. A conformity is adhered to in which individuation is discouraged. Over a period of time under the conditions of this system, we become fearful of moving on. We forget our dreams, hopes and desires and believe we must conform to get tenure, financial and job security, good insurance and a retirement plan. In this system what we really have is pseudo-security. Debra felt trapped in such a system.

■

Debra teaches sixth grade, loves her job and is very conscientious. For the past three years, she has been teaching an honors class for exceptionally bright students where the curriculum is more advanced. She spends each summer preparing the lessons for the upcoming year. Though some of the material is repeated from past years, she spends a good amount of time preparing new material, absorbing the costs.

Within the first week of school, Debra establishes a great rapport with her students. They like her, and she likes them. The second week of school, the principal tells Debra that he has decided to give someone else the honors class and she will teach an average class. There is no explanation, no reason for his decision. Debra has no recourse and no voice. The principal is the boss. She tells him of her unhappiness about his decision and explains that the curriculum in the new class is different and that she is not prepared. He is not concerned. Like an obedient child, she is expected to do what she is told and feels she has no other option. Debra is angry, frustrated and discouraged.

Having worked in the school district for twenty-two years, Debra has accumulated a comfortable salary with good insurance and a solid retirement plan. This is not the first time she has been shuffled to a different class. The decisions for her teaching schedule and moves are done with no concern for her or her students. Neither she nor the other teachers are consulted about administrative decisions. It seems that the administration is more concerned with procedures and record keeping than encouraging learning. Debra loves teaching but hates the system and feels trapped.

■

In the past, employers often treated employees as children who received rewards for good behavior and were chastised for unacceptable behavior.

There was a measure of almost familial loyalty to employees. Today we continue to relate to companies and bosses as if they are parents and assume that they will reward us if our performance measures up. From small to large corporations, however, most employers are less benevolent, tend to be more impersonal and lack human concern for employees now than in the past. Employees are seen as part of a functioning operation, and they must fit into a particular slot or be eliminated. Loyalty is expected but not reciprocated.

The fear of unemployment is very real. This fear keeps us in jobs that we have outgrown, that we are bored with and even hate. We are often paralyzed in abusive situations and become dis-eased with the constant daily struggle. Today, just getting older brings up fear of unemployment. In a 1997 court decision in California, one company was allowed to lay off a male executive over a certain age while keeping younger men with lower salaries for economic reasons. Previously, age discrimination laws made this illegal. Now companies can get around this by claiming economic cutbacks. Men over forty years old who have been loyal to a company, who have increased their skills and knowledge in their field along with salaries that they deserve, are now let go. The prospect of going to another company at the same status and salary is almost impossible. We have become a disposable society in which human lives hold little or no value.

This kind of thinking places the responsibility for our worth outside of ourselves. There is an external authority that knows more about us than we do and has an agenda that we must follow and that will reward us if we measure up. Then and only then will we be worthwhile. We will be disposed of if we fail to meet expectations. This taps into our unmet dependency needs that we never outgrew in our childhood. We may have grown up physically, but emotionally we are still dependent, as children, on our external caregivers.

If our dependency needs were met as children, we were able to move into independence. We could think for ourselves, listen to our own needs and meet them. We began to learn what our beliefs were and what our parents' beliefs were. If we get stuck here, however, we are unable to move to the next level of interdependence and thus will have difficulty working in cooperation and collaboration with others in personal or professional relationships. The goal of healthy relationships, personally or professionally, is to relate interdependently with others.

THE OPEN SYSTEM

In the workplace, the open system provides options and choices for resolving issues. Collaboration, not control, dominates negotiations. The rules are flexible and changeable as needed, and communication and ideas are welcomed. Differentiation is encouraged and validated. Communication is direct and clear and encourages dialogue. Individual goals are matched with company goals.

David Packard, co-founder of the Hewlett-Packard Company, will be remembered for his management style, which combined teamwork with an entrepreneurial spirit. He believed in dispersing power throughout the company, allowing employees to work in teams, free of management intervention. He encouraged an open-door policy in which people could interact with one another on all levels. He believed in meeting with his employees individually to encourage their contribution to company policies and changes. Practical goals are set by management and implemented and reached by the employees. Packard's management skills have become a model for business and are currently being taught in most business schools.

Companies, corporations and businesses are changing. Many companies are hiring consultants and psychologists to teach interactive ways to dialogue. Communication skills are more accepted as opposed to the old, authoritative ways. Interaction is invited. Today many employees are shareholders in the company they work for. Thus their contributions are really for themselves. Their commitment to the company becomes a personal involvement. A collective consciousness is emerging that is slowly changing attitudes about work and creating healthier environments in which there is concern for everyone.

SUBPERSONALITIES IN THE WORKPLACE

The workplace is a great environment to observe subpersonalities. As we have discussed, our behaviors are based in our beliefs. Therefore, our leading or following style is based on our belief in our own self-worth. In a 1986 study done on personality, culture and organizations, Manfred Kets De Vries of the European Institute of Business Administration and Danny Miller of L'école des Haute Etudes Commerciales and McGill University examined several heads of companies and found that the personality of the top executive influences the whole organization. As in the structure of the dysfunctional family, dysfunction exists in corporations, businesses and organizations as well. Disturbance unfolds from the top down. If those in authority have emotional or addictive problems, this will affect the entire structure. The organization will be in a constant state of inconsistency, confusion and chaos.

Each of us has our own way of reacting to our life experiences. We have different ways of thinking and acting based on our belief system. Our adaptations and maladaptations from childhood are triggered in different circumstances. As in all relationships, personal and work, our subpersonalities complement each other. If there is a Controller, there are always those who feel they need to be controlled. If there is a Caregiver, there are always those who believe they need care. The study revealed that parallels could be drawn between individual dysfunction at the executive level and organizational dysfunction. This model was found in those firms whose decision-making power was in the hands of a top executive. In firms that were not directly influenced by top management, the dysfunction was considerably less.

THE PERSECUTOR

If the top executive is a Persecutor, his belief is that nobody can be trusted and that the major preoccupation of the executive is to be on guard and ready for an attack, real or imagined. He tends to be a high reactor. This CEO also has a subpersonality of a Critic, always looking for hidden motives in the actions of others that they easily misread and distort.

There is a general feeling of suspicion, mistrust, hypersensitivity and hyperalertness in all his interactions, and he easily takes offense and responds in anger. Envy and hostility are present in all his negotiations.

With a Persecutor personality in the executive position, the culture of the organization will be fearful and paranoid. The boss will act hostilely to those beneath him and react with attack and abuse. His reactions come from a fear of mistrust learned in childhood. The leader sees his employees as malingerers and incompetents. He will exert harsh punishment on subordinates. The employees will feel protective of themselves and react by fearing the same things as the top executive does. Fearing attack, they become paranoid with each other, which in turn affects interpersonal and even interdepartmental interactions. In this environment, no one is *ever enough* from the top down.

Remember Susan from chapter 1? She worked in the film industry as an executive secretary to a woman who had ruthlessly worked her way to the top. Susan's boss is a Persecutor. She is highly critical of everyone and abuses her power. Susan could never please her. And if she ever did please her, her boss never acknowledged it. Instead, she found fault in everything Susan did and verbally attacked her. There was constant tension in the air. Her boss could be heard chewing someone out in her office every day. Everyone in the company feared her. The stress kept Susan anxious and constantly on guard. It brought up Susan's People Pleaser and Good Girl subpersonalities. She kept trying to be enough so her boss would approve of her.

By exploring her own beliefs that kept her in this abusive relationship, Susan was able to leave it. We can never allow ourselves to be abused for any reason, anytime by anyone. We must learn to stand up for ourselves. Our path is ours, and how we express our potential is ours. We must trust ourselves to find our way.

THE HELPLESS/DEPRESSIVE

Leaders with this personality lack self-confidence and self-esteem. She feels dependent on others for approval and affection and looks to others to bolster her ego. This depressive leader has feelings of guilt, worthlessness and inadequacy. She tends to abdicate responsibility and authority and is subject to feelings of powerlessness. Such an executive tends to be ingratiating to others she idealizes and is a People Pleaser. Passive and often reclusive, she is also a low reactor.

The culture under this leadership is avoidance. There is a pervasive feeling of futility because the leader sets a tone of negativity and lethargy. A depressive atmosphere prevails. This situation can occur when there is a loss of a previous strong leader, or when a conglomerate takes over, leaving healthy executives with no sense of control, authority or self-esteem. An avoidance culture is characterized by lack of motivation, absenteeism, buck-passing, delays and an absence of meaningful communication. Permeating the atmosphere is a lack of confidence, a purposelessness and a lack of competition. Suggestions for change are resisted, and action is inhibited. The sense of the organization is aimlessness, and apathy and the goal is the status quo. In this environment, people give up because it is a no-win situation.

THE NARCISSIST

With this CEO there is a need for grandiosity. He has a dramatic style that draws attention to himself. He exaggerates his achievements, talents and "who he knows" connections. Relationships are unstable and alternate between overidealization or devaluation. This leader is dramatic, charismatic, and often superficially warm and friendly. However, he often lacks sincerity and is inconsiderate of others. In fact, he is exploitative and takes others for granted. More often than not, he lacks self-discipline, is impulsive and has a tendency to be a high reactor.

Those subordinate to this dramatic leader tend to idealize him. People who idealize others have feelings of insecurity and worthlessness and need a power figure they can identify with and admire. They ignore the leader's faults, accentuate his strengths, never question his authority and are easily manipulated. Their lives revolve around him. Such involvement with the leader masks the employees' basic sense of inferiority and inadequacy and not enoughness. This kind of work environment gives its employees a false sense of worth.

THE CONTROLLER

The executive who is a Controller sees all relationships as power struggles. The Controller insists that others submit to her way of doing things and steps over other people to enforce control. She can be ingratiating to superiors but autocratic to subordinates. A perfectionist and rigid in organization, she fears making mistakes and is quick to point out mistakes in others. Basically, the Controller is trying to protect herself and is driven by her own buried feelings of low self-esteem and inadequacy.

In this compulsive, hierarchical organization, there is mistrust, suspicion and manipulation between employers and employees. Subordinates tend to be dependent, angry, fearful and compliant. With no sense of discretion, involvement and personal responsibility, those who work in this atmosphere are depersonalized and often feel victimized. They are directed by rigid rules that leave little room for initiative or self-expression. Control emanates from the top. Formal and elaborate policies are established, including dress code, lifestyle and employee attitude. Change in this atmosphere is difficult, for in this atmosphere the employees will be enough, according to management, only if they obey the rules and agenda dictated from above. Unfortunately, enough is never enough.

THE DETACHED AVOIDER

According to Kets De Vries and Miller, the Detached Avoider stays away from interactions and is mistrustful. He has experienced interpersonal rejection in the past and avoids close relationships, yet he longs for closer attachments and greater social acceptance. A pattern of noninvolvement and withdrawal can be found in this leader type. The Detached Avoider prefers to be alone, pursuing noninvolvement as a defense against being hurt. To others, he appears cold and aloof.

Where there is detachment in upper levels of management, members of the second tier, none of whom is clear about his or her own responsibilities, jockey for position and power. Problems of cooperation and coordination are quite common. Changes happen as second-tier management achieves power, but that is reversed whenever a new group of managers wins favor with upper management. The structure of the organization is fragmented by ineffective communication and collaboration. Everyone from the top down feels inadequate, inferior and not enough in an environment that makes everyone crazy.

THE MEANING OF WORK

Our growth is an inner process that is expressed in what we do. Work is the way in which we express who we are. It is an opportunity to nurture the seeds of potential that lay dormant within us. In this sense, work does not refer to a job, a profession or a career, nor does the amount of money we earn equal our success in life. Our work is how we direct our life's energy. It means being engaged in something we value, something meaningful that brings us pleasure and growth. Most of us spend the better part of our lives working for someone else, and it leaves us frustrated. Our job often feels like an obligation, a responsibility that is burdensome and stressful.

There is a direct flow between what we do and our inner process. If there is harmony between what we do and who we are, we experience joy, peace, happiness and well-being. If there is a lack of harmony in our outer experience, it creates disharmony in our inner process, and vice versa. Disharmony can lead to illness, break us down emotionally and spiritually and leave us cut off from ourselves and our loved ones. When we locate that source of joy within ourselves and express it in what we do, we will find fulfillment.

We should love each and every day, and wake up to delight in our relationship with our work. Instead, most of us dread going to work, seeing it only as a way to attain status and success, which we believe will eventually give us self-worth. Unfortunately, it rarely happens. Self-worth is never negotiable. It is not dependent on how much we do or how much we achieve. Our worth is already there, at our very core. We were always worthwhile and enough, but this truth has been contaminated over years of limiting and false beliefs. We bought into the system and jumped on the merry-go-round of success. We find out, sometimes too late, that the ride took us nowhere and we ended up with nothing except grief over the losses that this illusion created.

We often chose our work based on someone else's idea of who we should be. A young man enters the military because his father was in the military, and his father before him. A young woman becomes an attorney because her parents want status and prestige in their family. In our teens we decide what we will do with our lives without really knowing the seeds of potential that lie within us. For some, the interest and desire is there from a young age to be an artist, a writer, a healer. If we are supported and encouraged by parents and society to develop this burgeoning potential, it will be expressed as our life's work. For others, though, we have no idea who we are because our lives have been about following a belief blueprint someone else created for us. Being financially successful in a prestigious job is often more important then expressing our true selves. Because success reflects the beliefs of society, our culture, our parents and our family about our worth, we are encouraged—and expected—to march to the beat of a different drummer.

■

It looks like all those long years of schooling have paid off. Catherine is finally invited to join a successful law firm. She proceeds to take every case assigned to her, devoting her full attention to each one in hopes of one day becoming a senior partner. Catherine's drive is intense, yet in therapy she shares with me her flagging zeal for what she does. She has come to hate her work. Her relationship with her husband is falling apart. Her law firm demands all her focus and her time, leaving little for herself, her home, her husband and the things she wants to do. Any thought of having a baby has to be ignored. It leaves her sad and confused.

Catherine admits she became a lawyer to please her father. She felt that it would finally get her the pat on the back he never gave her, that it would make up for not being the son he wanted. Catherine is the elder of two daughters. Her mother died when Catherine was eight years old. From that point on, she did everything to please her father. Somehow, she never felt she could measure up and be enough. At a young age she decided she would be a lawyer like he was. At the same time, Catherine had also discovered her artistic talents, but they went unrewarded, and she was made to feel that they weren't as important as a real career like law or medicine. Catherine is resigned to her decision but feels trapped, empty and filled with despair.

■

Finding what we want in life is to find what matters to us. What do we love? Do we put our energy into what we love? Our job, profession, or career is a big chunk of our lives. When we spend time doing what we love, life is timeless, and we are filled with creative energy. When we hate how we spend our time, our energy is drained. What would it be like to fulfill our potential and be a full expression of all that we are?

We have each come into this world with our own potential and gifts ready to be expressed. If our environment was supportive, we are left with better tools to allow that potential to be expressed. If our environment was too controlling and coercive, we tend to go the way of others' agendas. Our inner potential, however, is a strong, natural energy that will struggle for emergence. Plant a seed, and the power of its growth can push up a sidewalk. Even if the soil of our environment was not cared for, we will continue to grow, though the growth may be crooked. Inside us lies a reason and purpose for our lives, and it will struggle to push forth in our lives to our last breath.

Potential is not just for those who are exceptional or extraordinary. In each of us is a potential that is uniquely ours. It was there before we took our first breath. We can recognize that potential early in life, and if we are encouraged to follow that potential, we will find our true purpose. If we ignore it, compromise and follow someone else's agenda, we will forever feel the distress of trying to fit a round peg into a square hole.

Striving to develop our potential does create stress, but with this stress there is a feeling of satisfaction. Our gifts will lay dormant and die without attention. An artist who doesn't express her gifts will suffer in her personal life. A musician who never plays his instrument or sings his song will feel an inner frustration. Not only is our relationship with work an expression that comes from our inner self, but the work itself affects our inner process. It is a dance, a flow, that moves back and forth, outward and inward. It is our life's process that is expressed in each moment. The inner change affects the expression, and the expression in turn changes our inner process.

In writing this book, I experienced a process that has been an accumulation from my childhood of my innate potential, my learning and my experiences that is being manifested in the moment. The book becomes a living, breathing, changing event that changes me as I write. As I change, so does my writing. When I was a child, I wrote the thoughts and ideas of a child. I sculpted, drew and painted in a child's way. Many of my gifts were glimpses of possibilities. Those gifts never left me; they just developed and grew, sometimes less, sometimes more. But the potential that was there had a life of its own. In each of us is an acorn that carries the blueprint for a full-grown oak tree. Our seeds of potential are glimpses into our life's work.

Take some time to observe children. You will see that their gifts are effortless. I saw it in my own daughter. I see it in my granddaughters. If these gifts are encouraged, it will change our life's commitment to what we call work. Doors will open unexpectedly, and opportunities will be given to us. In our bodies is the flow that is our natural potential. If we go against the flow and choose to follow someone else's agenda, or the agenda that equates our innate worth to our net worth, we will grow tired, frustrated and dis-eased.

THREE STEPS TO CHANGE

Knowing our intention to express our potential keeps us conscious of our journey to self-discovery. If we continue to function from old, limiting belief patterns, we will stay unconscious. To wake ourselves up and start to change our lives, we need to follow three steps: intention, attention and detachment. Deepak Chopra discusses intention in his book *The Seven Spiritual Laws of Success.* What is our intention? Is it to continue to be stuck in patterns that no longer serve us? Or is it to clean house and let go of old, outmoded thoughts, ideas and beliefs? Now is the time to look at the intention of our lives.

No one will create change for us. No amount of money, no career or job, not even great success, not even the greatest discovery in the world will bring us the lasting joy, peace and fulfillment we long for. Look at the lives of people who we believe have made it: multimillionaires, lottery winners, rock stars, famous actors and athletes, even the late Princess Diana. They may have moments where they feel joy and peace, but many of them experience emptiness and pain and live—or lived—lives of quiet desperation.

We can push ourselves to attain every imaginable success in life, but it will never fill the deep, dark hole created by our false belief that we are not enough and inadequate. Only *we* can change that belief. Intention means taking full responsibility to free ourselves from the burden and bondage of the oppressive beliefs that constantly remind us that we can be enough if we acquire money, material possessions, importance or fame. If we don't make the necessary changes in our life, our children will continue to perpetuate the same beliefs in themselves. Even the belief that we *can't* change is just another false belief.

With *intention,* Chopra says, we must have *attention.* This means staying in the moment and making choices based on our conscious intention and awareness. We must focus on what we are, right now, so that we may begin to work on what we want to change. The point of change and power is in the present. We must stop repeating the same patterns over and over. *Now* is the time for change.

The final step to making successful changes in our lives is *detachment.* Too often we let go of something in order to get something else. To detach means stepping into an unknown experience free of attachment, to let go just for the sake of letting go. In truth, this can be scary. The reason we stay in old, outmoded belief patterns is because it gives us the illusion of stability and security. It feels familiar, and from it we can predict the outcome. Detachment asks us to enter into an unknown experience without knowing the outcome. But if we make intention, attention and detachment our goals, it will lead to change and the fulfillment of our intrinsic potential.

Our work need not be merely a means to an end. Let us nurture and sow the seeds of potential that are implanted within us all, and we—and our children and our children's children—will reap the rewards for eternity.

EXERCISE

Our society sends strong messages that our worth is judged by how we earn our living. How much are you influenced by society's pressures? This exercise helps you find the answer by looking at the messages you received as you grew up. Work is a way to fully express our inner potential. Limiting beliefs block that potential. What are the messages you heard from your parents, your educators, your society, your culture and your peers about work and careers?

MESSAGES ABOUT WORK

Answer the questions below. These messages make up your belief blueprint and are possible blocks to your potential. This is the first step to unlocking your potential and creating your vision.

Messages and Beliefs from Your Mother

Did your mother work outside of the home? If so, what did she do?

_____

_____

If she worked at home, caring for the home and family, what were her beliefs about that?

_____

_____

What were her messages and beliefs about money?

_____

_____

What were her messages and beliefs about people who had money?

_____

_____

What were her messages and beliefs about buying and having material possessions?

_____

_____

What were her beliefs about success?

_____

_____

What were her beliefs about education?

_____

_____

What were her messages to you about what you should do for your career/work?

_____

_____

What was her first priority in life?

_____

_____

Messages and Beliefs from Your Father

What was your father's line of work?

_____

_____

What were his messages and beliefs about his work?

_____

_____

What were his messages and beliefs about money?

_____

_____

What were his messages and beliefs about people who had money?

_____

_____

What were his messages and beliefs about buying and having material possessions?

_____

_____

What were his beliefs about success?

_____

_____

What were his beliefs about education?

_____

_____

_____

What were his messages to you about what you should do for your career/work?

_____

_____

What was his first priority in life?

_____

_____

■ In your False Belief notebook write down the beliefs you carry about work. Note whom or where they come from. Do these beliefs still control your life?

■ Based on the messages and beliefs you wrote down above, fill in the blanks below.

1. From the messages I received from my childhood/adolescence about my career/work, these were the decisions I made:

_____

_____

_____

_____

2. The results of my decisions are:

_____

_____

_____

3. My greatest desire for my life's work would be:

_____

_____

_____

4. What I need to do to reach my work potential:

_____

_____

_____

5. The limiting beliefs I have about reaching my potential are:

_____

_____

_____

6. What I do to keep myself from reaching my potential:

_____

_____

_____

7. I am not living up to my full potential because:

_____

_____

_____

8. What I am waiting for to express my full potential is:

_____

_____

_____

■ Now, in your personal journal, write freely of your memories from childhood. What brought you pleasure? What were your interests? What creative things did you enjoy doing? What were your favorite subjects in school? What memories of past experiences bring up good feelings? What did you daydream about? What were your fantasies? Who was your hero or heroine? Whom did you admire? What were your favorite stories or TV shows? Who did you pretend you were? What were the games you played?

■ Next, create a vision. To get what you want out of life, you need a vision. This is your intention. It helps you to set the direction for your life. What is your vision of how you would like to express yourself in your work? Be creative and give your imagination free rein. Your ideas will come from your childhood memories. In your journal, write down how you envision your perfect career. Write it in the present tense, as if you are experiencing it at the moment. What are you doing in your job? Do you work alone or with others? How do you interact with others? Are you a leader or a follower? Do you work in an office? What kind of an office? Do you travel? Do you work indoors or outdoors? What is your growth plan? How much money do you make? Express what you want out of your work.

This same vision can be created for retirement. What do you want to do that you have never had the time to do? Where would you do it? Envision your life doing exactly what brings you enjoyment and a true sense of your own worth. What unexpressed potential is there, dormant within you, waiting to be expressed?

■ Finally, create goals. Again, be totally creative as you picture what it is you want in life. Start with the end results in mind. Then, ask yourself what behaviors you need to get there. Break these behaviors down into small steps. To help you clarify your goals, ask yourself what you have and don't have now, and what you want and don't want. Use the worksheet that follows to help you organize your thoughts.

	HAVE	DON'T HAVE
WANT	What do you now have that you want? (HAVE & WANT)	What do you want that you don't have? (DON'T HAVE & WANT)
DON'T WANT	What do you now have that you don't want? (HAVE & DON'T WANT)	What don't you have and don't want? (DON'T HAVE & DON'T WANT)

Chapter 9

OUR SPIRITUAL QUEST

Lisa was raised in a strict, religious home. Her family lived by the Bible, with firm rules about right and wrong. They believed their religion was the only way. Though Lisa's parents seemed to express their love for her, there was always an undercurrent of control, manip- ulation and coercion. In a way, their love was conditional. Their hidden agenda left Lisa feeling unsure of her interactions with them. She weighed everything she said to protect herself from their judgments and control, which were often couched in loving words. They were invasive with their questions, wanting to know what she thought, what she was doing, where she was going, whom she was going with. Lisa's parents explicitly and implicitly lectured her daily about rights and wrongs. As she grew older, they were very strict about how she dressed and where she went. Everything she did had to meet her parents' approval. Lisa felt smothered, suffocated and trapped.

When Lisa was very young, she had a deep love of God. She tried hard to be a good girl and live up to her parents' expectations, which she was told were also God's expectations. Lisa learned to get approval by pleasing others: her parents, her aunts and uncles, her Sunday school teacher, her minister and God. In her family, anger was never allowed. God didn't approve of it. If Lisa got angry or upset about something, she was told to go to her room and pray to God for forgiveness. Soon she internalized all the beliefs of her parents' religion about being a sinner and of not being good enough. She followed their beliefs and rules, prayed every day, read her Bible daily and went to church three times a week. She developed a ruthless inner judge and critic who told her she was bad. Lisa developed subpersonalities to survive in this repressive environment: a Good Girl, a People Pleaser, a Follower, a Worrier and a Rebel. Though she followed the rules as best she could, she always felt confused, frustrated, shamed and guilty. She tried to be good, but she was never good enough.

By the time she started high school, Lisa had compartmentalized her life. One part of her followed the religious beliefs that were expected of her: always have pure thoughts, be obedient to the Bible's teachings and to your parents, go to church regularly, refrain from sinning, don't express anger, please others, don't break any of the Ten Commandments, pray to God every day to ask for forgiveness and for help in being a good person. To Lisa, God was a God of judgment, not of mercy But as a teenager, there was another part of her that rebelled against the constant judgments she received from her environment. Around her parents and others who held the same religious beliefs, Lisa pretended to be whatever was expected of her. When she was away from them, however, she smoked, drank, did drugs and became sexually promiscuous. She lived in a constant state of guilt and shame. She would act out, judge herself harshly and feel guilt, shame and hate for herself. She would then beg God for forgiveness and to help her sin no more. Riddled with feelings of anxiety, fear, even craziness, at times, Lisa had no idea who she was.

When Lisa left home to go to college, she felt liberated. She met other young adults who had beliefs and ideas that were different from those she grew up with. It was confusing at first, and she had guilty feelings about being with others who were different from her. But in time, she felt a deep sense of relief. Though Lisa liked her new friends, she became fearful. She discovered that if she got too close to them, she would start judging them or would become whatever they wanted her to be in order to get their approval. She couldn't stand up for herself for fear of being abandoned and was filled with many negative beliefs about herself. Once she got too intimately involved, she would feel scared and leave the relationship. Sometimes her boundaries were weak; other times she put up rigid boundaries to protect herself.

Lisa was continuing to compartmentalize her life. The beliefs she developed from her childhood were: I am basically bad and a sinner; there is something wrong with me; I have to do what others want or they won't accept me; if I don't follow my parents' rules, I will be punished; I am not safe with others, nor am I safe with myself; the world is a scary and confusing place; I can't ask for what I want; I am helpless and can't stand up for myself; It is not OK to say no; I am basically not enough and inadequate; God will punish me if I am bad; I will never measure up in God's eyes no matter what I do.

Like Lisa, many of us carry unexplored beliefs from childhood about the spiritual part of our lives. As young children, many of us had a pure, innocent love for the divine. The connection with our Beloved filled us with bliss and rapture, and we often had mystical experiences. But there was a rupture in our rapture when the dogmas, rules and rights and wrongs of our parents' religious beliefs were imposed on us. Because we believed whatever our parents believed, we followed their path. Soon their limiting beliefs became ours, and the rapture and bliss was gone.

Our beliefs about God are usually the same as those of our parents and of our parents' parents. As children, we automatically accepted these beliefs. It gave us a structure, a model and a path to follow. But as we grew and matured, there came a time when we questioned the path on which our parents directed us. We made choices to follow the same path as our parents, or we chose to find our own path. Or, like many, we live by default, never deciding what our path is until we have a major crisis in our life.

What is the difference between religion and the spiritual? Religion, for the most part, usually holds a belief in a higher power or supreme being, such as God. It is an institutionalized, organized system of beliefs with dogmas and rituals. Religions are usually founded on the teachings of a particular teacher or master such as Moses, Jesus, Mohammed, Buddha, Krishna, Ram and many others.

The spiritual refers to the relationship that a believer has with the Creator, God or nature. It is not tangible and is a private experience. The spiritual may not be observable such as in rituals. It is not based on dogmas or rules. It is a deep, soullike experience that is not necessarily related to a religion or religious belief. Our spirit is always there, whether we are in a religious setting or not. We can connect with it in the quiet of our room, in nature, in our loving relationships, in reading a poem or listening to music. It is always there because we are spiritual beings on a human path.

The forms that religion has taken are endless, and the names we have given our gods and goddesses are countless. Each religion has its own set of beliefs, rules, regulations and rituals for protection, life's passages, blessings and ways of conducting our lives. Many of these teachings bring value and meaning to our lives. Some, however, have restricted our ability to grow. Even in traditional religions, there are hundreds of subgroups and factions. The religious beliefs that were passed down have become a part of our belief blueprint and influence our thinking, our feelings and our behavior.

In humans, there is an inherent desire, dating back to prehistoric times, to understand and worship the infinite. Archaeologists continue to dig up and study artifacts from the religions of long ago. We also have an intrinsic longing to understand the mystery of life. We long to make sense out of our lives, to determine what our purpose is, and so we join others in following a particular religious path. Though there are similarities among all religions, the beliefs that come from each individual religious path are usually exclusive and limited to those who are its followers. Religion often is based on egotism that perceives others who have different beliefs as the enemy to be destroyed or won over. Throughout history, hate, murder, atrocities, abuse, violence, prejudice and wars have all been committed in the name of religion.

RELIGION AS A HIERARCHY

Like other institutions, religion is a hierarchy. And more often than not, it has been a patriarchy. Men hold the power, and women are considered weaker because God deemed it so. God, at least in Western religions, is referred to as Him, or Father. In pictures, God is always male. The pope and most members of the clergy have been males. There was and still is in many religions no room for women in positions of power.

Religions, like families, have both closed and open systems. In a closed religious system, members must maintain and accept the same beliefs and practices. The ruling is from the top, and all those below must comply. Closed systems are more fundamental, with very little room to change and no room for differentiation. Members believe that "there is us, and then there is everyone else." These groups tend to be xenophobic, full of fear and contempt for others that are not of the same faith.

The closed system demands conformity. Though this agenda may be visible through its rules, these rules are usually based in fear and guilt and enforced through coercion and manipulation. The goal in this system is to indoctrinate and influence its members and often to proselytize others outside of the particular faith. There are rigid rules for behaving, thinking and feeling and anything that does not comply with these expectations is forbidden. This belief system encourages and demands dependency and reliance on religious authority. The more a religion follows a hierarchy, the more rigid its rules, beliefs, dogmas and regulations. Members may contribute to changes in updating policies, but basically followers have little or no influence on the beliefs. The rules and dogma that are the foundation for each particular religion have probably been the same for generations.

Open religious systems are less formal. The main difference is their openness to growth and change. There is unity with diversity, and individual differences are taken into consideration. Communication and open dialogue are encouraged and validated. Members work together to resolve differences. Laymen in such a system have jurisdiction over the clergy. Leadership is more flexible, and the roles of the leader are more diverse.

The clergy serve as teachers, preachers and liaison to the community and as pastoral counselors to those in conflict. Unlike closed religious systems, in which ruling comes down from the top, responsibility for leadership in an open religious system is divided among several people.

THE PURPOSE OF RELIGION

Religion was established because it served a purpose. Throughout history, humans have sought communion with God in their spiritual search. Buddha sat with his followers and shared his wisdom. Jesus gathered his disciples and others to feed the hungry not only in body, but also in spirit. Religion can feed our souls and address our needs. Although much hate and violence has been perpetuated in the name of God, a deep concern and charity for the downtrodden has also been carried out in the name of God. In Judaism the phrase *Tikkun Olam* means "to heal the world." Religion brings awareness to all of us of the suffering in the world.

The social mores, ethics, values and sense of what is right and wrong (based on the times) that religion teaches can be an asset to our society and our world. Sometimes, however, religion limits our growth and stifles our desire to explore and learn. Nevertheless, it is a way that people survive. It brings people together to support one another when isolation would only create struggle.

During my early childhood, my father taught at a rural school. The focus of the community was the little nondenominational church. People gathered there for support during hard times and joyous times. It was a spiritual and a social place where marriages were celebrated and babies were baptized, including myself. This community cared, rejoiced and cried together. For those in need—both in the church and in the extended community—parishioners prayed, brought food and shared in the burdens. Where there was conflict, the church encouraged and supported resolution and healing. It was here that I experienced the love of God. I felt joy and bliss. Even today, the songs we sang of love and grace are with me and comfort me in my times of need.

Religious life nowadays has become more secular. Many churches, temples and synagogues in larger communities are impersonal, and the individual often goes unnoticed. Smaller religious communities, with their emphasis on church attendance and proper lifestyle, had more influence and probably more control over people's lives. The notion of religion as a kind of extended family is becoming less prevalent. However, even traditionally closed religions today are incorporating more ways to socially involve its members and the community.

Our churches, synagogues and temples have been our guideposts for living. The messages we hear can strengthen and encourage us. It is here that we go to renew our faith in something more than our mundane lives. It is here that we are reminded of our purpose. It is here that we are inspired. It is here that we can feel the Divine in a new way. We come as a community of souls longing to find the Divine, to find God. We find spiritual fellowship with other seekers. It is not in the buildings that house our religious beliefs that we find God. We bring our intrinsic God with us to any common place of worship. *Wherever we are, God is.*

The soul's language is not a human language, it is a sacred language. We can connect to our souls through sacred music and rituals. Rituals provide divine order to our lives that honors our transitions and processes. They are the rites of passage that help us move to the next level of our journey: from infancy into a community of souls, from childhood into adulthood, in the union of two souls in marriage, and in death and the release of our souls. The sacred music, the incense, the candles, the mantras, the prayers and the meditations are all ways to bring us in harmony with the Divine.

GOD AS PARENT

We have many names for God, including Mother-Father God, Father, Yahweh, Creator, Lord, Universe, Divine Spirit, Divine Intelligence and Great Spirit. Each religion views its God in a particular way: a masculine energy, wrathful, punitive, abusive, destructive, controlling, rigid, critical, judgmental, withholding, violent, prejudiced, yet benevolent, loving, kind, wise and caring. We usually accept the God that our religion teaches us. If our religion is rigid, judgmental and controlling, we view God in the same way. If we have a religion that sings and speaks of love and kindness, we see God as benevolent. These are all qualities we recognize in one another, in our parents and in ourselves. They are also the qualities of our subpersonalities. Consequently, we see God as having human qualities that are often like those of our parents. We have "created" God in our reflection and image. This practice is called anthropomorphism.

Often we carry fears of an unknown, judgmental God who we believe will love us only conditionally. Likewise, if we feared our parents' punishment and abuse, we believe God will also be punitive and abusive. If we got our needs met from our parents by manipulating, bargaining and begging, we relate to God in the same way. "I promise I will change if You give me what I want," we tell God. "I'll give up smoking if You will give me healthy lungs."

Many people enter religion to fulfill the unmet needs of their inner child. They look to religion to give them the self-worth that they lack because they are unable to love themselves. Like the proverbial genie in the lamp, we beg God for more money, happier relationships, new cars, better jobs and cures for our illnesses, believing that if we measure up and are good enough, God will grant us our wishes. Most religions, past and present, encourage a parent/child relationship with God. Like children, we comply to the religious beliefs, dogmas, rules and regulations that have been imposed on us, hoping all our needs will be met. We believe all our sins will be forgiven and we will have eternal salvation.

Through our particular religious teachings, we strive to meet what we believe are God's expectations: to be good, to be obedient, to repress our negative or bad side, to internalize the rules. Yet because of the core messages programmed into our belief blueprint, we believe we are basically unworthy, bad, inadequate and not enough. We struggle to obtain God's favor, but we continue to feel powerless, helpless, hopeless and guilty, filled with feelings of shame.

When we have struggles and difficulties, we often blame God for abandoning us. If we are in a crisis, either we blame ourselves because we have somehow failed, or we question why God is punishing us. We wonder what we have done to deserve this discomfort and pain; perhaps we are suffering from karma or bad deeds from other lifetimes. Our anger is directed at God, who we believe should take care of us like a good parent. We feel forgotten, left to die, and helpless and desperate.

Just as we react to our parents' authority, at times we defy God and refuse to obey the rules. Like Lisa at the beginning of this chapter, we rebel out of anger because of the pressure we feel is being placed on us to conform. We want to break away from the intense, trapped feelings that come from having an external control on our lives. The internalized judgments we hear in our heads, which we believe is God's voice, haunt us with blame and shame, and we feel angry. To escape from these beliefs, we rebel, act out and end up hating both God and ourselves. We see ourselves as bad, as unlovable sinners. Then, like frightened, insecure children, we return to this external authority called God and beg Him for forgiveness. In pleading for help for our failures and our weaknesses, we are often left with deep despair and an alienation from our inner selves. Great confusion and doubt about our relationship with God ensues.

At other times, to deal with the pressure, we withdraw. We back away as far as we can to avoid any imposed control over our lives. We don't act out and rebel, we don't comply—we simply avoid anyone or anything that reminds us of religion or God. Sometimes we take on other philosophies that are more laissez-faire: "You live your life, I'll live mine." "You do your thing, I'll do mine." Or we call ourselves atheists and maybe even believe that God is dead. We live our lives by default. We refuse to commit to anything because we have been raised to believe our choices are limited to complying with or defying a fearful, powerful force. We choose not to think about it. If the topic of religion or God comes up, we change the subject to something else we feel more comfortable with. Making no decision is the best decision. This reaction, however, is just as powerful as compliance and defiance. The fact is, no decision *is* a decision. No choice *is* a choice. When we avoid taking responsibility for the choices we make, we also avoid fulfilling our innate potential.

Pierre grew up in a French Canadian Catholic environment. He attended Catholic school from first grade through five years of college. Growing up, he knew only Catholics and believed that only Catholics went to heaven. Non-Catholics were not favored in God's eyes and were perceived as morally inferior. They were lost sheep. Pierre's beliefs were so deeply ingrained that whenever he had to walk past a Protestant church, he would cross the street so as not to be "contaminated" by them.

As a child, whenever Pierre hurt himself, his mother told him God must be punishing him for having done something wrong that his parents didn't know about. His parents and God were in collusion with each other, he was told, and that was why God created the Fourth Commandment: Honor thy father and mother. In his religion classes in elementary school, Pierre learned that God gave His authority to the pope, the clergy, the heads of state, law enforcement, bosses, teachers and parents in order that they may rule in His stead. Pierre always held a deep-seated belief that he was in God's hands, and if something tragic happened, it was the will of God. Feelings of shame and guilt were a constant for Pierre.

For his own salvation, Pierre observed all of the church rules, including his parents' interpretation of these rules. He did what was expected of a good Catholic. He thought that if he was a very good Catholic, his shame would lessen, and then he would, of course, be acceptable to God.

When he entered the teen years, masturbation became a common practice for Pierre. Although it was carried out in shame and secrecy, the shame was never strong or powerful enough for Pierre to give up his most enjoyable and comforting activity. Confession became a weekly practice so that God could forgive him for his pleasures. Pierre believed, though, that carnal pleasure with a woman was the equivalent of carnal pleasure with Mother Mary and equal to murder in God's eyes.

By the time Pierre married in his early twenties, he had left most of his Catholic beliefs and practices behind. He married outside of his religion, and although logically he knew it to be absurd, he half expected to be struck by lightning while coming out of the Protestant church after his wedding ceremony.

The day Pierre's daughter was born was traumatic, as his deep-seated beliefs came back to haunt him. Because he had married a Protestant, he could not shake the fear that his daughter would be born a cripple. As a child, Pierre had been told by one of the nuns that the marriage of a Catholic and a Protestant is displeasing to God. To show his displeasure, God punishes the parents by sending them crippled children. What lent this belief so much power was that one of Pierre's aunts had married a Protestant, and two of her children were born with minor physical deformities that were, fortunately, surgically correctable. But nevertheless, the proof was there for an impressionable child.

Although the beliefs of a punishing and vengeful God were absurd to Pierre as an adult, they had been implanted so deeply in his unconscious mind that they surfaced as a grown-up in spite of his attempts to rationalize them. Of course, Pierre was greatly relieved when his daughter was born free of physical abnormalities, and this defused much of the power of his early beliefs about God.

VENTURING BEYOND OUR 8-BY-10 WORLD

Our beliefs tend to form in clusters. If one belief is proved to be untrue, then the hierarchy of beliefs tumbles. Pierre had an 8-by-10 space that held his beliefs about himself and his world. Like the panda story at the beginning of chapter 2, each of us creates an 8-by-10 space that holds our limiting beliefs about ourselves, our religion and our relationship with God. If we choose to move beyond these traditional, imposed beliefs, we experience confusion and fear. When we break free of religious beliefs that we have carried since childhood, we have doubts and disillusionment. In adolescence, our budding urgencies to experience that which is forbidden pushes us to challenge the beliefs of our parents. In the adolescence of our spiritual lives, as we recognize conflict and doubts within ourselves, many of us choose to push ourselves beyond our 8-by-10 world. To find our truth, we must break free of the limiting beliefs we have placed on our relationship with God.

Moving toward any kind of clarity in our lives at first brings up feelings of immense confusion as we try to reconcile our need for safety and security with our desire to break free. To redefine our relationship with God, we must let go of everyone else's beliefs and find our own way. Carl Jung, the great psychoanalyst, said, "I used to believe in God, but now I know God." We, too, must take the responsibility of knowing a relationship that is free of anyone else's influence. In adolescence we begin to individuate from the family, sorting out their beliefs and coming to know what is right for us. From everyone else's truth, we glean our own. To have a relationship with God means stepping into the unknown so that it can be known. To go there, we must leave all our baggage behind. It is a process of growth that can only lead to a kind of knowing that exceeds the limiting beliefs we have at this moment.

Even in adulthood, many of us choose to stay where we are, following the traditionally held beliefs of our forefathers. To explore outside the 8-by-10 parameter is much too frightening, especially if our religion tells us that forsaking our beliefs will be catastrophic. Beliefs give us a sense of security, and if we open up to the possibility of something different, our security and our relationships with parents, relatives and friends are threatened. A leap into the unknown can fill us with terror. Any crisis can bring us to this place: a life-threatening illness, the loss of a loved one, a reversal of fortune or in my case, a traumatic accident. These are wake-up calls that can shatter the structure of beliefs about ourselves, our world and our relationship with God. In Scripture, we are reminded in Corinthians (1 Cor. 13:11–12): "When I was a child, I spoke like a child, I thought like a child, I reasoned like a child; when I became a man, I gave up childish ways. For now we see in a mirror dimly, but then face to face. Now I know in part; then shall I understand fully, even as I have been fully understood."

SHOWING US THE WAY: PROPHETS, TEACHERS AND MASTERS

Masters and teachers such as Mohammed, Moses, Buddha, Christ and Rumi have shown us the truth about our lives. Throughout history, messengers have come to awaken us, because in our humanness we fall asleep. Their messages were told as parables and stories in the context of their time. Those stories were based on the collective beliefs of the people, on how they lived and on the culture that was the foundation for their beliefs. The messengers used these cultural beliefs as references to bring the people to a clearer understanding. The core message from each teacher and prophet held the same basic truths: that we should seek a spiritual path to find fulfillment, and that this path was and is already within ourselves.

When teachers spoke of rights and wrongs, it was to enlighten people of that time. When Jesus said, "Love thy neighbor as yourself," he was speaking to people who hated and coveted their neighbors. These messages were used to bring awareness to people who were ignorant and totally unaware. As religions were formed around these messages, they included health, dietary and family laws for protection. Even today, it is difficult to separate the chaff from the wheat as we search for the truth in all of the beliefs, dogmas and doctrines.

These messages have been translated from generation to generation, but much has been lost in the process. Myths have been interwoven with the truth. Historically, many prophets, teachers and masters came from the Middle East, which is a crossroads of cultures. There was an infiltration and contamination of societal and cultural beliefs that often distorted the purity of the message as it was passed down. When a belief was carried from one seaport to another, it was commingled and fused with other cultural beliefs. Our religions today often carry outdated beliefs filled with myths. Usually, the myths have become more real than the actual events in history.

Prophets and teachers come to tell us things of which we are often ignorant. Many of us follow deceased teachers and masters. Others follow living teachers with modern parables. From the relationship between student and teacher, a new awareness develops, an awakening and a feeling of great joy and gratitude. We often feel love and gratitude for our teacher.

Born-again Christians project onto Jesus the image of a lover. For others it is a guru or a spiritual teacher with whom the "in-love" relationship happens. They think the relationship with this teacher is what will free them from their sinful unworthiness. I believe the born-again experience is similar to the in-love phase in relationships, which we discussed in chapter 5. The in-love phase is a preview of the real love that perhaps lies ahead. It is an introductory stage that can lead to the unconditional love we long for. The in-love phase creates a natural endorphin in our bodies that makes us feel high, even blissed out. This endorphin, called phenylethylamine, or PEA, is triggered whenever we see a picture of our beloved, hear him or her, or sing our beloved's praises in a love song. With our spiritual teachers, we project wonderful, positive qualities onto them and fall in love with our projection. It is like projecting a movie onto a blank screen and reacting to the image.

This high lasts for about six months to two years. We tell everyone about our beloved. We want everyone to have a similar born-again experience. But as in human relationships, when the high wears off and the bloom of love fades, we begin to feel confused and disillusioned. *There is no disillusion without an illusion*. At this point, many will leave this spiritual relationship and look for new prophets, teachers or gurus. If we don't move to the next level, real love, we will keep repeating the same experience of searching and never finding.

There are many followers who remain dependent on the teacher and never find their own way. Their whole life is about following, and they sacrifice their own Divine potential and purpose. Our spiritual teachers, like good parents, want us to move from being dependent and helpless to being fully mature. Though we can remain students, there comes a time when we must manifest our intrinsic gifts and live our lives with courage and enthusiasm. In fact, the word *enthusiasm* means to be filled with the Spirit.

Real love develops when we return to our inner home and connect with that part of ourselves that holds our bliss, joy and happiness. What we have longed for is the experience of our homecoming. But often we confuse the message with the messenger. If we attach ourselves only to the messenger, we will never truly complete our journey. Wholeness and well-being is not only in the messenger, it is also in us. The message that the master or teacher offers us is the key to gaining the knowledge we need to go home. We must look to ourselves to use that key.

The path to our source, and the truth of who we are, is within. When we find that wonderful place within ourselves, we find unconditional love. Real love creates other endorphins. In the maturity of our spiritual experience, the endorphin for real love gives us feelings of peace, contentment and well-being. It is void of good or bad qualities. In this place, there are no rights or wrongs. When we embrace ourselves, free of judgment, we will experience what we have always longed for. These are the qualities of our true existence. It is here that we find God.

OUR DUALISTIC BELIEFS

James's father left his mother when James was four years old. His maternal grandfather then became the male role model in James's young life. By the time James was eight years old, his mother had remarried. His stepfather was kind to him, but it was Grandfather whom James loved the most. They had a close bond. He believed his grandfather had all the answers and was a saint. James tried to be like him and lovingly obeyed him.

Grandfather was very fundamental in his religious beliefs. He strongly admonished those who didn't follow his beliefs and verbally chastised James's mother for everything he believed she did that was sinful and bad. He piously spoke of virtues that he strove to achieve and prodded James to do the same. Grandfather's influence stayed with James long after the man himself died.

James developed a subpersonality that was like his grandfather. It judged and criticized him constantly, reminding him of all his sinful way and thoughts. That part also judged everyone else's behavior. James also created another subpersonality he called the Saint. It, too, was like his grandfather. When he hung out with the Saint, he felt virtuous, spiritual and holy. James liked that. He felt superior to others and believed he could save others. If he got out of line, however, the punitive and judgmental subpersonality would come down harshly on him.

James decided to dedicate his life to a spiritual path. He went to seminary to become a minister. All through seminary he lived a monastic life. As long as he watched his thoughts and his behavior, he felt OK with himself. It created a balance between the two parts he had created to keep him in line. After graduation, his first assignment was as the assistant pastor in a small Pentecostal church. James had waited all his life to spread the message to others of what was the right and only path.

It was at evening Bible study that James met Sarah, a lovely, spiritual woman to whom he was immediately attracted. They began a casual friendship and shared their love for God. His attraction to her grew. Gradually their relationship turned sexual. James was constantly torn between right and wrong. He believed having sex without marriage was a sin—even thinking about having sex was a sin. He longed for Sarah and thought about their sexual encounters often. Just the thought of her brought up in him intense shame and guilt. This inner conflict kept James in a constant state of anxiety, worry, fear and sleeplessness. He was so overwhelmed with this internal dualistic turmoil that it began to affect his ability to do his job. He felt he had to make a choice either to end his relationship with Sarah or to leave his spiritual path.

In our therapy sessions, we explored the battle of the two subpersonalities that James had created, the perfect Saint and the punitive and abusive Judge and Critic. His life has been about following the ingrained beliefs of his grandfather, which had become part of his blueprint. Under it all, James didn't know who he was and what he wanted. The longing for a spiritual connection was within him, but it had been masked in

duality. I asked him, Do you know what it is like just to be? To be free
of judgment and rights and wrongs? His eyes filled with tears, and he
replied that sometimes he experienced this state and it was what he really
longed for. He said that when he was there, he was very much in the
present and allowed things to be just as they were. In that state, he felt
peace, joy and contentment.

Most religions view life as good or bad, right or wrong, and view people in one of two ways. According to some religions, we are basically
sinful and imperfect and must be saved from this inherent dilemma. Other
religions see us as basically good, perfect and angelic, and the purpose
of religion is to bring out our goodness. We learned this dualistic way of
thinking in infancy and have established it as the foundation of our belief
blueprint.

If we perceive the events in our life as good, we feel virtuous and
believe we are being favored by God. If we experience the events as bad,
we believe we have fallen out of favor with God. If we believe in a punishing God, we analyze our failings to find what we have done wrong.
And, when we view others' lives from this perspective, we believe that
those who are ill, in poverty, in distress or exhibit behaviors on the wrong
side of the ledger have somehow failed and are out of God's favor. We
equate poverty, illness and suffering with sin.

Dualism gives us a false sense of security. If we can neatly line up
things in life as right or wrong, good or bad, positive or negative, it gives
us the illusion of control in our world. Our belief blueprint is made up
of opposites that come from our dualistic beliefs. On one side of the
ledger are the *not enoughs,* and on the other side are the *enoughs.*
Traditionally, our religions teach us that if we follow the right path, we
will be saved from our intrinsic sinful nature. Dualism keeps us stuck in
a polarity of limiting and false beliefs that prevent change and growth.

As we collectively repress parts of ourselves that we as label bad or
wrong, we also project them onto others whom we label as bad people
and sinners. We try to rescue them from their sins and bring them into
our way of thinking, which is the *only* way. Rescuing those who we believe

are lost is a way of avoiding the darkness within ourselves. If we see the world as "either/or," we create a schism in our own selves and in the world. If we hold tenaciously to only one side and cut ourselves off from the other side, we split off from our wholeness. As long as we believe in a duality in our external world, we will maintain a split in our own being.

NEW AGE THOUGHT

Duality is also the foundation for the New Age thought movement. The belief is that through positive thinking, we can eliminate the negative aspect and circumstances of our lives. Like traditional religion, the message is that there are negative forces that must be controlled. Instead of repressing them, however, New Age thought believes—mistakenly— that they can be controlled through positive thinking.

New Age thinking says that through positive affirmations, we can manifest what we want in life. If we think positive thoughts often enough and long enough, we believe God or Creative Intelligence will change our feelings of unworthiness to worthiness and our not enoughness to enoughness. Balancing duality *can* in turn create a balance in our lives. But until we recognize that the belief in our inadequacies and in not being enough is false, our lives will never be truly transformed.

When we experience negative events and tragedies in our lives, positive thinking, like negative thinking, can prevent us from seeing that the events in our lives are neither good nor bad, but something we need to become aware of. If we try to repress, pray away or think away the signals we are receiving, it is like removing the warning light on the dashboard of a car. And, if we deny or ignore our feelings, we will never know the messages that they hold for us. Our crises, our struggles, our dis-eases are a wake-up call. What is being revealed is what needs to be healed.

There is an appropriateness to our feelings. If we are busy denying them, we will not get to the source. It is appropriate to feel emotional pain when our friends betray us, when one of our parents dies or when we have health concerns. To be stoic in a time of understandable crisis is ludicrous. We need to embrace ourselves, free of judgment, and stay open so that we can make sense of the experiences we are having.

To connect with the Divine within, we must move into a nondualistic place. Between negative and positive beliefs lies a state in which we experience such nondualistic qualities as clarity, harmony, wisdom, faith, love and grace, as shown in the chart in figure 6. Use this chart to explore and recognize the duality we live with. We will address this natural state in the next section.

The Polarity of Opposites		
Negative Qualities	Nondual	Positive Qualities
NEGATIVE	GRACE	POSITIVE
BAD	CLARITY	GOOD
ANXIOUS	WISDOM	RELAXED
DARK	TRUTH	LIGHT
MEAN	HOPE	KIND
IMPATIENT	FAITH	PATIENT
SAD	LOVE	HAPPY
POOR	WELL-BEING	RICH
SICK	JOY	WELL
FAT	CONTENTMENT	THIN
FAILURE	BLISS	SUCCESS
DEPRESSED	SPIRIT	FEELING UP
OLD	GOD	YOUNG
IGNORANT	SOUL	EDUCATED
STUPID	CONSCIOUSNESS	SMART
GREEDY	WHOLENESS	GENEROUS
WITHHOLDING	BALANCE	GIVING
WRONG	HARMONY	RIGHT
UGLY	KNOWLEDGE	BEAUTIFUL
POWERLESS	INFINITY	POWERFUL

IMPERFECTION AND WHOLENESS

A Chinese proverb says, "The opposite of imperfection is not perfection. It is wholeness." Within us are a perfection and wholeness that are always in a state of becoming. Moment to moment we are in a state of process and evolution. Our wholeness comes from the integration of all that we already are. It is the Yin/Yang principle. Where there is the integration of the two sides, there is balance. And in that space between opposites, there is well-being and wholeness.

The space between opposites is a natural state. It is neither good nor bad. *It just is.* Each quality—peace, joy, love, contentment and so forth—has no opposite. These are unconditional gifts that are and have always been in each of us. We don't have to earn these gifts by being good enough, by repressing our negative side, or by following anyone else's beliefs. No one outside of ourselves, including religion, can grant us these gifts. They were with us when we were born. We experienced this bliss and joy in infancy before the rupture. We split off from this bliss because we were ignorant, as was everyone else around us. Very soon in life, we began to absorb everyone else's beliefs because we thought they were ours. We believed that in order to survive, we had to adapt.

The longing to reconnect with our wholeness has been with us since the beginning of time. What separates us from this peaceful, loving place is our dualistic beliefs. Though we may not experience it at every moment of our lives, the bliss and grace are always there. It never leaves us, we leave it. It is in this state that we find the energy and essence of what we call God, the Divine, our Creator. It is here that we are in God's image. This place is limitless and filled with infinite possibilities. We search to find that which we long for. The Scripture says, "Ask and it will be given you; seek, and you will find; knock, and it will be opened to you" (Matthew 7:7). The place we long for is as close as our next breath. Jesus said, "The Kingdom of heaven is within."

The question is, how do we get to this place when we have drifted so far away? We must awaken from the deep sleep we have been in, a sleep that is thousands of years old. To find our way, we must accept that the long-held beliefs of our not being enough is not the way. We already are enough and will always be enough. Until now, if we had known differently, we would have acted differently.

OUR RELATIONSHIP WITH OUR CREATOR

Many of us see God as an external figure with a long white beard, an invisible entity outside of ourselves. We project onto this image all of our fears, hopes and dreams. And as we discussed in earlier chapters, we look for ways to be enough by acquiring more money and material things, by being successful in a profession or by having a relationship with someone who loves us. We also believe that in a relationship with God, we will be enough. But can we have a relationship with God?

How do we know God? We seek, we search and often we don't find. Yet at other times we experience the deep knowing of this experience when we least expect it: in a sunset, a morning sunrise, in the stars at night, in the birth of a child, in the feeling of love. We feel that presence *because it is always there.* And in that experience is clarity, wisdom and a deep feeling of love—in truth, all that is. Life, birth, death, the rain, the ocean contain the presence of God. And like the vast ocean, one cup filled with God's presence is the same as an ocean of it. We each are a portion of what God is. God does not dwell in us, like a raisin in a bun. God is within us, in every cell of our being. We are God manifesting as us. If we deny our own worthiness, we also deny God's worthiness.

We are spiritual beings on a human journey. We can find what we long for wherever we are, because wherever we are, God is. We can find God in nature, in our children's laughter, in our beloved's touch, in our daily chores, in music that touches our soul and brings forth tears of gratitude and joy. We can feel God in our synagogues, temples and churches. We can experience God in the rituals and ceremonies that mark the passage of time. In every experience of our life, God is there. But to seek that presence, to connect with our Creator, the Divine within us, we must divest ourselves of any rights and wrongs, beliefs, dogmas or concepts. In Matthew 19:24, Jesus says, "It is easier for a camel to go through the eye of a needle, than a rich man to enter into the Kingdom of God." To come into the Kingdom, we must leave our baggage behind.

A scripture that often comes to me in meditation is *"Be still and know that I am God,"* Psalms 46:10. My gifted friends Tara (Liz) O'Driscoll and Stuart Hoffman wrote the following poem that is set to music about knowing God in the stillness.

In the Stillness

When you were young you played with your gifts
Your gift of innocence, your gift of simplicity, your gift of trust
And I danced with you everyday
Together we would play

In the stillness you knew ME
In the stillness you knew you
In the stillness we were one and always would be
Can you listen still?

In your first breath
When you walked your first step
I was there with you
In your first thought
When you spoke your first word
I was there with you

In the stillness you knew ME
In the stillness you knew you
In the stillness we were one and always would be
Can you listen still?

Slowly and slowly, unknowingly you were taught
That you were apart from ME, separate and alone
I have watched you wander from your home
I have felt your longing to be one with ME

In the stillness you know ME
In the stillness you know you

In the stillness we are one and always will be
Can you listen still?

When your feet touch the dew in morning
As you watch the sun set in evening
As you seek me so I seek you
As you gaze in wonder at the universe of stars
And dream of other worlds I am there with you

In the stillness you know ME
In the stillness you know you
In the stillness we are one and always will be
Can you listen still?

Through the wisdom of the ages
The gentle reminder of a friend
I am there with you
In your last moment
Thru all eternity
I am there with you

In the stillness you know ME
In the stillness you know you
In the stillness we are one and always will be
Can you listen still?

OUR SOUL'S BLUEPRINT

I believe each of us has a soul that is nameless and faceless and has a purpose. We are in this life to evolve and to nurture the seeds of our potential so that we may express the gifts they hold. Many of these seeds were repressed in the environment in which we grew up, but they are so powerful that they will sprout and push through the soil of great adversity to be expressed.

Our soul directs our path and our life; it even selects for us our place of birth and our parents to learn the lessons we need to learn. Our evolution is about bringing us into consciousness individually and col-lectively. Throughout history there have been those who had the courage to move beyond collective beliefs. Often these few were criticized and judged by the belief system of that time and were executed. Later we realized they came to teach and show us new ways of seeing the world.

We are spiritual beings on a human journey. The human journey lasts a short time, within a parentheses in eternity, but our spiritual being is and has always existed. Our path or journey will be revealed as we embark upon it. We are both the teacher and the student, the parent and the child, the loved and the beloved. The lessons we need to learn that will show us the way home are already within us. We have been given freedom of choice, and we can choose to take the path or not. It is never forced on us.

Awareness is the beginning of change. That awareness comes at many points in our lives. There is something that happens, an experience, an encounter in which we know without a doubt that "this is what I want to do with my life. This is my purpose." Again, it is a wake-up call to who we are. We will experience a glimpse of the true blueprint our souls hold. That blueprint is not determined by our parentage, heredity or envi-ronment. We each have a unique blueprint that, like an acorn, carries in its code a full oak tree. This actualization, or *entelechy*, holds the master pattern for our lives. Like a gardener who shapes a bonsai, our beliefs have shaped us in a certain way that is not the natural pattern for our spiritual growth. The pains and disruptions in our lives individually and collectively come from the external and internal repression that our imposed beliefs have created. Until we uncover this imposed blueprint, we shall never see our true nature.

THE HOMECOMING

How do we connect to ourselves and return Home, where we find our divinity and potential? Our mind and ego can never go there, for it holds our core belief blueprint, duality, judgments and interpretations. The ego is responsible for our subpersonalities, which are based in rights and wrongs. We can take none of these with us to that place inside where our wholeness exists, that nondualistic place that holds all that we are.

We can't find our Home in our past accomplishments or achievements, or in our future goals and plans. We can only know the experience of Home in the moment, in the eternal *now*. We will always know what we need to know when we need to know it. The source of our lives is within us at every moment. We hold the innate wisdom, strength and courage to make wise decisions and choices. The healing is always here for our physical body, our mind, our emotions and our spirit. Within ourselves we find grace, the unconditional gift of life that was given to us with our first breath and continues to give to us with each breath. It is in our breath that we find the pathway to our center, our heart, our Home. To live our lives moment by moment, and to set aside time daily to connect with our Divine source is to experience joy, contentment and bliss. It is what we have longed for all our lives. When we remember who we are, we awaken and know. We have remembered that which we have forgotten.

My dear friend and colleague Hugh Beaton, Ph.D., wrote about Awakening:

> *You have been preparing for this Awakening for eternity.*
>
> *Who could have guessed it would be now?*
>
> *It has to take this long and has been this hard so you*
>   *will take it seriously.*
>
> *You are here to Awaken, transcend suffering, and*
>   *participate in the indomitable joy of life.*
>
> *You are not here to suffer.*
>
> *Purgatory is the temporary suffering you encounter when*
>   *you begin to Awaken to the deep meaning of your life.*
>
> *It comes between the stupor of unawareness and the*
>   *rapture of Awakening.*
>
> *The things you encounter in this world are the scenery*
>   *of your soul's journey.*

Each one is a teacher, that is why it is your life.

Life does not tell you what you need to know. It shows you.

Your life is your soul's journey through the world.

When you Awaken to this, you have returned home
  from your most distant wanderings.

Only then can you see that your wanderings were
  your way home.

EXERCISE

To make changes in your life, you must begin by exploring where you are now. This exercise helps you examine your beliefs about the spiritual side of your life.

YOUR SPIRITUAL BELIEFS

What was the religion of your childhood?

_____

_____

What were your childhood beliefs?

_____

_____

_____

Describe your father's beliefs.

_____

_____

_____

Describe your mother's beliefs.

_____

_____

How powerfully did these beliefs affect you? Why?

_____

_____

_____

Were the beliefs of your religion practiced at home? How?

_____

_____

_____

What influence did your extended family have on your beliefs?

_____

_____

_____

How were your religious beliefs supported in school or in your neighborhood?

_____

_____

_____

How did you perceive your rabbis, priests, ministers or spiritual teachers as a child?

_____

_____

_____

Who was most significant person in your spiritual direction?

_____

_____

What are your beliefs about God?

_____

_____

Did you feel the desire to follow a spiritual path?

_____

_____

_____

What experiences led you to pursue a spiritual path?

_____

_____

_____

Have your beliefs changed since childhood? How?

_____

_____

_____

What was the turning point for the changes in your beliefs?

_____

_____

_____

Throughout your life, what spiritual or mystical experiences have you had?

_____

_____

_____

_____

_____

_____

_____

Chapter 10

THE RETURN TO WHOLENESS

The death of Princess Diana in August 1997 was a terrible shock to many. The tragedy touched the hearts of people from every walk of life. Her life—and her death—brought up in these individuals thoughts, emotions and beliefs about their own lives. People were shaken out of the complacency of their everyday lives and were forced to confront the fragility of life itself. We tend to forget that life is temporary. We view it as a permanent experience and often shut out the bigger picture.

Diana's death reminded people of their own life's struggles and victories. In spite of a difficult childhood, the divorce of her parents, her shyness, her bulimia that kept her physically and emotionally fragile and the nonacceptance of her husband and the royal family, Diana persevered with courage and honesty, and she gave lovingly of herself to others. The world watched her struggles and her victories and silently cheered because they identified with her. Her struggles were their struggles, her death, their personal loss.

Though she had all the wealth and material possessions she could ever want, Diana still suffered. She became the princess that every little girl dreams of being. In his eulogy, her brother, Earl Spencer, said, "For all the status, the glamour, the applause, Diana remained throughout a very insecure person at heart, almost childlike in her desire to do good for

247

others so she could release herself from the deep feelings of unworthiness." Even Diana, who seemed to have everything, harbored a deep feeling of unworthiness. She believed she could release herself of those feelings of unworthiness by proving her worth through her good works.

Diana is no different from any of us. In spite of everything she had, she continued to believe in her inadequacies. Each of us is stuck in the same place, longing and hoping, some way, somehow, to overcome this basic feeling of unworthiness that we carry around. We learned in childhood the beliefs that we were taught; we experience it in all of our life's tragedies, a belief that if we were lovable enough, we wouldn't be hurt, abused and abandoned by our parents and others. Somehow we have always felt we could never measure up. Throughout our lives we have struggled to achieve what we believe we can never have. We have exhausted ourselves in the trying and continue to feel stuck and confused. Though we want change, at the same time we fear it.

THE FEAR OF CHANGE

In his book *Escape from Freedom,* Erich Fromm discusses our basic fear of freedom. We look to totalitarianism, be it governments, corporations or religion, to tell us what to do and how to think. Even if we choose to leave one form of external control, we often continue to encounter it elsewhere. First, we leave our family system where parents are controlling and whose beliefs leave little room for our individuation. Soon we go to school in an educational system with beliefs that dictate to us how we should think and learn. We join religions that have rigid beliefs, dogmas and rules for behavior and thought. Later we join corporations that establish agendas for us that leave little or no room for personal growth. We marry a partner to whom we give our power or who gives his or her power to us. Finally, we re-create in our new family the same system of our birth family by placing ourselves in the power position and expecting our children to comply with our agenda.

Our fear of change keeps us repeating old patterns that give us the illusion of security. We sell out our freedom for a pittance. But if we give our power away to an authority that we believe holds our truth, we block the natural flow of our own existence. It is like interrupting the flow of a river by damming it up. In time the backed-up dam will stagnate or eventually break through with such tremendous force that it shakes up our whole existence. If we ignore this wake-up call, we will gradually begin to break down physically, emotionally and spiritually. Signaling that we have stopped the flow are the physical and emotional symptoms that inform us that something is blocked. These symptoms speak to us from our psyche, if only we will listen. We can ignore them, but the signals will persist.

A popular bumper sticker reads *Shit Happens.* Things happen in our lives that are awful and difficult to deal with. I think the bumper sticker would be even more frightening if it read *Shift Happens.* Change is scary but necessary. Everything changes: our physical body, our emotions, our relationships, our work. We experience seasons, tides, storms, earthquakes, hurricanes, fires, cloudy days and sunny days. Some changes are natural and evolutionary, some are catastrophic, but nothing stays the same. To resist change creates pain. In every area of life, we are locked into systems with limiting beliefs that attempt to maintain the status quo. Though we succeed in making some changes, often we are unable to make the most important change: that of the limited belief system that creates our personal reality and our core belief of not being enough.

CHOOSING TO CHANGE

Life is about choices, and some of the choices we make are better than others. Our experiences, our beliefs and our awareness determine these choices. Every moment is a crossroads to learning. Each moment builds on the previous one, and each choice is the foundation for the next choice. Life truly is a process that never ends.

That voice in our head, our self-talk, carries all the limiting beliefs that tell us what we should and ought to do and be. There is another, deeper, inner voice that holds all the answers for our life. All we have to do is learn to recognize this voice and listen. The answers are already within us even before the questions are asked. They will guide us in our soul's journey.

We often believe that we will fail if we take risks, but if we stop risking, we stop growing. We perceive as failures the choices that didn't turn out the way we expected. In criticizing and judging ourselves so harshly, we stop our process and our growth. It sets us up for dis-ease.

Our beliefs are like toxic waste that must be cleared away. If we put a pitcher of poison under a dripping faucet of clear, fresh water, in time the whole pitcher will be filled with fresh water. The poison will flow out as the fresh water fills the pitcher. As we make conscious choices for our life, we will release our toxic beliefs and our lives will automatically change.

Everyone who comes into our lives is our teacher. We attract what we need to learn in order to evolve. Every experience is also our teacher, and we can learn from each if we choose. Life is never static. If we learn our lessons, we can graduate to the next level. We evolve by committing to a return to wholeness. These choices can mean making major changes in our lives. Trusting and honoring our individual sacredness, and the voice within that directs us, will guide us in making choices that are for our highest good.

Life's experiences propel us in whatever direction we are willing to go, based on our limiting beliefs and decisions or on our conscious choices. If we consciously choose to learn and grow we will excel emotionally and physically. If we choose not to listen and learn, we will stagnate and stop growing physically and emotionally, and spiritually we will break down. We must trust the natural, intrinsic growth process in ourselves that comes from our wholeness. It is the same growth energy that is in a child. We couldn't stop that growth even if we tried. In growth there is ease, but if we resist it out of our fears, it will lead to dis-ease. I often tell my clients that their growth in therapy and in their belief work is like getting into an elevator and riding to levels that they have never been on. They leave behind old, limiting beliefs about themselves and their world that no longer fit. Sometimes we find ourselves stuck between levels. We can no longer relate to the one we left behind, and we have not yet experienced the next level. It can be a confusing time, but it is part of the changing process. Before we experience change and transformation, we may experience chaos and confusion. If the commitment to change is there, however, we will move from our confusion into clarity.

When as we make new choices for our lives that are no longer the same as our parents' and friends' choices, our relationships will change. Our friends and family may become uncomfortable with us and want us to continue to hold the same beliefs. In turn, we may be uncomfortable with them. It is like being a stranger in a strange land, and sometimes we will have periods of emptiness and loneliness. But we must realize we are learning a new language that up until now very few people in our lives have been able to understand and communicate. It is like the alcoholic who chooses to quit drinking, and his old drinking buddies can no longer relate to him as they used to. As we choose to change, we create change in all of our relationships. It is an opportunity to relate to those in our lives in new and healthier ways. We can forgive the past hurts from others, and we can ask for forgiveness from others. Eventually, our inner changes can and will improve relationships in ways that we never dreamed were possible.

WHO ARE WE?

We are multidimensional. There are many parts to our existence. We are not limited by our past or our history. We are not limited by our beliefs, our reactions or our adaptations. We are not defined by our subpersonalities. We are more than what we can imagine. Our personal reality is limited by what we are able to see and experience. We are like the proverbial iceberg of which only the tip of our existence is exposed. Within each of us is a longing for the knowledge of our totality.

There are three major realms of our existence. The first, the "*This is me*" realm, is the historical part of ourselves that was born on a certain day in a certain year, in a particular city, county and state, in a particular country. We are a female or a male. Our parents have a lineage of nationality, race and color. We are born into certain ethnic and religious families.

At the time we were born, our family had certain dynamics that were unique, and we inherited physical attributes and proclivities. We live only so many years within a certain time frame and space with multiple experiences.

The *This is me* part of ourselves has had many experiences. It is the part in which we connected with family, went to school, got married, made love, moved to a new home, made friends, had children, worked through conflict, experienced financial struggle, accumulated things, lost friends and lovers, were wounded, were betrayed, dealt with crises, accidents and illness, healed, had a career, a profession, traveled, retired, read books, enjoyed music and poetry, failed, succeeded, laughed, rejoiced, played, cried, felt anger, hate, despair and hopelessness and faced the deaths of ourselves and others.

This is me makes up our ego and has its own personality with certain habits, thoughts and ideas. Consequently, it creates the many subpersonalities to survive. It carries the belief blueprint of our culture, ethnic background, parents, society and religion. At its core is the limiting belief of our not enoughness. *This is me* reacts to events in a particular way, feels, thinks, interprets, judges and adapts. It is our flesh, our bones, our blood, our humanity. *This is me* is a temporary, finite existence that will end in death.

Many people believe that we live this life and then we die. Many healers in the medical and psychological professions believe this same aspect as well, and seek to heal our dis-ease only from this dimension. They define our reality, diagnose us, label us and treat our symptoms from this awareness. Our humanness is viewed as body parts that can be replaced or altered to sustain life. Like an automobile, doctors look to create new, more efficient parts to replace the damaged ones. Even now, scientists are experimenting with cloning new human body parts. The view of life limits our ability to access and connect with that part of ourselves where transformation and healing can happen.

In the Old Testament, God says, "I am, that I am." That same *"I am"* is the second realm of our existence. It is that nondualistic place where the Divine exists. When Jesus said in John 14:6, "I am the way and the truth and the life," I believe he was speaking of the *I am* in all of us. Yet the *I am* cannot be reached through our ego, that part of us called *This is me,* which is limited by the duality in our beliefs. To enter the *I am,* we must embrace both our negative and positive qualities and transcend the ego into a nondualistic state of unity and balance (see chapter 9).

In that place of the *I am* is wholeness, peace, joy, contentment, well-being and the infinite. The *I am* is permanent, eternal and changeless. Though the *This is me* goes through constant change, the *I am* never changes. It was there before our first breath and will go on after our last.

It is here that we find wisdom to make the right choices and decisions for our temporary life. In the *I am* there are no judgments and criticisms. Here we can ask for clarity and the revelation of what we need to know. Here we find healing and direction for our soul's journey. The crises in our lives and the confrontation of death can bring us Home to our true selves, the *I am* within us. We find our way to this sacred place in our prayers and meditations. It is here that we find God's grace. It is here that our lives can be transformed.

Finally, we come to the extended part of ourselves, the "I that is we." This is the third realm, the *"We are."* We are all connected to one another, and from these experiences—falling in love, having an intimate relationship with a partner, being a parent, sharing a crisis—we learn, grow and evolve. In this human environment is the opportunity to find our wholeness. Life's experiences are catalysts that force us to grow and change. There is a web of connectedness between us all. Each of our acts affects the lives of others in this web of *We are.*

Our individual change in consciousness can indeed influence others. One candle can light thousands. But it is also in the community of those who seek and choose to live a conscious and intentional life that our personal lives will change. In a conscious community, great physical, emotional and spiritual changes can happen as we tap into the depths of our collective resources and integrate them individually. When we are in a spiritual community, we can support each other through prayer and rejoice in the miracles, and we can gift each other with a spiritual wake-up call when we fall asleep.

One member of a family who awakens through a crisis can change the whole family. I have seen it in my practice. A person will come in and move through his personal challenges, tap into his extended self and know that he is more than this period in his life. He will experience a healing on a deeper level where transformation takes place and other family members automatically change. We are energy that interacts and influences others.

Albert Einstein said, "Our separation from each other is an optical illusion of consciousness." And in the words of the Hebrew philosopher Hillel,

> *If I am not for myself, Who is for me?*
> *If I am only for myself, What am I?*
> *If not now, when?*
>
> (Pirke Avot 1:14)

THE RETURN TO WHOLENESS

The *American Heritage* dictionary defines *heal* as: "to become whole and sound, to restore to health, to return to spiritual wholeness." To heal our wounds means a return to wholeness. There is nothing to fix, because nothing is broken. Nothing needs to be removed, and no parts are missing. To heal is to allow the wholeness that is already there to be revealed. Our belief work is not for the purpose of fixing anything; it is about clearing away that which covers up our true nature. It is the dark cloud that covers the sunshine. Like the sun, our true nature is always there. It has just been covered up. We are wiping away the dust and dirt that has covered the beautiful mosaic that is our life.

How do we find what we are longing for? How do we return to the wholeness within? It is the same question asked by seekers and realized by saints. It has been asked by generations past. We must embrace ourselves where we were in our past and where we are today. We can change our past and our future right where we are now. The point of change is in the present. The power for our healing is in the moment, this moment.

Returning to wholeness is about staying in the present. If we stay aware of our experiences as an observer, we always know what we need to know in the present. The answers are always there. Our beliefs come from the past, a past that was undergoing constant change. But our beliefs did not change, so we projected these beliefs onto our current experiences and judged them accordingly. We also project these same limiting beliefs into a future that we have not yet experienced. In doing this, we perpetuate the same experiences because they have been contaminated by our belief system. Each new moment will then be contaminated by old beliefs.

Many times we believe we need to prepare for the next moment because we don't trust our ability to handle it. But there is no need to prepare for each new moment. We have what we need without preparing because we are always prepared. Life is our preparation. We forget that the system called life works perfectly without our monitoring it with outmoded limiting beliefs that belong to other people. We have an inner authority, an intrinsic wisdom that guides us in making the right choices. Every moment is an opportunity to make choices that can bring us health, well-being, joy, peace, love, happiness, wisdom and fulfillment. Each choice we make directs our life in a particular way. If we make conscious choices, it keeps us in a state of wholeness. If we see life as a process in which the lessons are taught as we go, we will also grow. "You realize that all along there was something tremendous within you and you did not know it," said Paramahansa Yogananda.

There are three aspects to returning to wholeness: validation, compassion and forgiveness. We explore these in the sections that follow.

VALIDATION

Before we can change, we must validate and accept ourselves *as we are.* That doesn't mean we are resigned to situations that are not what we want. To change, we must see things as they are now. We are experiencing, at this moment, unconscious past choices based on our limiting beliefs. It is through self-acceptance and validation of ourselves and others that healing can happen, not through judgments and criticisms.

Validation is necessary for healing. In validation there is no judgment, no rights or wrongs about ourselves or others. Our beliefs are the source of our analysis. We judge and criticize not only ourselves, but also others from the same perspective. Validation and acceptance will bring about healing in our lives and in our relationships. It is seeing another person's point of view, seeing their actions and behavior as being based on the beliefs they hold. By learning to listen to what other people are saying, free of our interpretations and judgment, their point of view will make sense, and we will understand. Until that happens, we will never hear others clearly. What they are saying will be processed only through our belief blueprint. Listening and validating is a technique we can learn. When another person listens to us in this way, we feel connected. Our reality has been validated. This is the foundation for healing. Who in our life has really heard us and validated us? No one, probably not even ourselves.

But how do we learn to listen and validate? It is often easier to validate others. Inside us is a powerful judge and critic that relentlessly blames and shames us. To validate ourselves means bypassing our criticism and looking at our lives from a nonjudgmental place. It is easy to determine what is wrong with ourselves and look for quick fixes. Validation, though, is looking at what is true for us. It is looking not at how we "should be," but at how we are. Self-validation and self-acceptance are the only ways we can understand ourselves. Through finding fault we will only find confusion; through validation we will find clarity. Looking at our past experiences and our behaviors in an accepting, loving way, free of blame, will heal us.

Often we blame others in our past for hurting us. We blame our parents for their legacy of limiting beliefs, for the critical voice we continue to hear within ourselves that was once theirs. To heal our childhood wounds, we must stop the blame and validate ourselves and our caregivers, who were also wounded. If they knew better, they would have done better. They, too, were limited by the beliefs that had been passed down to them. They were unconscious of their own wounds and unconscious of how they had wounded us. It makes sense that we feel violated, angry and resentful. We can, however, honor and embrace our anger and bring it into healing. Staying angry will stop the flow of healing. We must validate our anger, forgive ourselves and forgive others so we can put closure on our past and move into the *now*.

Each of us has a need to be validated and accepted. This is usually why we express our hurt to others instead of going directly to those who hurt us. We have the mistaken idea that if we can find allies to support our blame, we will feel validated. We join in bashing parents, husbands, wives, bosses and friends. Allies in blaming only perpetuate the wound. Usually the people we seek to recruit have the same beliefs as we do and have difficulty bringing us into consciousness. Perhaps having these allies makes us feel good and accepted, but we soon know on a deeper level that all we have done is perpetuate the unresolved hurt. Blaming and avoiding is often how we deal with our conflict. Our beliefs tell us it's too scary to communicate directly with those whom we feel have wounded us. But to heal all our wounds from the past, we must confront these people. What we don't heal we will re-create. I call it returning to the scene of the crime. Healing will happen only when we make sense of life in the context in which it has been lived.

COMPASSION

Compassion comes from a deep awareness of the suffering of another, coupled with the wish to relieve it. It is the feeling of another's sorrow or hardship. The word *compassion* comes from Latin and means "to suffer with, to be with." We all have tried ways to avoid hardship and suffering. But suffering, dis-ease, aging and death are part of our human existence. Compassion is necessary to embrace our woundedness and the woundedness of others. For some, our wounds occurred in childhood and were inflicted by parents who ignorantly abused, violated and harmed us. Others were wounded in our growing years or in adulthood. Suffering is part of our lives. When we have been abandoned and betrayed by loved ones, it forces us to reassess our sense of trust, which was based on our old belief system. When we experience great loss and life-threatening changes, we move into deeper levels of awareness. These wake-up calls open up opportunities to reach the potential of our souls. They break us out of our complacency and help us move into a deeper awareness of our meaning and purpose in this life.

For the ovum to create a fetus, it must be penetrated by a sperm. For a seed to grow, it must break open to sprout the potential in its innate pattern and blueprint. To heal, there must be a death of our attachments to where we have been and our view of the world and a letting go of the unconscious conditioning of our beliefs. Life-threatening crises separate us from our familiar moorings and send us adrift into an unknown. However, to sail beyond our familiar spaces, we must be willing to lose sight of the shore. It is necessary to break from the old limited structure for our souls to be expressed.

Many individuals who remain neurotic or psychotic have not healed the deep rupture that came from their suffering. They have never made sense of their wounds. It is in experiencing deep compassion that our mental, emotional and physical wounding can be transformed individually and collectively. Compassion must be for ourselves, for our intimate others and for the collective other called the *We are.* In this consciousness we will heal our lives and heal the world. The Greek word *agape* means "a compassionate love where union and healing can happen." Sharing the suffering of others through compassion can lead to healing and transformation. In our religions, agape is the compassionate foundation for charity to those in need.

FORGIVENESS

From compassion comes forgiveness. To put closure on our past hurts, we must forgive ourselves and others. Holding on to past suffering, hurts and bitterness only creates dis-ease in our physical body, our emotions and our spirit. Old wounds cannot be undone or canceled, but they can be forgiven. In forgiving, we move on.

Forgiveness enables us to release ourselves from blame, shame and guilt, and absolve others of the same. Sometimes we have intentionally or unintentionally wounded others out of our own fears and the need to protect ourselves. These others may not be the target of our abuse, but they still experience the pain of our unconscious acts. Our wounding of others can come from our ignorance and lack of awareness. More often than not, we refuse to take responsibility for our hurtfulness toward others. Instead, we get defensive and rationalize why we did what we did, sometimes even blaming the other person for causing us to hurt them. To heal, we must forgive ourselves of all the hurts we have caused others and ask others to forgive us. The ability to forgive ourselves and the courage to ask for forgiveness is necessary to experience peace, joy and wholeness.

When we are unable to forgive ourselves, we close off a part of ourselves, and we try to hide that part from others for fear they might judge us as bad or sinful. We even judge our own behavior as dark and evil and fear ourselves. Unconsciously, we punish ourselves and sabotage our accomplishments, and we see ourselves as unworthy, not enough and not deserving. To cover our feelings, we act out with compulsive behaviors. We project an "I don't care" attitude and act out by having sexual affairs, overeating, drinking and taking drugs, or we withdraw into noncommunication. We stop honoring our gifts and deliberately deprive ourselves of the good in life.

How do we forgive ourselves when we have carried the guilt and shame for our deeds for so long? How can we relieve ourselves of the deep shame we carry? Forgiveness involves taking full responsibility for our actions and, at the same time, recognizing our humanness. Sometimes we do make choices that are not for our highest good. Those choices may hurt and harm others. We not only must forgive ourselves for our past transgressions and ask for forgiveness from others, but we also must commit to changing our behavior so that our harmful acts will not be repeated.

If we confess what we have done to someone who will unconditionally accept us and embrace us, we will feel validation and relief. This someone may be a therapist, a pastor, a rabbi or a dear friend. Next, we must ask for forgiveness from those whom we have harmed. Judaism suggests we ask for forgiveness at least three times, so that we may be released from the pain of our injustices toward others. It is never too late.

How do we forgive others who have hurt us? This, too, is a difficult but necessary act to bring about our healing. Holding onto bitterness and revenge destroys and damages us far more than the person who we feel has hurt us. Forgiveness frees the forgiver. To cling on to our anguish and pain only creates emotional suffering for us and keeps us stuck from moving on with our lives.

The other person may not ask us to forgive them. In fact, they may not even know what they have done to wound us. Often we suffer in silence needlessly and never share our hurts. For our own good, we must forgive others. Wounded by our parents, we carry the bitterness of these hurts into our adult lives. Even though our parents may be dead, the painful relationship often continues. Relationships last beyond the grave. Though others may be responsible for hurting us, we are responsible for continuing to hold onto the hurt by our unforgiveness. Our thoughts are filled with rumination, going over and over the injustices in our head. We feel confused, disappointed, lost, rejected, betrayed and abandoned. It is the closest relationships that bring about the deepest agony and hurt: parents who neglect us, abuse us and lie to us, a friend who betrays and abandons us, a lover who leaves us for someone else, a business partner who abandons our joint effort. The agony and pain is the greatest with those we love the most.

How we deal with this pain is often to deny it. We put on our false self and pretend that we are not hurt. We repress within ourselves the searing pain that often leaves us with a depression that doesn't make sense. We avoid dealing with the ones who hurt us and cut off our relationship by never seeing them or staying distant and disconnected in their presence. People who have cut themselves off from family members for years continue to harbor anger over painful events that have long been forgotten. Often we use our wounding from our past as excuses for our failures and difficulties in the present. We act as if the event is still happening and blame others from our past for our addictions and our problems.

To forgive others, we must take responsibility for our own unforgiving nature. There is the old adage that time heals all wounds. This is a false belief. Wounds will heal only when we take responsibility for healing them. Ignoring hurts and trying to forget them only intensifies the pain. We must release others from owing us anything, from being responsible for the act or even from giving us an apology. Only then will the gift of forgiveness free us and others. Accept others where and as they are. They may deny any wrongdoing; they may be defensive. It matters not. This experience is for our own release. It must be a gift with no strings attached.

We must own our part in all of the events that happen in our lives. An abuser will always find a participant that allows herself to be abused. I am not talking about children. We as children trusted in the care of our caregivers. Any abuse of those who are vulnerable and helpless is difficult to understand. Most often our caregivers acted out of their own abuses by their caregivers. These actions are passed down from generation to generation. But to abuse others when we know we are harming them, or when we allow others to harm us by betraying and abandoning ourselves, requires the deliberate act of forgiveness. The willingness to forgive and change allows our lives to be transformed.

LEARNING TO LET GO

Once we have learned validation, compassion and forgiveness, we can work on letting go of what we know is no longer our truth. An inventory of what we need to let go of is a good way to begin the healing process. It is a way of cleaning out all the toxic waste we have carried around from unresolved and unhealed experiences and relationships. If we are caught up in believing that things should have been different than they were, that people should have been different and that even we should have been different, we will stay in the same limiting belief blueprint. The past cannot be changed. We can, however, change our future by putting closure on the experiences of our past and letting them go so we can be healed.

The moment we decide to see life the way it is and not the way we believe it should be marks the beginning of change. It requires a basic shift in our consciousness. The key is the willingness to let go of the past hurts we have done to others and that others have done to us. The energy we need to hold onto the past keeps us from moving forward. It is time to let go of any unresolved conflict with our parents, our siblings, our mates, our children, our friends, our bosses. If we are still mourning the loss of someone, it is time to let go to make room for new, loving relationships. When we release the pain from our past, we will have closure. It will give us renewed energy and enthusiasm. Letting go will bring about a major shift in our consciousness.

What is consciousness? Consciousness is the ability to step outside of ourselves and observe our beliefs, thoughts, emotions, interpretations, judgments and actions. It is the part in us that is the witness. Witnessing ourselves brings about the awareness that is necessary to make changes in our lives. Its role is dual in that it can assess data and conditions from both inside and outside of ourselves. This clear, nonjudgmental part of ourselves gives us the ability and the clarity to make decisions for our highest good and set the course for our lives.

At the 1993 national convention for the Association for Imago Relationship Therapists in Chicago, Illinois, the introductory address was given by Harville Hendrix, founder of the Imago movement and author of *Getting the Love You Want.* His topic was consciousness. "To understand consciousness," he said, "we must look at what it is not. We must look at what is unconscious." These are his ten indicators of unconsciousness:

1. When we do the same thing that doesn't work over and over again. To become conscious is to quit.

2. When there is blaming. When we relinquish the responsibility for whatever is wrong and assign it to someone else, and relish in their suffering.

3. When we make excuses for our behavior, blaming someone or something outside of ourselves: "This happened because . . ."

4. When we use the word *you* instead of *I* when talking to another person about ourselves.

5. When we describe the character and motives of another: "You are bad and intended to hurt me because that is how you are." "You are dangerous."

6. Believing our experience is the only reality.

7. Believing we live in the present (an illusion), when in fact we live in memory. Where there is no awareness that there is a connection of the present to our past experiences.

8. Believing that others experience things the way we do. (This is the source of symbiotic illusion.)

9. When we devalue those people who don't experience things as we do.

10. Believing that we are autonomous and that we occupy central space, and that we are separate and self-sufficient by ourselves. Being conscious is knowing we are all connected.

Consciousness is moving from being reactive to being intentional in our lives. There is an old saying, "If I always do what I've always done, I'll always get what I've always gotten." We are responsible for our reactions and choices and their consequences. Until we take responsibility for being the cause and not the effect, we will remain powerless victims. Once we realize that we create our own reality, we feel liberated, knowing that we can make profound changes in our lives.

OUR TRUE DESTINY AND HOW TO GET THERE

If each of us has a blueprint that carries our true destiny, how do we find it? This blueprint is like the acorn that holds the pattern for the full-grown oak tree. It is waiting to be expressed. It doesn't matter how old or how young we are; the longing for its revelations will disrupt our lives until we stop and listen. Our potential lies beneath the false beliefs we have been conditioned to accept as ours. To find diamonds and gold requires digging, and digging is what we must do to reveal the most precious gem of all, our true self.

Our true destiny has many aspects. It will bring us fulfillment in many areas of our lives. If we follow it, it will bring us the joy, peace and happiness we long for. We will experience happy and harmonious relationships, enjoy optimum health, have success in our profession. We will then bring joy to others and to the world. The gifts we have in our potential are waiting to be fulfilled. When we go against what is intrinsically ours, we experience stress. But when we follow our destined path, our work is effortless. Everything falls into place, and we marvel at its ease. The ease comes from going with our natural flow to bring about a feeling of satisfaction, fulfillment and gratitude.

We search for magical ways to overcome the flawed parts in ourselves. Like the fairy tales we heard in childhood, we believe if we are pretty and sweet enough, someday a prince or princess will come and love us, and we will be healed. That is what Princess Diana believed, only to discover that the fairy tale was wrong, and her wound of unworthiness never healed before her untimely death. We think that once we are rich and famous, our inadequacies will disappear. If we get married, have children and make a wonderful home, this deep pain will go away. Diana felt the same. How about good deeds and good work? Diana will be remembered for her good deeds but went to her death never feeling enough. The message of our inadequacies can haunt us and hound us until our last breath, all of the prestige, status, riches, fame and even good works can never overcome it.

Under one belief lies another, and under that, another. That is why the process of belief work takes a lifetime. When we pull on the string of beliefs, we find often more than we bargained for. Everything that comes up as we move through the awareness process is a revelation of stuff that needs to be healed. But as the Chinese philosopher Lao-tzu says, "A journey of 1,000 miles starts with the first step."

Our journey in life is guided by our intuition and inspiration. Inspiration means the spirit within, and guidance comes from within. To find the answers, we must look where they can be found. We search for the answers in all the wrong places. If I want to buy a dozen eggs, I don't go to the hardware store. I go to the market, where I know eggs are sold. We must go where the source of our wholeness lies. The place where we can find our true nature and our true destiny is within ourselves.

MEDITATION AND PRAYER

The act of contemplating and reflecting on that within us is called meditation. It will come about directly or indirectly according to our own individual practices. Some of us may have never experienced prayer or meditation. It seems foreign, something that mystics do. We don't know where or how to start. Prayer is how we communicate with that presence within.

In meditation we listen to the voice of guidance that is within. The key to going inside is to follow the path of something outside that comes inside us moment to moment. That is the breath. By deliberately watching and following our breath, we experience our life moment to moment. We become still.

Meditation happens when we keep our mind fully focused on one thing, such as our breath. It happens when the mind becomes quiet. The mind is usually never quiet; it interprets, judges and analyzes everything and constantly demands our attention. But if we shift our attention from its chatter to something else, it becomes quiet. This quietness creates a deeply relaxed environment where healing can take place. In that quiet space, a calmness and stillness exists where in time even the thing we focused on fades away. And we simply experience what is. It is in this space that we realize everything and connect with our true nature.

Try focusing on your thoughts. Watch them as you would watch a cloud passing by, and stay detached. Ask yourself, Who is thinking? Who is troubled? Who is worried? In time your thoughts will stop and you will experience stillness.

Another way to meditate is to stay focused on sounds. If your mind begins to wander, gently return it to the single focus. Put on some spiritual music and try focusing on that. We can also use one word or a series of words to bring us into a meditative place. This can be a sacred name, a sound, a verse or a mantra. A mantra is a made up of sounds that vibrate with our own energy. Just the words "Be still, know that I am God," quietly repeated, will still the chattering mind. In time the words, sounds and mantra will fade away, and what is left is silence.

It is important to prepare yourself for meditation. There are many wonderful books and teachers to help you. Preparation begins with a strong intent. Commit to it daily. Set aside the same time every day to practice meditation—morning and/or evening, whichever time works best. Sit in the same place and in the same position every day. Being regular in your practice will condition the mind and body. The body and mind are like little children, and they will respond to your inner authority. Soon you will notice a subtle change. You will sleep better at night. Physical symptoms will slowly begin to disappear. Your health will improve. You will feel happier, more contented and loving. Your life will begin to change. (See the end of this chapter for an exercise in meditation.)

THE ROAD AHEAD—AND BEHIND

In this book, I have sought to convey the importance of learning to recognize your old limiting beliefs and how they affect your personal reality—your perception of men, women, relationships, family, work and spirituality. Only then can you embrace and know these beliefs in order to break free of those that have held you back, that have kept you stuck in the feeling of being not enough.

Awareness is the beginning of change. Creating a False Belief notebook (see the exercises in chapter 1), in which you record your limiting beliefs, and writing in your personal journal daily will keep you aware of your distortions. Creating new beliefs balances the energy in your psyche. You can create positive beliefs and act "as if" until the change begins to happen. You can set new goals with new behaviors that will in time change your attitudes. This process is slow, and the steps are often small, but you can persevere.

Doing the exercises throughout this book will help bring you into an awareness of your true destiny and return you to wholeness. If you begin to meditate daily and read from the wonderful selection of spiritual books that are available, you will shift your awareness and come closer to Home. By connecting with others who are on a spiritual path that supports your individual growth, you will return to your wholeness. Life itself will lead you to the teachers, groups, seminars, books and other ways to find what you are seeking. *When the student is ready, the teacher will come.* Trusting your own process will bring you Home; when the intention is clear, the path is made available. Seek and you will find, knock and the door will be opened, ask and you will receive. It is a promise.

Changes will happen through belief work. As a result, your life will become more liberated from the beliefs that have kept you locked in fear. But you must remember that what is being revealed through awareness needs to be healed. Healing leads to transformation. What transforms your life will also transform those around you. With your individual light, you can light the world. The healing of the world's wounds must start with your own. Healing begins at Home.

EXERCISES

THE HEALING PROCESS

■ To be free of guilt and pain from the past, you must bring up the memories of unfinished business that still needs to be healed. Unresolved hurts from your past halt your ability to move forward. When you heal these old wounds, you will experience a release of energy that had been used to repress these old issues. We made decisions about others—family members and friends—that now need to be released. These decisions become part of our belief blueprint and limit our experiences. Dealing with the issues that you have avoided will take effort and may bring up pain and tears. But remember, to *heal* it, you must *feel* it. Now is the time to take an inventory of your life and lovingly let go of old hurts, decisions and beliefs.

Before you start the healing process, find a quiet place where you will not be disturbed. Set aside a period of time that is free of inter-ruption. Turn off the ringer on your phone. Bring your journal, a pencil or pen, a writing pad, a box of tissues and a glass of water. Now, go into a brief meditation. Focus on your breath, following it as you breathe in and out. Imagine you are resting in a big hammock and your breath is gently rocking you with each inhalation and exhalation. Feel your body relax with the movement of your breath. If your mind begins to wander, gently bring your focus back to your breath. Begin to feel the stillness around you. Let your body absorb the stillness. Feel your mind and body becoming calm. During this process, lovingly allow your pain, sadness and tears to happen. In this safe place, you no longer need to repress them.

Now, in this quiet space, remember your childhood. Remember the house you lived in. The house that comes to you will be the house to remember. There is something special about this house—good times, bad times. Go to the place that was your room. Look around the room. See your toys, books, dolls, teddy bears. What do you remember of these possessions that held special meaning for you? Take that meaning with you and find your mother. Where is she? Once you have found her, look at her closely. Notice her eyes. What color are they? Observe her hair, her face, every part of her. Is she frowning or smiling? Notice her body. Is she tall or short? Fat or thin? What is she wearing? How does she smell? What do you feel when you see her? What are the things you needed to say to your mother but didn't? What are the things you wanted but didn't ask for? Share these with her. Now, write in your journal the things you shared with your mother.

Go back into the quietness within. Return to your childhood and find your father. Where is he? Look closely at him. Notice his eyes. What color are they? Look at his hair, his face. Does he smile or frown? Is he tall or short? Fat or thin? What is he wearing? How does he smell? How do you feel when you see him? What would you like to tell him? What are the things you needed to say to your father but didn't? What are the things you wanted but didn't ask for? Share these with him. Then write in your journal what you shared with your father.

Close your eyes and return to that quiet place again, focusing on your breath. In this stillness, remember all of the people with whom you have unfinished business. Who hurt you? Whom did you hurt? For which relationships do you seek healing and closure? In your journal, write the names of the people you have hurt, lied to or harmed in any way and the people who hurt, harmed or betrayed you. After each name, answer the following:

> Lies I told
>
> Things I did
>
> Things you did to me that hurt me
>
> Things I needed to say but didn't
>
> Loving words I didn't say
>
> Things I wanted but didn't ask for

Forgiveness is the next step. In the spaces below, describe your relationship with each person in one sentence. Then write what you need to forgive and release: all of your hurts, grievances and resentments, and all of the hurts and grievances you committed against each person.

1. Mother:

_____

_____

I forgive you for:

_____

_____

I ask you to forgive me for:

_____

_____

2. Father:

_____

_____

I forgive you for:

_____

_____

I ask you to forgive me for:

_____

_____

3. Brother(s):

_____

_____

I forgive you for:

_____

_____

I ask you to forgive me for:

_____

_____

4. Sister(s):

_____

_____

I forgive you for:

_____

_____

I ask you to forgive me for:

_____

_____

5. Lover(s):

_____

_____

I forgive you for:

_____

_____

I ask you to forgive me for:

_____

_____

6. Marital partner:

_____

_____

I forgive you for:

_____

_____

I ask you to forgive me for:

_____

_____

7. Friends:

_____

_____

I forgive you for:

_____

_____

I ask you to forgive me for:

_____

_____

8. Business partners:

_____

_____

I forgive you for:

_____

_____

I ask you to forgive me for:

_____

_____

9. Bosses:

_____

_____

I forgive you for:

_____

_____

I ask you to forgive me for:

_____

_____

10. Others (specify):

_____

_____

I forgive you for:

_____

_____

I ask you to forgive me for:

_____

_____

11. Me:

_____

_____

I forgive myself for:

_____

_____

Write a letter to each person on your forgiveness list. Describe your relationship with each, naming the negatives, the positives, the desires, dreams and hopes. Share your forgiveness of anything you believe they have done to harm you. Ask for forgiveness for what you have done to harm them. Thank each person for being a part of your life. At the end of each letter, write "I now release any pain, hurt or discomfort our relationship has brought us," and lovingly let go. You may have lost contact with some on your list; some may have passed on. Remember, our relationships go beyond death.

Send the letter to everyone you can, or use the communication process given in chapter 5 with those on your list. This may be difficult at first, but once you begin, you will gain an inner strength and a feeling of great relief.

■

Freeing yourself from the past and letting go of old decisions and beliefs will change your life. Change can happen the moment you decide for it to happen and the moment you commit to the process of change. It takes intention, attention and detachment. If change is your intention, it will happen. But it also requires your daily attention and a letting go of any attachment to the end results. Your inner map already has a plan for your life, and life itself will show you the way.

CREATING A VISION

From the work you have done in the exercises in the previous chapters, you can see where you have been and where you want to go. In your journal, write your vision as a narrative. Focus on how you would like to experience wholeness, joy, fulfillment and the expression of your potential. Describe your life positively and in the present tense. Imagine you are writing to a friend and telling it as if it is happening now. Use the chart of priorities you made in the exercise "Where are You Now?" in chapter 1 as a guide. Rearrange your priorities and the amount of energy and time you give them to create a balance in your life. Cover all eight areas: self, family, friends, work, pleasure, spirituality, health and exercise.

Write to your imaginary friend about where you live, how you live, who is in your life, how you relate to them, what you do, how you express yourself in your work. What are your enjoyments and pleasures? What are your goals in terms of growth, spirituality and emotional and physical health?

After you have finished, read this vision every night before you go to sleep. In your vision, how do you appear? How do you feel? How do you act? As new information comes to you, edit and rewrite your vision.

Explore the behavior changes and choices that are necessary to bring this vision to fruition. Create doable and measurable behaviors. Start with small steps you can do every day. Example: *I meditate every morning for twenty minutes.* Then adjust your daily schedule to accommodate these steps. Soon your life will change in a way you never expected. Claim this path for your life, because it is already yours.

The Persian poet Rumi, writing more than 700 years ago, revealed a greater possibility for humanity:

> *Out beyond ideas of rightdoing and wrongdoing,*
> *There is a field.*
> *I will meet you there.*

INDEX